Young Adult Literature in the Classroom

Reading It,
Teaching It,
Loving It

Joan B. Elliott
Indiana University of Pennsylvania
Indiana, Pennsylvania, USA

Mary M. Dupuis
Penn State University
University Park, Pennsylvania, USA

EDITORS

INTERNATIONAL
Reading
Association

800 Barksdale Road, PO Box 8139
Newark, Delaware 19714-8139, USA
www.reading.org

The International Reading Association attempts, through its publications, to provide a forum for a wide spectrum of opinions on reading. This policy permits divergent viewpoints without implying the endorsement of the Association.

Director of Publications   Joan M. Irwin
Editorial Director, Books and Special Projects   Matthew W. Baker
Senior Editor, Books and Special Projects   Tori Mello Bachman
Permissions Editor   Janet S. Parrack
Production Editor   Shannon Benner
Assistant Editor   Corinne M. Mooney
Editorial Assistant   Tyanna L. Collins
Publications Manager   Beth Doughty
Production Department Manager   Iona Sauscermen
Supervisor, Electronic Publishing   Anette Schütz
Senior Electronic Publishing Specialist   Cheryl J. Strum
Electronic Publishing Specialist   R. Lynn Harrison
Proofreader   Charlene M. Nichols

Project Editor   Shannon Benner

Cover   Design, Donna A. Perzel
          Illustration, Creatas

Credits   begin on page 231 and are considered an extension of the copyright page.

Library of Congress Cataloging-in-Publication Data
Young adult literature in the classroom : reading it, teaching it, loving it / Joan B. Elliott, Mary M. Dupuis, editors.
       p.   cm.
Includes bibliographical references and index.
    ISBN 0-87207-173-1
1. Young adult literature—Study and teaching.   2. Young adult literature—History and criticism.   I. Elliott, Joan B.   II. Dupuis, Mary M.
    PN1008.8 Y68 2002
    809'.89283'071—dc21

                                                                    2001006204

To our parents,

Paul and Freda Elliott
Bob and Nelle Miles

our first role models, who taught us the value of an education and who instilled the love of reading within us.

CONTENTS

SECTION III
Studying Authors

ACKNOWLEDGMENTS

The development, writing, and publishing of this book would not have been possible without the patience, enthusiasm, contributions, and thoughtful and positive suggestions from many individuals. This has truly been a collaborative effort.

We are grateful to the chapter authors—our colleagues around the United States—for their patience, perseverance, and dedication to seeing the book to completion. We also thank the teachers who contributed "Teacher Ideas" in order to make this a practical and useful resource for teachers. Our appreciation is additionally extended to the following individuals:

- Suzanne Mateer for compiling the list of websites in the Appendix, contributing to and field testing some of the Teacher Ideas, doing some editing, and assisting in a variety of other ways.

- Audrey M. Quinlan for providing the annotations in the Glossary of Teacher Ideas and for assisting in the editing.

- Alberta Dorsey for reading and assisting in editing.

- Joan Irwin, Director of Publications; Matt Baker, Editorial Director, Books and Special Projects; and Shannon Benner, Production Editor, of the International Reading Association for making this book possible and for their guidance and patience.

- M. Jerry Weiss for all his interest, dedication, and support for this book and for promoting young adult literature.

JBE and MMD

CONTRIBUTORS

Christine Carlson
School Library Consultant
St. Charles, Illinois, USA

Rosemary Chance
Assistant Professor of Library Science
University of Southern Mississippi
Hattiesburg, Mississippi, USA

Jan Cheripko
Author and English Teacher
The Family Foundation School
Hancock, New York, USA

Lynne R. Dorfman
Codirector, Pennsylvania Writing
    and Literature Project
West Chester University
West Chester, Pennsylvania, USA

Mary M. Dupuis
Professor Emerita of Education
Penn State University
University Park, Pennsylvania, USA

Joan B. Elliott
Professor of Literacy
Indiana University of Pennsylvania
Indiana, Pennsylvania, USA

Carol J. Fuhler
Associate Professor of Literacy
Iowa State University
Ames, Iowa, USA

Barbara A. Illig-Avilés
Assistant Professor of Literacy and
    Curriculum & Instruction
Indiana University of Pennsylvania
Indiana, Pennsylvania, USA

Teri S. Lesesne
Associate Professor of Library Science
Sam Houston State University
Huntsville, Texas, USA

Suzanne Mateer
Classroom Teacher
Homer-Center School District
Homer City, Pennsylvania, USA

Arlene Harris Mitchell
Associate Professor of Literacy and English
    Education
University of Cincinnati
Cincinnati, Ohio, USA

Barbara Moss
Professor of Literacy
San Diego State University
San Diego, California, USA

Elizabeth A. Poe
Assistant Professor of English Education and
    English Education Program Coordinator
West Virginia University
Morgantown, West Virginia, USA

Laura Robb
Teacher, Author, and Consultant
Powhatan School
Boyce, Virginia, USA

Barbara G. Samuels
Associate Professor Emerita of Language,
    Literacy, and Library Science
University of Houston-Clear Lake
Houston, Texas, USA

Jerry Spinelli
Author
West Chester, Pennsylvania, USA

INTRODUCTION

Mary M. Dupuis

Young adult literature, which is usually written for readers in grades 6–10, is a relatively new part of the literary spectrum. Adult literature is as old as writing. Children's literature has been around for more than a century. But young adult literature (known as YA literature) is only a few decades old. However, in that short time, it has developed a great following. Teachers and librarians use it regularly, and many parents and community librarians seek it as a way to keep young people reading when reading is not always "cool."

Why is YA literature so popular? How can we use it in classrooms at many levels and in many subject areas? That is, how does YA literature help us to teach and learn across cultures, across genres, across disciplines, and across grade levels? These are the central questions this book aims to answer. Our goal is to help teachers identify reading materials and ways of teaching that will retain students as readers—or bring them back if they have stopped reading.

Who Are Young Adults?

Young adult literature is written for readers whose reading interests and skills are not yet mature but who are themselves maturing. Adolescence is often identified as the time when students—even those who are effective readers—stop reading because they do not identify with the types of reading, the types of characters, or the problems and issues that are found in traditional reading materials.

Who are these young adults, anyway? They are people, in the most basic sense. They are young people who are becoming aware of the problems facing them as they mature. They are becoming aware of the problems facing their friends, their families, and their communities. Some of these issues are beyond their control, such as their own developing sexuality or their parents' potential divorce. Some of these issues are broader, such as changes in ethnic groups living within communities or changes in interaction among racial groups. Much of growing up is learning how to handle feelings about these issues.

Young adults are also concerned about making decisions and solving problems that will affect their adult lives, such as identifying and choosing a career, deciding who and when—even whether—to marry, and choosing where to live. Young adult readers are of both genders and at all levels of reading skill. They are of all racial, ethnic, and religious groups. They are living in urban, suburban, and rural or small-town environments. They are, in short, all children.

Young adult literature is popular with students, and is therefore an effective teaching tool, because it deals with the issues and problems that confront students as they approach and live through adolescence. It deals with issues that have been described as "growing up" problems, some of which have been part of literature for a long time. Dickens dealt with class concerns in *Great Expectations,* Twain with racial issues in *The Adventures of Huckleberry Finn.* These important contributions to the genre of "growing up" books gave the authors a chance to consider many of the social issues of their times, issues that are alive today—issues that concern young adults. As YA literature has developed, authors such as Lois Lowry and Walter Dean Myers have made dealing with such issues a central part of their writing.

A few topics that attract YA readers focus on individual issues in growing up, such as potential career choices, parents and their expectations, relations with siblings, and sex and developing sexual attractions. Other popular topics focus on the reality of adult life: death and dying; drugs, alcohol, and substance abuse; divorce; spousal and child abuse; race and class discrimination. The list could go on. All of these issues are full of moral and ethical questions. As adolescents struggle to understand how different people and cultures deal with the issues that are important to each of us, they can explore a range of options through YA literature.

Students also need to learn more about the world around them. Through nonfiction materials, they study different cultures and countries, sometimes included as social studies; the way the world works, often included as science; and the explosion of information, including the Internet, on all sorts of topics that concern adults. Diversity, and the inclusion of different cultures and groups, is a current focus for middle schools and junior high schools throughout the United States. At this age, students begin to see the differences among us, and they are often in school with students from different cultures for the first time. Learning about those cultures and others not represented in their school is an important developmental task for students. How can we include the diversity represented in the United States within a single curriculum? Each chapter in this book contains examples of books that include racial and ethnic diversity. The number and quality of books by and about people of diverse ethnic and cultural backgrounds is increasing rapidly. Including such books in today's classrooms can be easier if teachers follow the suggestions given in this volume.

What Do Young Adults Choose to Read?

One of the International Reading Association's responses to the growing interest in YA literature was the establishment of Young Adults' Choices, an annual project to determine which new books, authors, and topics excite young adults most. The Young Adults' Choices program allows students to read books by new authors and determine whether they like them. The resulting annual list of books selected by YA readers is a good barometer of the interests and preferences of YA readers. The Young Adults' Choices program has been in effect since 1985, so we now have more than 15 years of Young Adults' Choices, involving thousands of books.

What have young adults chosen to read? Young adults are interested in books with main characters they can relate to—people of similar ages, facing similar problems. They are interested in both fiction and nonfiction. They are intrigued by how people solve problems, often problems they have not caused but feel they must resolve. Interestingly, topics in which students are interested include the Holocaust, Vietnam, facing and dealing with homosexuality, and understanding and responding to racial and ethnic differences. These are hot topics among young adults today, and controversial in the larger U.S. society.

Hot topics could also join the definition of YA literature. The positive side of this reality is that, contrary to public opinion, YA readers are interested in some of the same topics as their parents and community members. However, some of these topics are also controversial, and they make some parents and community members uncomfortable. As a result, YA literature is among the most challenged in schools and libraries. Teachers and administrators may be wary of including YA literature in the curriculum, even in school libraries, for fear of offending members of the community. Handling this situation is an important issue for all educators: We need to defend students' right to read, but we must be aware of the community's attitude, as well. Although this book does not contain a chapter on challenges to literature, there are many helpful resources for teachers available, including the International Reading Association's *School Censorship in the 21st Century: A Guide for Teachers and School Library Media Specialists* (2001) by John S. Simmons and Eliza T. Dresang.

The Organization of This Book

Following is an outline of this book, including a quick overview of each chapter. Read the section introductions for more specifics on each section.

Section I: Responding to Reading

Responding to literature in general has become a fixture of good classrooms everywhere. Response can involve oral discussion in small or large groups, creative dramatics, and writing of all kinds.

Elizabeth A. Poe opens the first section with a focus on writing book reviews and offers a host of ways to elicit student response to books. In "Reader Response, Process Writing, Young Adult Literature, and the Art of Book Reviewing," Poe notes, "Because they are grounded in the reader's personal relationship with the book, book reviews are a valuable form of reader response." One sixth grader wrote that his book "is one of the coolest, funniest, and most addicting books I have ever read." What review could be better than that?

In "Thinking About Books on Paper," Laura Robb explores a number of teaching techniques she has used with YA literature. She starts with talk of all kinds and progresses to writing in numerous formats. For Robb, "When talk precedes writing, it can clarify thinking and enable students to write in order to discover what they think and understand." She uses examples of student writing to help teachers see the possibilities.

Diversity is central to helping our students mature into thoughtful, responsive adults and citizens. Barbara G. Samuels summarizes and solidifies our attention to diversity in "Somewhere Over the Rainbow: Celebrating Diverse Voices in Young Adult Literature." Promoting diversity has long been a goal for many schools and many teachers. Samuels reminds us that "literature provides one important resource for all students to learn about themselves and others." Although all the chapters in this book refer to books that represent different cultures, Samuels's chapter brings this issue into focus. She includes selection processes and lists of fine books recently published.

Section II: Exploring Genres

In order for teachers to feel comfortable using YA literature in the classroom, it must be seen in the context of the larger curriculum. How does YA literature encourage greater reading skill development? Better language understanding? Better writing? How does YA literature fit with the standard English literature curriculum, the traditional canon? And finally, how have teachers used YA literature in other subject area classrooms, and with what effect? These are all questions answered in this section.

Historical fiction is an important genre for YA readers. Barbara A. Illig-Avilés discusses how it works as "a bridge between content curriculum and the social/

emotional needs of young adults." Her chapter, "Great Moments in History: Engaging Young Adults Through Historical Fiction," focuses on why historical fiction attracts young adults and how we can use that attraction to engage them in both the personal and the historical issues included in those books. She provides methods of selecting historical fiction, including books that are not specifically written for YA readers, and concludes with several specific teaching suggestions to incorporate historical fiction in the classroom.

Nonfiction is the fastest growing area of publishing for YA readers, just as it is for adults. Barbara Moss discusses nonfiction in "Nonfiction Trade Books for Young Adults: A Complement to the Canon and Content Area Texts." Moss reviews the plethora of nonfiction trade books currently available and compares them to the standard middle school and junior high texts in social studies, science, and other areas. She concludes that students will read trade books more easily and willingly than they will read conventional texts. Moss writes, "Today's nonfiction can enhance adolescents' understanding of an array of topics and may even cultivate interests that last a lifetime. It can deepen students' knowledge of real people, places, and phenomena of the present and the past." Hence, it is in teachers' best interests to include some trade books in their reading materials. How do we select such trade books? How do we teach with them in the classroom? How do we ask students to respond to them? Moss has some interesting suggestions for teachers. She also includes a list of excellent recently published nonfiction.

In "Using Nonfiction Books to Launch a Successful Research Project," Christine Carlson focuses on using YA literature to revitalize the infamous research report. This discussion focuses on teaching the skills of research writing while using interesting and informative nonfiction. Student involvement in selecting a topic, careful planning, and help from the school librarian are the critical elements in the project. As Carlson notes, "Choosing and reading a nonfiction book is the critical piece that has made this project so successful."

Biography is a special and important subset of nonfiction. Teri S. Lesesne focuses on this genre in "Whose Life Is It, Anyway? Biographies in the Classroom." Lesesne reminds us that biographies are as old as history and as new as this year's Nobel Prize winners. Biographies are full of athletes, musicians, and contemporary heroes, as well as people with historical value and everyday folks. According to Lesesne, a biography "extends [students'] opportunities to identify with a diverse group of people." She discusses how students can respond to biographies, such as creating biographies and autobiographies of their own. She includes a list of excellent writers of biographies and good biographies published recently.

Rosemary Chance presents poetry as an important opportunity to allow students to read material about things that interest them. In her chapter "Poetry Pathways for Teens," Chance suggests working with poetry on topics in which most teens are interested, such as love and death. She writes, "In recent years, more poets are writing for teens and selecting poems for a teenage audience. These collections make it easier and more pleasurable for teens to find paths to poetry for their constantly changing lives." She emphasizes contemporary poetry and gives examples of recent poets and poetry, especially those from different cultures. However, she also shows how to connect recent poets with those from the past. Finally, she gives us several examples of good teaching ideas using poetry.

Arlene Harris Mitchell presents poetry in an exciting and inclusive way. In "When I Hear a Poem, I Want to Write," Mitchell includes both traditional and contemporary poets and poetry as she moves her students from studying poetry to writing poetry. She shows YA teachers how to introduce students to selecting poetry, encourage them to read a lot of it, and then to write it.

A new type of book for YA readers, the picture book, has been used for many years with younger readers. In "Picture Books for Older Readers: Passports for Teaching and Learning Across the Curriculum," Carol J. Fuhler outlines the values and joys of picture books for YA readers: They grab you instantly and provide immediate information and response. Fuhler defines picture books as those "where the pictures and text work to present a unified whole, one enriching and blending smoothly with the other resulting in a story that is somehow greater than the sum of its parts." This definition helps us identify good picture books, as Fuhler points out; she also shares how to use these books in many classrooms across the curriculum. The chapter includes references to sources of picture books and a recommended list of recently published picture books.

Section III: Studying Authors

Young adult authors are well aware of the problems and the rewards of writing for YA readers. The authors have much to tell us about the responses they receive from readers and their own sense of how to handle challenges of all kinds. How do authors read changing community tastes? How do they decide the right topics to include? How do they write for YA readers? Is it different from writing for adults? We can learn a lot from listening to authors.

Bringing YA authors into classrooms and studying their works is the topic of Lynne R. Dorfman's chapter, "Empowering Young Adult Readers and Writers Through Author Study." Dorfman helps us understand why focusing on one author may be useful. She describes her use of Patricia Polacco's work as a microcosm of such a study. As Dorfman notes, "Author studies move children closer to our goal of creating lifelong readers and writers. Middle school children need the familiarity and comfort of voices they have come to know and love, and who nudge them into reevaluating their lives in the light of literary experiences."

The final chapter, "Getting the Most Out of an Author's Visit: Multiple Perspectives," brings together several angles on studying authors: the teacher's, the author's, and the publisher's. Joan B. Elliott and Suzanne Mateer, working with author Jerry Spinelli and publisher and author Jan Cheripko, have considered how author visits can influence teachers and students, and how those visits can be developed into maximally effective experiences for everyone. Elliott and Mateer provide essential planning steps so that both students and teachers are well prepared for the author's visit. Spinelli enjoys visiting with students and reminds us that "your favorite author has already communicated with your students in the best way he or she knows how—by writing them a book." He reminds us that students can communicate with authors in other ways such as writing letters. An author who is also a publisher, Cheripko notes how valuable author visits are and gives valuable suggestions about planning these visits. His contributions underscore the reality that advance planning is necessary. A list of websites for making these contacts is included in the Appendix.

Using This Book

Teachers reading this book will reasonably ask, "How can we use YA literature in the classroom?" Our contributors have included suggestions for teaching the literature they discuss in each chapter. In addition, we have asked other experienced teachers how they successfully use YA literature in their classrooms. Their responses, which we have labeled "Teacher Ideas," are included in each chapter and described briefly in the Glossary of Teacher Ideas at the end of the book. Many of these ideas are useful in various areas of YA literature. Be sure to check the Appendix, too, for a list of useful YA literature resources on the Web, including new and exciting teaching ideas. Be creative and use these ideas wherever they work for you!

We hope this book will provide you with new ways of looking at and teaching YA literature. We especially hope you will see some new authors, some new books, and some new teaching ideas that will inspire you to use YA literature in the classroom. Everything that is included here has been used in someone's classroom, but the true test is whether it will work in yours. Happy reading and happy teaching!

Responding to Reading

Response to literature is a hallowed feature in young adult classrooms. Since noted reading educator Louise Rosenblatt focused us on it, teachers have tried to keep young adults intimately involved with reading materials across genres. We encourage students to respond to literature in ways that enrich their lives, advance their skills in reading and writing, and broaden their perspectives.

Chapters in this section focus on responding to reading, from talking to writing. The authors explore new methods of reaching students from differing cultures and explore new ideas for helping all students appreciate many cultures. In addition, the chapters offer fresh ways for us to help students tackle book reviews and critical essays. Teacher-tested ideas are embedded in these chapters to show how real teachers have used teaching techniques such as these.

CHAPTER 1

Reader Response, Process Writing, Young Adult Literature, and the Art of Book Reviewing

Elizabeth A. Poe

After students have read a piece of young adult literature, they are frequently eager to share their thoughts about the book with their peers. Many will enthusiastically talk about the book's content, discuss what they like and dislike about it, and make recommendations about who might like to read that particular work. Initial comments on these topics may be part of a journal entry or class discussion, but students can crystallize, extend, and deepen their responses to a literary work by writing a book review. As a book reviewer for several professional journals, a past book review editor for *The ALAN Review* journal (published by the Assembly on Literature for Adolescents of the National Council of Teachers of English [NCTE]), and the current editor for the *SIGNAL Journal* (published by the Special Interest Group Network on Adolescent Literature of the International Reading Association [IRA]), I have a high regard for the skill involved in writing book reviews, as well as for the value that book review writing holds for students of all ages. Because they are grounded in the reader's personal relationship with the book, book reviews are a valuable form of reader response. They are also an excellent vehicle for practicing summarizing and developing higher level critical thinking such as interpretation and evaluation. And because they demand concise, focused, and interesting writing, book reviews are a superb way to hone writing skills.

As a high school English teacher, I had my students write reviews of short stories from Donald Gallo's *Sixteen: Short Stories by Outstanding Writers for Young Adults* (1982), because the stories are accessible for 10th graders and provide interesting subject matter while fulfilling the curriculum objective that requires students to write a critical review. (Other teachers had students critique movies, musical recordings, or restaurants.) Reviewing young adult short stories proved a pleasant way to meet this objective. I compiled the reviews from all three classes and printed them in a booklet that celebrated not only the diversity of the stories in Gallo's collection, but also the voices and views of my 75 high school sophomores. Ever since this first success, I have introduced the art of writing a book review to middle school, high school, undergraduate, and graduate students whenever possible. (See Chapter 3 for information on reviewing multicultural literature, Chapter 8 on reviewing poetry collections, and Chapter 11 on reviewing works by a writer featured in an author study.)

Over the years, I have coordinated several book review projects that involve students in my college-level young adult literature courses and sixth graders at a nearby middle school. My university students, who are preservice or practicing teachers, prepare for the project by selecting and reviewing a work of young adult literature. They first read the books and write a three-part response that includes a summary, personal connection, and evaluation. Then they read a variety of reviews in professional journals, examine reviews I have written, and discuss a list of guidelines and techniques for writing book reviews that sixth-grade language arts/social studies teacher Nyanne Hicks and I developed for a conference workshop (see Figure 1.1).

Next, they draft their own book reviews, peer edit these drafts (using the format provided in Figure 1.2), and submit their book reviews to a volunteer class editor, who holds individual editing conferences with each student. The students submit their revised reviews to the class editor, who compiles them into a class publication. We share these book review booklets on the last day of the semester as a way to celebrate our work together and inspire continued reading of young adult literature. While my university students write their own book reviews, they also observe and help sixth graders at a local middle school who are learning to write book reviews.

A Successful Collaborative Book Review Project

During the semester that I was putting together a *SIGNAL* issue featuring humor in young adult literature, I wanted to see what books middle schoolers thought were funny. Why not ask them to write reviews of books they found humorous? Nyanne Hicks liked the idea and agreed to collaborate on this undertaking. Her

FIGURE 1.1   *Guidelines and Techniques for Writing Book Reviews*

1. Give complete bibliographic information:
   Title of book
   Author(s) or editor(s)
   Illustrator or photographer if there is one
   Publisher(s) (both hardback and paperback)
   Publication date(s)
   Number of pages
   ISBN(s)

2. Include information about the book:
   Essential information for understanding the nature of the book (genre, topics, setting, etc.)
   A brief summary that includes enough information to make someone want to read the book, but not so much that they do not need to read the book:
       Names and ages of main characters
       Age group for whom the book seems appropriate
       Recommendations for type of reader who might enjoy the book
       An evaluation of the book's primary literary strengths

3. Write in such a way that:
   The opening line grabs the reader's attention
   The review demonstrates good, concise, tight writing
   The reviewer's voice is evident
   The writer shows an awareness of the audience
   Comments are honest, but kindly stated
   The tone reflects the nature of the book
   The review is pleasurable to read

4. Give the reviewer's name, affiliation, and professional status or grade.

Adapted from a conference workshop handout developed by Elizabeth A. Poe and Nyanne Hicks.

50 sixth graders at Blacksburg Middle School in Blacksburg, Virginia, USA, also agreed to participate.

Nyanne began by having her students conduct a humor hunt in the classroom and school library. They came up with quite a few young adult books they thought might qualify, and I supplied a number of titles from my own library. Books by authors such as Paula Danziger, Gordon Korman, Stephen Manes, Louis Sachar, Jon Scieszka and Lane Smith, and Jerry Spinelli were piled on classroom tables. (See the annotated list at the end of this chapter for a selection of books that the students thought were funny.) Students browsed,

FIGURE 1.2   Guidelines for Peer Editing of Book Reviews

In groups of three, read each person's book review and respond to the following questions. (Remember: civility and truth with kindness. To critique does not mean to emphasize the negative.)

What do you think this book is about?

What is the reviewer's attitude toward the book?

Which parts of the review impressed you the most?

Based on this review, do you think you would like to read this book? Explain why or why not.

To whom would you recommend this book?

Which parts of the review were easy to understand?

Which parts of the review could benefit from some revision?

Was the review itself interesting to read?

Did the tone of the review fit the content of the book?

What are some specific words that seemed particularly appropriate for this book?

Do the comments seem to be honest, but kindly stated?

Is all of the biographical information included and accurate?

Did you notice any mechanical errors? Discuss them with the writer.

skimmed, read first chapters, and chatted as they chose the books they wanted to read for the project. Then they settled down to reading the books. As students read their books, they kept response logs, a procedure they were in the habit of doing. They wrote about how the book was affecting them, recorded questions they had about it, discussed their feelings about the characters, and identified notable passages.

When the students finished their books, Nyanne conducted a series of minilessons about various aspects of book reviewing. She began by reading them book reviews from professional sources such as *SIGNAL*, in which reviews are written by educators, and *Voices From the Middle* (published by NCTE), in which reviews are written by middle school students. Following this overview, students met in small groups and mapped words and phrases that aptly described humorous books or situations. Each group had a thesaurus or two to help them find great words. The group shared with the class such words as *hilarious, silly, funny, amusing,* and *delightful.* They came up with phrases such as "side-splitting humor," "drop-dead funny," "slap stick," and "dangerously humorous," and statements like "It was so funny I laughed out loud" and "I laughed until I cried." Nyanne put these on a chart and posted it on the wall for future reference. She also discussed the importance of using socially appropriate words when describing a book's humorous effect on the reader.

In other minilessons, students discussed the importance of leads that grab the reader's attention, experimented with summaries that tell just enough to get the reader interested, reviewed the importance of a strong writing voice, and practiced making recommendations for potential readers. They also learned how to present bibliographic information, reviewed revision strategies, and worked on proofreading skills. After each minilesson, the students met in writing groups to work on that particular aspect of book review writing. My university students and I served as facilitators for these writing groups, adding our experience with writing book reviews and learning from the students about individual reading interests and literacy skills. Each student's book review was read and commented on several times by group members before best drafts were submitted to Nyanne.

Nyanne wrote comments on the students' best drafts and returned them for revision. After they revised their reviews to Nyanne's satisfaction, she graded them. The students then submitted their reviews to Margaret Christle and Jay Dodson, student editors from my class, who edited and formatted them for publication in the class book review booklet.

Examining Multiple Reviews of the Same Book

A quick glance at the annotated list of young adult literature at the end of this chapter shows authors who have the knack for capturing middle school humor. Several of the books received multiple student reviews, indicating they were particularly popular. Multiple reviews also provide the opportunity for students to read different reviewers' perspectives on one book or to compare reviewing styles. The following excerpts from reviews of Paula Danziger's *Remember Me to Harold Square* (1988) submitted by Blacksburg Middle School sixth graders illustrate the individuality of students' responses to the same book.

Kate McQuail begins by asking, "So what do you do when your friends ditch you for the summer, your little brother pesters you, and you are sharing your house with a kid from Wisconsin you never met? Just try to live with it."

Sallie Johnson leads in with "Yuck! that's exactly what teenager Kendra Kaye thinks when she hears the news. She is spending her summer with a boy."

Michele Spraque summarizes the book by writing,

In this hilarious book, Paula Danziger tells about [Kendra,] a 14-year-old girl living in New York. This summer her parents really give her a surprise when they tell her she has to live with a 15-year-old boy for the summer. Then she gets another surprise when she hears that Frank (the older boy) and Oscar (her annoying little brother) get to go on a scavenger hunt in New York City. Now that's a summer.

Michele recommends this book for girls in fifth through seventh grade "if they like to laugh," and concludes her review with, "So as Kendra would say 'be still my heart' because this book will blow you away."

Nathan Mutispaugh comments that "this book has plenty of humor and a little bit of love to touch it up."

Will Gunner identifies the scene when Oscar asks if "the Statue of Liberty put on underarm deodorant" as a humorous part of the book. He thinks "all readers should read this book if they like humor."

Publishing Student Book Reviews in a Professional Journal

For the part of the project that related to the *SIGNAL* issue on humor, I asked Margaret and Jay to select well-written reviews from the stack submitted by 50 Blacksburg Middle School sixth graders and a few Blacksburg Middle School eighth graders. Margaret and Jay selected a cross-section of reviews that conveyed a strong sense of enthusiasm for and enjoyment of a variety of books and authors.

TEACHER IDEA

GRAFFITI

- Provide a "wall" for the students to write on. Brown butcher paper or dark red paper can be used to simulate a brick wall.

- Students should use chalk, paint, markers, or crayons to write events in the story or favorite parts of the story on the wall. Remind your students that each idea can be written only once. They need to come up with many different thoughts and choices.

- Continue this until the entire wall is covered with colorful graffiti.

Suzanne Mateer is a sixth-grade teacher in the Homer-Center School District, Homer City, Pennsylvania, USA.

Although only quasi-research, we believed that this informal sampling of books could serve as a valuable resource for teachers interested in young teenagers' perspectives, so we printed it in the "Research Report (of a Sort)" column of the Fall 1995 issue of *SIGNAL*. Margaret and Jay served as guest editors for the column, which was titled "What Books Do Middle Schoolers Think Are Funny?" The issue was dedicated to humor, so the column's topic fit well. Included here are some of the reviews published in that column.

Beware the Fish!
by Gordon Korman
Scholastic, 1980. 173pp.
ISBN: 0-590-44205-8 (PB)

How can two kids and 40,000 soda cans help save Macdonald Hall from going bankrupt? Bruno and Boots are two teenagers, who go to the boarding school, Macdonald Hall, and want to save it. To get school publicity, they decide to set the world record for the tallest soda can pyramid in the world. The girls in the neighboring school, Miss Scrimmage's Finishing School for Young Ladies, help them collect the cans. But when Bruno and Boots sneak out to the apple orchard to get the girls' cans, Miss Scrimmage catches them red-handed.

I would suggest *Beware the Fish!* to all middle schoolers who like hilarious books.

Bill Rodriquez
6th Grade
Blacksburg Middle School
Blacksburg, Virginia, USA

Boys Against Girls
by Phyllis Reynolds Naylor
Delacorte, 1994. 141pp.
ISBN: 0-385-32081-7 (HB)
      0-440-41123-8 (PB)

Who is the abaguchie? What is the abaguchie? That's what the Hatford brothers want to know. Unfortunately, so do the Malloy sisters. The Hatford brothers and the Malloy sisters are sworn enemies. And once tricks start, it's hard to stop. But that's not the worst part. The worst part is that Caroline Malloy and Wally Hatford are in the same class, and so are Jake and Josh Hatford and Eddie (Edith) Malloy. There is a constant irritation in this class also.

This book does not relate to my life because I have never played tricks on people I don't like. I usually try to ignore them. But in this book, the Hatfords and the Malloys can't ignore each other. That's what makes this book so hilarious. I would recommend this book to anybody who likes funny books. I couldn't stop laughing at all the pranks that were played, or at how Phyllis Reynolds Naylor describes somebody being embarrassed. It's a great book for anybody who wants to read for fun, or just for a good laugh.

Poosa Phaltan
6th Grade
Blacksburg Middle School
Blacksburg, Virginia, USA

Dealing With Dragons

by Patricia C. Wrede
Harcourt Brace Jovanovich, 1990/Scholastic, 1992. 212pp.
ISBN: 0-15-222900-0 (HB)
0-590-45722-5 (PB)

In *Dealing With Dragons*, 16-year-old Cimorene watches her parents wheel and deal her into marrying the wrong prince. Her parents obviously don't know a good prince when they see one. When they try to get Cimorene to marry the geek of the castle, she runs away to a nearby cave of dragons. I highly recommend this humorous fantasy book to all readers 10 years and up. It is the first in Patricia C. Wrede's Enchanted Forest Chronicles.

William Riegert
6th Grade
Blacksburg Middle School
Blacksburg, Virginia, USA

Earth to Matthew

by Paula Danziger
Delacorte, 1991/Dell, 1992. 148pp.
ISBN: 0-385-30453-6 (HB)
0-440-40733-8 (PB)

Matthew Martin is just like any 6th grader. He does no school work, plays practical jokes on people, and tries to survive the G.E.T.H.I.M. Club (Girls Eager to Halt Immature Matthew) which was started by Vanessa Singer, his worst enemy. But Matthew's family is anything but normal. Why do his parents have to be so weird? His mother is a health food freak, and she and Matthew's father dress up in weird costumes (duck costumes, hamster costumes, chauffeur costumes, you name it) and hand out balloons to preschoolers. That's not all.

His sister, Amanda, keeps doing questionable things to her hair. Can Matthew survive 6th grade with such a strange family?

This book is very funny. It cracks me up. Some of the parts I like are when Matthew's class starts a serious discussion and ends it with a lot of bad puns. I would recommend this book to anybody, unless they can't read or they're at the point where they think the 6th grade is boring. I would especially recommend this book to a 6th grader with a taste for humor.

Emily Bracker
6th Grade
Blacksburg Middle School
Blacksburg, Virginia, USA

Math Curse

by Jon Scieszka; illustrated by Lane Smith
Viking, 1995. 32pp. (But you have to count them yourself.)
ISBN: 0-670-86194-4 (HB)

Math Curse is about a girl who acquires a "math curse" so that everything she hears or thinks about becomes a math problem. I thought it was funny because the kid in the story gets things mixed up a lot when she is trying to figure out these math problems. She comes up with questions like "How many yards in a neighborhood?" and "How many M&M's would you eat if you had to measure the Mississippi in M&M's?" She also devises multiple choice answers to her questions which are sometimes even more confusing than the math problems themselves. By the end of the story, she almost stops doing things in fear of them becoming a math problem. I got a real kick out of the clever math humor, but even people who do not like math will laugh when they read this book.

I also like Lane Smith's construction-paper-collage-type pictures because they add to the confusion and chaos of the book. This book is one of my all-time favorites because it is an intersection of math, art, and humor—three things I thoroughly enjoy.

Trevor Oakes
8th Grade
Blacksburg Middle School
Blacksburg, Virginia, USA

Misery Guts

by Morris Gleitzman
Pan Macmillan Publishers, Australia, 1991/
Harcourt Brace Jovanovich, 1993. 122pp.
ISBN: 0-15-254768-1 (HB)

Do you have sad parents? Well, 11-year-old Keith Shipley does. His parents are what he calls "misery guts" because they always look and act so sad. He will do anything to cheer them up. He has all kind of silly ideas, but they almost never work. That's what I like about Keith. He is funny and almost seems stupid at times. Keith tries everything. He paints his father's fish and chips shop "tropical mango" orange. He hopes his parents will come back from the errands they are running and be surprised and happy and start smiling. Only half of Keith's wish comes true. His parents are very surprised, but they are also furious.

If you would like to know more about this book, you'll have to read it for yourself. As for me, I thought it was very funny. Keith did some pretty dumb things, but I don't blame him. I would recommend this book for anyone who likes realistic humor.

Melissa Christman
6th Grade
Blacksburg Middle School
Blacksburg, Virginia, USA

The Stinky Cheese Man and Other Fairly Stupid Tales
by Jon Scieszka; illustrated by Lane Smith
Viking, 1992. 56 action packed pages.
ISBN: 0-670-84487-X (HB)

The Stinky Cheese Man and Other Fairly Stupid Tales is a collection of well-known fairy tales revised and disguised by Jon Scieszka. The collection includes stories such as "Little Red Running Shorts" and "The Princess and the Bowling Ball," which are all put together in the book by the narrator, Jack, who is working day and night to make sure the table of contents is in the right place, the dedication page is right side up, and trying to keep the wolf and Little Red Running Shorts from walking off the set. In this Caldecott Honor picture book, Lane Smith uses oil and vinegar to paint intricately bizarre and humorously intriguing illustrations which completely capture the comical effect created by Jon Scieszka's vivid imagination.

I found this book mildly amusing—okay, even hilarious—but mostly I thought it was fairly stupid. ☺

Ryan Oakes
8th Grade
Blacksburg Middle School
Blacksburg, Virginia, USA

A TO Z BOOK ACTIVITIES

A   Write and perform an *advertisement*. Write an *advice* column.

B   Create a *book jacket* or a *bumper sticker*.

C   Make a *collage* of events in the story using magazine photos. Design a *cartoon* or *comic strip*. Write a *cinquain*.

D   Make a *diorama* of an event from the story. Write a *diamante*.

E   Write a new *ending* to the story. Write an *editorial*.

F   *Finish* the story by rewriting the chapter in a different way.

G   Make a *game board* that follows the plot of the story. Design a *greeting card*.

H   Make a *handmade* filmstrip of a book. Write a *headline*.

I   *Interview* a character from the story.

J   Write *journal* entries from a character's point of view.

K   *Keep* a reading response log.

L   Write a *letter* to a character in the story or to the editor.

M   Create an aerial *map* of the setting. Construct a *mural*.

N   Write a *newspaper* article.

O   Design an *overhead* transparency. Give an *oral report*.

P   *Plot* the events of the story on a timeline. Design a *poster* or a *pop-up* book.

Q   Develop a *quiz* about the book.

R   Write a *review* of the book. Create *riddles* about the characters.

S   Write a *skit* based on a chapter or scene from the book. Have some peers act it out with you for the class. Create a *slogan* to advertise the book.

T   Design a *T-shirt* or *television commercial* promoting the book. Create a *travel brochure*.

U   *Use* the computer to type your opinion of the book.

V   Complete a *Venn diagram* comparing two characters from the story.

W   Create a *word find* puzzle including characters, setting, and other important words from the story. Make a *want ad*.

X   Take an *X-ray* of a main character. Describe the character's personality and physical traits, part in the story, and likes and dislikes.

Y   *You* become a prosecuting attorney. Place one of the main characters on trial for a crime or incident related to the book. Present your case to the class.

Z   *Zoom* ahead. Write an epilogue explaining what characters are doing in 10, 15, or 20 years from the ending of the story.

Joan B. Elliott is a professor at Indiana University of Pennsylvania, Indiana, Pennsylvania, USA. Suzanne Mateer is a sixth-grade teacher in the Homer-Center School District, Homer City, Pennsylvania, USA.

TEACHER IDEA

Celebrating the Publication of Book Reviews

On the day before Christmas vacation, there was a celebration at Blacksburg Middle School. The students in Nyanne's language arts/social studies classes were celebrating the publication of their book reviews. All of the reviews had been printed in their class publication, making every voice heard, every response appreciated. A few had also been published in *SIGNAL*, and the whole team recognized this accomplishment with pride. Each student received a copy of both publications as well as a copy of the booklet of book reviews by the university students with whom they had worked during the book review project. Each student left with numerous suggestions for other young adult books to read and enjoy.

Although this was not the first or last time I did a book review project with Nyanne's classes, it was the only time we had the opportunity to publish student reviews in a professional publication. But of course there are many other ways to publish student book reviews. Classroom, school, or community newspapers, along with student-produced booklets, provide excellent means for book review publication. Student reviews can also be read over the loudspeaker during announcement time, they can be posted around the classroom and library, and they can be included in school newsletters to parents. Amazon.com also provides a book review forum. However it is done, it is important to make book reviews public.

Thoughts About Book Reviews

Each time students write book reviews, I am reminded of the value this form of response holds for readers. Because each review is different, even from readers who chose the same book, the value of individual responses to literary works is emphasized. Writing a review demands that readers deepen and sharpen their initial responses in order to articulate their experiences with a book. Writing a review also forces readers to think beyond themselves and consider the effect the book will have on other readers. In addition, writing a review requires tight, interesting writing with particular attention to tone and diction. Because reviewers do not find revision of book reviews to be a daunting task, they are more willing to rework a short piece of writing until it is worthy of publication. Thus book reviews provide excellent opportunities for integrating process writing with reader response. Young adult literature is particularly suited for this type of written response because it is accessible, interesting, and enjoyable for teenage readers—it

DESCRIPTIVE POEM

Think about the story you have read recently. Create a simple five-line poem about an event from the story following this format:

One word about the main character

Two words describing the setting

Three words telling the problem

Four words explaining the event

Five words telling the solution

Tracey Beard is a sixth-grade teacher in the Indiana Area School District, Indiana, Pennsylvania, USA.

can even make them laugh. Book reviews, young adult fiction, and humor—I highly recommend all three!

AUTHOR NOTE

Thanks to Rebekah Moore Smith, graduate student in English education at West Virginia University, for supplying book annotations, and to the Blacksburg Middle School students and their teacher, Nyanne Hicks, who helped make this book reviewing project a success.

YOUNG ADULT LITERATURE CITED

Danziger, P. (1991). *Earth to Matthew.* New York: Delacorte.

Danziger, P. (1988). *Remember me to Harold Square.* New York: Dell.

Gallo, D. (Ed.). (1982). *Sixteen: Short stories by outstanding writers for young adults.* New York: Delacorte.

Gleitzman, M. (1993). *Misery guts.* Orlando, FL: Harcourt Brace Jovanovich.

Korman, G. (1980). *Beware the fish!* New York: Scholastic.

Naylor, P.R. (1994). *Boys against girls.* New York: Delacorte.

Scieszka, J. (1992). *The stinky cheese man and other fairly stupid tales.* Ill. L. Smith. New York: Viking.

Scieszka, J. (1995). *Math curse.* Ill. L. Smith. New York: Viking.

Wrede, P.C. (1992). *Dealing with dragons.* New York: Scholastic.

ANNOTATED LIST OF BOOKS CONSIDERED
FUNNY BY MIDDLE SCHOOL REVIEWERS

Coville, B. (1991). *My teacher glows in the dark*. New York: Turtleback.

Peter Thompson discovers his alien teacher's plans for Earth after following him onto his spaceship. Peter heads for a destination beyond his wildest dreams where only he, Susan, and Duncan can stop the aliens from taking over Earth.

Danziger, P. (1982). *The divorce express*. New York: Delacorte.

After Phoebe's parents divorce, she is forced to ride the Divorce Express. While spending time with her dad in the country, she must deal with separation from her boyfriend, with a new school, and with watching her father date. Just as Phoebe is adjusting to everything, her mother makes a decision that will bring more changes into Phoebe's life.

Danziger, P. (1985). *It's an aardvark-eat-turtle world*. New York: Delacorte.

Because Rosie and Phoebe are best friends, everything seems perfect when Rosie's mom falls in love with Phoebe's dad and decides to move in with him. The girls soon discover that being friends and being sisters are very different and will require much more work than they originally thought.

Danziger, P. (1988). *Remember me to Harold Square*. New York: Dell.

At first the summer-long scavenger hunt around New York City seems likely to be disastrous. Kendra soon discovers that it is packed with adventure and that Frank, a virtual stranger who is now staying with her family, turns out to be as interesting as their adventure.

Danziger, P. (1989). *Everyone else's parents said yes*. New York: Dell.

Sixth-grader Matthew Martin has a knack for getting into trouble with his family, teachers, and several female classmates. He looks forward to his 11th birthday sleepover, believing that things will improve.

Danziger, P. (1990). *Make like a tree and leave*. New York: Delacorte.

Matthew Martin and his friends cover one of their classmates in bandages for a class Egyptian unit project. When they try to remove the cast, they discover that things have not gone as planned.

Danziger, P. (1991). *Earth to Matthew*. New York: Delacorte.

Matthew's life becomes even more complicated when he discovers his crush on Jill. As the book draws to a close, Matthew cannot wait to see where Spaceship Earth takes him next.

Danziger, P. (1992). *Not for a billion gazillion dollars*. New York: Delacorte.

Matthew Martin and his friends open their own business in what seems to be a surefire way to make some quick cash.

Erikson, J. (2000). *The original adventure of Hank the Cowdog*. New York: Nairi.

As the "Head of Ranch Security," Hank uses his sleuthing skills to investigate a suspicious death on his ranch—only to discover that he is the top suspect.

Gleitzman, M. (1993). *Misery guts*. New York: Harcourt Brace Jovanovich.

Keith realizes that his parents are downtrodden from their economic problems at the shop that they own. He decides that a move to Australia is just what they need. After an initial rejection of the plan, his family is forced to move there after their shop burns down. In Australia, they find that the tropical location does indeed lift their spirits.

Gleitzman, M. (1993). *Worry warts.* New York: Harcourt.

In another attempt to solve his parents' problems, Keith paints their car bright green and yellow. After several well-intentioned attempts with disastrous outcomes (such as opal mining), Keith realizes that his parents should separate.

Haynes, B. (1986). *The great mom swap.* New York: Bantam.

Swapping mothers seems like a great solution to best friends and next-door neighbors Lorna and Scotti. They enact their plan only to discover that their perfect solution may have been a big mistake.

Konigsburg, E. (1971). *About the B'Nai bagels.* New York: Atheneum.

Mark Seltzer believes that his life is complex enough without his mother becoming the new manager for his Little League baseball team. He soon discovers that the team is improving due to "Mother Bagel's" helpful hints.

Korman, G. (1978). *This can't be happening at Macdonald Hall.* New York: Scholastic.

The prank-loving Bruno and Boots team has been split up by Macdonald Hall's headmaster. Now they must plot to get back together as roommates.

Korman, G. (1980). *Beware the fish!* New York: Scholastic.

Bruno and Boots attempt to earn money to save Macdonald Hall from bankruptcy by building the tallest soda can pyramid in the world.

Korman, G. (1984). *No coins, please.* New York: Scholastic.

Artie Galter is a genius at making money, but his money-making schemes get him in trouble all over the United States.

Korman, G. (1985). *Don't Care High.* New York: Scholastic.

Tenth-grade student Paul Abrams transfers to Manhattan's Don Carey High School only to discover a lethargic school that has renamed itself Don't Care High. Paul and his new friend Sheldon concoct an ingenious and humorous plan to reawaken the school's spirit.

Korman, G. (1987). *A semester in the life of a garbage bag.* New York: Scholastic.

Sean's junior year has not turned out as he expected it to. Believing himself the unluckiest guy around, he tries to win a trip to the luck-bringing Greek island of Theamelpos.

Korman, G. (1990). *Losing Joe's place.* New York: Scholastic.

Joe's older brother is letting Joe and his two friends stay at his place for the summer. Everything is perfect, except for Mr. Plotnick, the landlord. When the boys try to play a hoax on Plotnick, it backfires and they find themselves in danger of losing Joe's apartment.

Korman, G. (1991). *Go jump in the pool!* New York: Scholastic.

Tired of being beaten in swim meets by their York Academy rivals, Bruno and Boots try to raise money for a swimming pool at Macdonald Hall. They hold a yard sale, enter sweepstakes, have craft sales, and hold a funny photo contest.

Korman, G. (1992). *The Twinkie squad.* New York: Scholastic.

Douglas Fairchild had big plans for the special discussion group, or the "Twinkie Squad," as the other kids call them. Before he is through, he is going to turn the school upside down, thanks to some help from his special friends.

Korman, G. (1993). *The toilet paper tigers.* New York: Scholastic.

Corey Johnson thinks his baseball team cannot get any worse—after all, they are sponsored by Feather-Soft bathroom tissue. Then Kristy, the coach's loudmouthed, opinionated granddaughter comes to town to help coach the team, and Corey realizes he was wrong.

Korman, G. (1994). *Why did the underwear cross the road.* New York: Scholastic.

Fourth-grader Justin Zeckendorf is determined to win his class's good Samaritan contest. However, his seemingly foolproof ideas always backfire, leaving his team in a mess of trouble.

Korman, G. (1995). *Something fishy at Macdonald Hall.* New York: Scholastic.

Boots and Bruno are suspected of setting the school upside down with a series of practical jokes. In order to save themselves from expulsion, they must unmask the mystery menace—and fast!

Manes, S. (1990). *Chocolate-covered ants.* New York: Scholastic.

When Max's little brother, Adam, gets an ant colony for his birthday, he becomes overly annoying with his newfound knowledge on ants. Max finds himself in the middle of a bet to find someone else to eat the chocolate-covered ants he has no intention of eating.

Manes, S. (1990). *Comedy High.* New York: Scholastic.

Ivan Carmody is less than pleased when he and his father move to Carmody, Nevada. Ivan finds comfort in fellow students who agree that the town is nothing more than tacky.

Manes, S. (1991). *Make four million dollars by next Thursday.* New York: Bantam.

Jason Nozzle follows the misguided advice of a get-rich-quick book and tries to get himself adopted by the richest family in town.

Naylor, P.R. (1993). *The boys start the war.* New York: Delacorte.

The first book in this series begins as the Hatford brothers begin a war with their new neighbors the Malloy sisters. Although the boys start the war, the sisters are quick to catch on and come up with their own tricks of retaliation.

Naylor, P.R. (1993). *The girls get even.* New York: Delacorte.

Picking up where the rivalry left off in *The Boys Start the War*, the seven neighbor children agree that the winner of the Halloween contest will be entitled to a month of "slavery" from the losing side. All of the children are disqualified after a series of tricks designed to sabotage the other team.

Naylor, P.R. (1994). *Boys against girls.* New York: Delacorte.

This third book in the series of the war between the Malloy sisters and the Hatford brothers revolves around tall tales of a monster in the woods. Through alternating view points, Naylor provides both comedy and suspense.

Pinkwater, J. (1994). *Mister Fred.* New York: Dutton.

After their teacher leaves, the students of My Dear Watson Elementary School are able to successfully scare off 5 weeks' worth of substitute teachers. When Mister Fred comes along and issues a challenge to discover if he is from outer space, the children cannot resist.

Robinson, B. (1972). *The best school year ever.* New York: HarperCollins.

> Beth can think of a lot of names to describe Imogene Herdman, but none are suited for the "Compliments for Classmates" project. Beth is able to eventually enlist Imogene's strengths despite her initial reluctance.

Robinson, B. (1982). *The best Christmas pageant ever.* New York: HarperCollins.

> The church's annual Christmas pageant turns into an amazing miracle when the five Herdmans play the unlikely parts of Wisemen.

Sachar, L. (1989). *The boy who lost his face.* New York: Knopf.

> Trying to understand why his popularity has taken a sudden turn for the worse, David blames the misfortune on an elderly woman whom he and his schoolmates have attacked.

Sachar, L. (1991). *Dogs don't tell jokes.* New York: Knopf.

> Gary tells jokes in order to adjust to problems in his life. He is determined to win the $100 prize in the school's talent contest with his stand-up routine.

Sachar, L. (1995). *Wayside School gets a little stranger.* New York: Knopf.

> When Mrs. Jewels, the fifth-grade teacher, leaves school to have her baby, a string of substitute teachers—each one a little stranger than the one before—try to take her place.

Scieszka, J. (1992). *The stinky cheese man and other fairly stupid tales.* New York: Viking.

> This book turns traditional fairy tales upside down. Both its stories and pictures are unconventional in every way. With characters such as Finger Lickin' Chicken and the Ugly Duckling who grew up to be an ugly duck, this book is sure to entertain.

Scieszka, J. (1995). *Math curse.* New York: Viking.

> A girl wakes up one morning to find everything in life arranging itself into a math problem. Oh, what a day!

Soto, G. (1994). *Crazy weekend.* New York: Scholastic.

> Seventh-graders Hector and Mando spend a weekend with Hector's uncle in Fresno, California. Things get exciting when Hector's uncle accidentally photographs a robbery, and the boys are quoted in the local newspaper.

Spinelli, J. (1984). *Who put that hair in my toothbrush.* New York: Turtleback.

> The sibling rivalry between 12-year-old Megan (Megamouth) and her older brother Greg (El Grosso) intensifies after she ruins his science project and he retaliates by throwing her favorite hockey stick into the pond. Their parents try to keep the peace, but this is a difficult pair to control.

Spinelli, J. (1988). *Jason and Marceline.* New York: Bantam.

> Ninth-grader Jason is surprised when Marceline rejects him in this funny sequel to the popular *Space Station Seventh Grade.*

Spinelli, J. (1992). *Do the funky pickle.* New York: Turtleback.

> Trying to win Sunny's heart, Eddie performs his new dance, the Funky Pickle. To his surprise, he instead attracts the attention of Angelpuss, a classmate with orange spiked hair and a nose ring.

Teague, S. (1987). *The king of hearts' heart.* New York: Little, Brown.

> Comical and serious at the same time, this is a book about the relationship between Harold and his mentally challenged friend, Billy.

Wrede, P.C. (1992). *Dealing with dragons.* New York: Scholastic.

   Cimorene, princess of Linderwall, is constantly criticized for being a tomboy. When she finds a nest of dragons, she decides that she would rather keep house for them than be bored in her parents' castle.

Zindel, P. (1983). *The Pigman.* New York: Bantam.

   Sophomores John and Lorraine begin playing pranks on strangers and unsuspectingly meet a new friend. They soon find themselves caught up in the world of Mr. Pignati—the Pigman.

CHAPTER 2

Thinking About Books on Paper

Laura Robb

> How can I know what I think till I see what I say?
> —E.M. Forster

Every writer, student or professional, can relate to E.M. Forster's quote because it pinpoints the revelation writers experience upon discovering what they know and think. However, I would amend the quote to read, "How can I know what I think till I *hear* and see what I say?" Hearing involves listening to an inner dialogue as well as listening to others talk. Seeing asks the writer to read what has been composed. When talk precedes writing, it can clarify thinking and enable students to write in order to discover what they think and understand.

Katherine Paterson (1981), in an essay on "Reading and Writing" from *Gates of Excellence: On Reading and Writing Books for Children*, expands Forster's quote by adding emotions and sensory reactions to reading and writing:

> Now the gift of creative reading, like all natural gifts, must be nourished or it
> will atrophy. And you nourish it in much the same way you nourish the gift of
> writing—you read, think, talk, look, listen, hate, fear, love, weep—and bring all
> of your life like a sieve to what you read. (pp. 26–27)

The first conversation about a book is the inner dialogue between writer and reader. In a classroom, responses that emerge from first readings are highly personal because each student brings unique experiences and knowledge to a text. According to Louise Rosenblatt (1983), the teacher's job is "to help the student realize that the most important thing is what literature means to him and does for him" (p. 67). By honoring students' personal responses, we encourage them to make emotional connections to literature. Such connections bond students to books and set them firmly on the road to making sense of the author's words.

Sometimes, personal connections are so bound to students' lives and experiences that they create their own text—one that embellishes the author's words. Early personal reactions are real for readers, even though they might not be part of the author's story. Lois Lowry calls this process "the paired creation of fiction"; writing about her love of *Mary Poppins*, Lowry observes,

> [Mary Poppins] lived there in my heart and imagination and in my own fictional world, half written by P.L. Travers and the other half a private book that was only mine, a gift from P.L. Travers to the child that was me. (cited in Robb, 1994, p. 62)

You can extend these personal connections to story by inviting readers to talk about books with a partner or in groups of three to six. A lively exchange of ideas will move students deeper and deeper into the meaning of a story, often enabling them to step beyond the limitations of their own thinking. Interactive talk clarifies understandings because it involves listening to alternate points of view and perspectives and offers readers opportunities to reevaluate information, raise questions, and identify parts that confuse them or seem hazy.

I called this chapter "Thinking About Books on Paper"; however, the ability to think critically about books on paper must be preceded by talk. Exploring ideas through conversations is a form of reflection that takes readers beyond personal connections with the text into an exploration of the layers of meaning in the text. "Reflection on the literary experience," Rosenblatt writes, "becomes a reexperiencing, a reenacting, of the work-as-evoked, and an ordering and elaborating of our responses to it" (1978, p. 134). By reflecting, readers rethink, sort, clarify, revise, reconsider, confirm, or adjust early responses to written and oral texts, then use what they have learned to organize an essay or critical paragraph.

Moving Students Toward Valid Interpretations

Teachers can help students move toward valid interpretations of texts, positions supported with facts and inferences from the story. This section highlights the recursive model I use in my eighth-grade reading-writing workshop. This model acknowledges the evolutionary process of reading, reacting to, discussing, and critically thinking about texts; writing; and rereading. As readers make meaning with a text, they revisit one or more parts of the model in order to construct an accurate interpretation.

Read and Reread

How students read books at school is equally as important as *what* they read. Chapter-by-chapter reading, followed by end-of-chapter questions, is frustrating and unnatural. It prevents readers from getting involved with a story and feeling that they cannot put the book down. Think of the way you read. If you are into a good book, you do not stop after each chapter to write a notebook response and answer questions. You want to read on. You want to share those "great parts" with a friend. You resent putting the book aside and try to carve out time to finish it.

To simulate natural reading as closely as possible, I work with my students to negotiate a reasonable due date for the entire book and ask them to decide on pause points. A pause point is a place to stop, react, pose questions, and discuss—usually every three to five chapters. This system works whether all students in the class read the same book or whether the class is divided into groups, each reading a different title.

Reading ahead is fine. If a book captures a student's imagination, then completing it is a necessity, and I encourage the student to finish. However, I ask students to refresh their memories by rereading sections before discussions. Rereading is another way students construct a rich array of connections to books, to self, to other books, to peer groups, to others' lives, to story structure, to movies and television, and to an author's style. All of these connections deepen and enrich the comprehension of a book.

DINNER AND CONVERSATION

Imagine that you are inviting a character from a book to your house for dinner. Construct a short paper that would include the guest list, a menu, and interesting questions that you would use for discussion at dinner. On the second page, write the thinking behind your choices. Be sure to include specific connections to the trade book.

Suzanne Mateer is a sixth-grade teacher in the Homer-Center School District, Homer City, Pennsylvania, USA.

Book Discussions

Students discuss their books at pause points, using questions they have raised and connections they have made. When they have completed a book, discussions continue for a few days or weeks, depending on the amount of time reserved and students' interest in pursuing the book's issues and themes.

Literature Notebooks

Using notebooks to respond to a book while reading is an effective way for students to explore the text's meanings. Most of my students use their notebooks to investigate intriguing words or phrases, note and react to a part that stirred them deeply, pose questions, or summarize a discussion.

Students explore ideas in notebooks after pause-point discussions and after completing the entire book. They revisit their entries to collect notes for critical paragraphs or to develop a position for an essay. I read some entries to evaluate discussions and to reflect on students' progress with thinking on paper.

The Critical Paragraph and Essay

Organizing thinking on paper is a challenge that students in grades 6–9 can meet. Students reread their notebooks to discover meaning and mine topics for paragraphs and essays. Through minilessons, I teach them how to develop a thesis or position, then compose an introduction, supporting paragraphs, and a conclusion.

Making Conversation Meaningful and Productive

"My students' discussions are never what I hope for," a seventh-grade teacher told me. "My students can't keep a book discussion going for more than 5 minutes. In my class, book discussions deteriorate into talk about the soccer game or meeting at the local mall."

Holding meaningful book discussions is not an innate ability; it is an art that requires posing open-ended questions and learning prompts that maintain the momentum of a discussion (Harste, Short, & Burke, 1988; Robb, 1994, 2000). I pause after daily read-alouds to model factual and open-ended questions, and I ask students to notice how the two types differ. One sixth grader observes, "Some questions only have one answer. But other questions, I want to talk to my group about."

"Why do you want to discuss some questions more than others?" I probe. If the students can express the difference, the questions they pose for discussion will improve.

"Usually, they can't be answered just by reading on," the student explains. "You got to think more. It's like this question I had about 'LaBamba' [Soto, 1990]: Why was Manuel relieved that the day was over? There's lots of answers, and I'm not sure which ones I believe."

"Some questions," I tell the class, "can be explained with a variety of events from the story. They're great to discuss because they generate a range of possible responses. These questions make you infer reasons from the events and dialogue, and that's what makes the reading exciting and meaningful."

I also want students to practice open-ended ways to discuss books so that a conversation can take place whether everyone is reading the same book or different texts. To model the process, I think aloud and demonstrate how I analyze a character's decisions or motivation, make personal connections to a conflict or an event, or discuss the genre's characteristics. Then I gather students' feedback and respond to their questions, recording notes on chart paper that I hang on a bulletin board or a wall. The charts are an important resource for students, who often refer to them prior to and during partner or group discussions. For example, here is a list of suggested discussion topics I generated with several groups of students.

- *Personal Connections.* What memories did a part of the story inspire you to reclaim as you read? Is there a character who had similar experiences to yours?

- *Other Books.* Show how the plot, characters, themes, and settings are similar to other books you have read.

- *Other Characters.* Explain how characters in your book are alike, different. Extend to other books.

- *Story Structure.* Does the author use flashbacks and/or foreshadowing? Is the text narrative or expository? What is the genre? Does dialogue dominate and drive the plot? Does the author use dialogue to show character, move the plot along, give background?

- *Author's Style.* How is the book like others by the same author? Are there similarities in structure, kinds of characters, settings, themes?

- *Questions the Book Raised.* What questions do you have about characters' decisions, motivations? Are there parts you found confusing?

- *Character's Personality.* What have you learned about this character? How and why has the character changed from the beginning to the end?
- *Link the Title.* Connect the title to one of the key themes, a character's actions, the settings, or a specific event. Explain how the title deepens your understanding of the point the author makes.

Before groups of students discuss their books, I also post on chart paper the prompts we have used during whole-group discussions to keep the dialogue going. The chart usually contains four questions that students can ask themselves and each other:

1. Can you find information in the book to support your idea?
2. Does anyone have another idea?
3. Is there additional support for this point?
4. Are there any questions about this issue?

During discussions, I circulate and listen to snippets of talk. I carry sticky notes and a pencil, jotting down some of the students' discussion strategies. Later I will review my notes to see what has worked well.

In one instance, after reading *To Kill A Mockingbird* by Harper Lee (1960), a group of eighth graders meet to discuss the book. The four students return to a question they have wrestled with at different pause points: Why did Atticus take on Tom Robinson's case? In the transcription that follows, note how the students help one another return to the book as well as search for diverse interpretations:

First, Kate summarizes all of the reasons the group has uncovered. She begins, "Atticus has strong values and he wants his kids to have them; he needs to *show* them [Jem and Scout] the right way to act by acting that way himself; he believes Tom is innocent and deserves a defense; he's independent and doesn't give a hoot about what his family or other people in town think; he couldn't live with himself and hold his head high if he didn't defend Tom."

"There's more," says Ryan, listening carefully to Kate. "There's got to be a reason bigger than Atticus and his values. Maybe we'll get some ideas if we reread our notes and skim that chapter again."

After the students skim through the chapter, Chris picks up the discussion: "Look here, page 153. I can't believe we didn't get it. You know how Atticus guards Tom Robinson and won't let the gang of men get to him?"

"Yeah, we said the men would have to kill Atticus to get to Tom," says Ryan.

"Isn't that the point—that Atticus stands up for what he believes in. Does anyone see it another way?" asks Chris.

"Maybe," Kate says, "maybe he was guarding more than Tom. Maybe, he was guarding the law."

"He is a lawyer and that's his job," pipes Ryan.

"I know," answers Kate. "I mean so that the law isn't broken."

"It's even more than that," says Chris. "It's like if Atticus lets the men take and punish Tom, then he's allowing men to make the laws and change them whenever they want to. In our country, men don't change laws whenever they want to."

"That's it!" Kate says. "Atticus knows that if he doesn't follow the laws that we have and if he lets men break them [the laws], then we will have chaos."

At this point, I join in. "Great job of supporting one another to discover a major theme in this book," I tell them. "I want you to share your thinking with the class—and explain what linked you to this idea."

Writing to Explore Ideas

When students record in notebooks the oral texts they compose after book discussions, they construct a permanent place to reflect on, test, and revise ideas. The notebooks become a thoughtful record of students' thinking journeys.

I view notebook entries as first-draft writing in which students explore new and shaky territory in order to construct meanings and make additional connections. That is why I do not grade notebooks for content or punctuation; I grade for organization and progress in transferring ideas from thoughts to paper. Many students, like eighth grader Ryan, for instance, write little in their notebooks at first. Near the end of October, I pull up a chair next to Ryan's desk to talk about his notebook.

Before we begin our conference, I ask Ryan to leaf through his notebook. "Tell me about your fast-writes," I say. Fast-write is a strategy students have been using after discussions for the past 2 weeks to summarize and explore discussion topics before partner or group book discussions. In 5 to 7 minutes, students write everything they recall and any new ideas that form in their minds. The pen never stops, even if it means repeating a word or phrase until ideas flow again. The strategy focuses students on the task of reclaiming memories and making connections.

"I don't say much," Ryan tells me. "Mostly I wrote the same word again and again." Grinning, he adds, "I'm getting better." He points to a half-page October entry. And I nod and smile, indicating my pleasure in Ryan's progress.

"I notice you talk about the book with your group," I say. "When I've listened to your group's discussions, you have so much to say. Can you tell me why you don't write your ideas?" I struggle not to fill in the silence that follows. Intellectually, I recognize that Ryan needs time to organize his thoughts. The 2 minutes, though, seem like an eternity.

Finally, Ryan responds. "I don't like to write. It's got lots of mistakes. The talking is easy. When I write, nothing sounds good enough. So I don't write much." Many students, like Ryan, censor their ideas while writing. Students' feelings that their hunches about a book are unworthy are common. I invite Ryan to read Meredith's notebook entry (see Figure 2.1), hoping he will feel relieved when he notices how unpolished most fast-writes are.

FIGURE 2.1   *Meredith's Notebook Entry*

Meredith   March 2
        Miss Caroline Fisher

Miss Caroline Fisher. First grade teacher -- not from Maycomb. Newcomer. First time in Maycomb. Brings a new type of learning. She doesn't know of families and town's ways. Just out of college -- 21-23. No life experience. Has no understanding of how they live. She doesn't even let the kids explain. Scared of their knowing more that she did? Stubborn, control, self-centered, single-minded, insecure. Victim of the town's traditions and her own ignorance.

Another way to spotlight notebook entries is to reserve time for students to read sections of their notebooks to the entire class. However, I never force a student to share. Observing how others use their notebooks opens diverse possibilities for students who struggle with getting ideas on paper. Once the mystery of what to explore in notebooks has been dispelled, students begin to write their ideas more freely.

I ask students to head each entry with a name, the date, and a title such as a topic or the name of a book, poem, story, or article. This helps students locate material quickly when they want to return to or enlarge an entry.

Once or twice a month, I look through students' notebooks to check organization and progress with writing ideas. Students choose a page for me to read, and I randomly select one to read. On a sticky note, I write comments that address organization and the quality of the entries. I always start with positive comments, then select one or two areas that need work; these comments I phrase as questions that I hope will provoke students to think about revision possibilities. Figure 2.2 shows two of my responses to students' notebook entries.

FIGURE 2.2 Responses to Student Notebook Entries

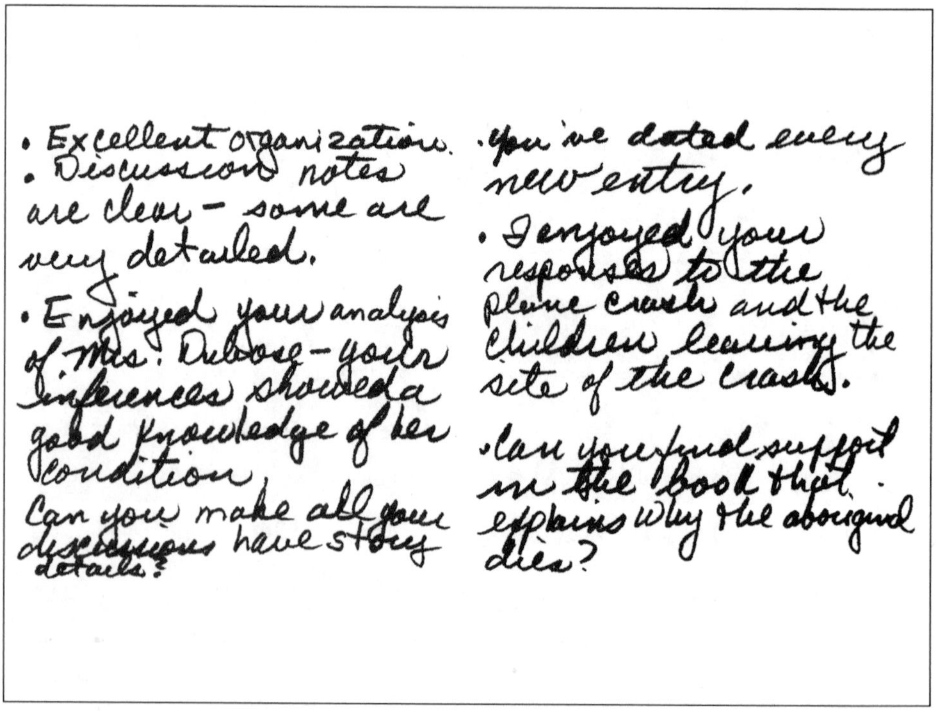
• Excellent organization.
• Discussion notes are clear - some are very detailed.
• Enjoyed your analysis of Mrs. Dubose - your inferences showed a good knowledge of her condition.
Can you make all your discussions have story details?

• You've dated every new entry.
• I enjoyed your responses to the plane crash and the children leaving the site of the crash.
• Can you find support in the book that explains why the aborigine dies?

MOVIES, HERE WE COME!

The book you just read became an instant bestseller. Now it is your job to sell it to a movie producer.

- Write a letter to persuade a movie producer to make this book into a film.
- Explain why this story would make a good movie by telling about the plot, characters, and setting in your letter.
- Suggest what actors should play the roles and where the filming would take place.

Who knows? Maybe you will be a star in the upcoming film!

Suzanne Mateer is a sixth-grade teacher in the Homer-Center School District, Homer City, Pennsylvania, USA.

Model by Thinking Aloud

Minilessons are ideal for modeling strategies for exploring ideas on paper. Start by thinking aloud and telling students how you organize your thoughts. Use large chart paper to show them how to set up a notebook page. Let them observe you writing so they can see you cross out and add ideas. Be sure to set aside time for students to comment on and question your process. This free outpouring of ideas is top-notch for gathering the specifics of a discussion. A list can include words that describe a character's personality, the problems the character encountered, the character's decisions and motivation, or a cause statement and a list of effects, themes, and outcomes.

After we read James Marshall's *Walkabout* (1959), for instance, I meet with sixth graders to model how I can use a list to summarize our discussion of Peter's and Mary's survival skills. When I am done, I ask students what they have noticed about my process. Some of their observations are as follows:

- Your ideas were not in any order.
- You didn't write down everything—but you had lots.
- You took time to think first.
- You stopped after the first five or six to think.
- After you read your list out loud, you added two ideas and crossed one out.

Often, students create two to three lists for a book, each grouped under a different heading. Chris's list of Atticus's personality traits offers a range of ideas that can be discussed with a partner or group and developed into an essay (see Figure 2.3).

FIGURE 2.3   Chris's List of Atticus's Personality Traits

Christopher   Atticus   May 22, 2001
- moral
- modest
- compassionate
- confident
- idealistic
- optimistic
- intelligent - rational
- clever
- clear thinking
- control of his emotions
- humble
- rises above what others say
- dry humor
- fair
- loving father
- can plan ahead
- can see life in others's shoes
- fair
- empathetic
- stands up for his beliefs
- loyal

Writing Critical Essays

With the teacher's help, students can move from analytical and inferential talk to critical writing. To begin, the teacher models how to organize a critical paragraph by composing in front of the class. A critical essay consists of an introduction, supporting details, and a conclusion. The number of supporting paragraphs depends on the guidelines that the teacher and students negotiate. If the process is totally new to students, I have them develop one piece of support. Once they can do that well, adding support is easy.

To introduce the process, I spend time during minilessons to model how I go about composing a critical essay. My demonstrations consist of three separate lessons:

1. I model how to form a thesis, evaluate the story, take notes, and write the introduction.
2. I highlight the general-to-specific-to-connection-to-thesis pattern of the support paragraphs.
3. I demonstrate how to write the conclusion and evaluate my work using guidelines.

During demonstrations, I identify each part of the essay so students can better observe and understand my goals. After each minilesson, students can pose questions that help them clarify what they have observed. Repeat these demonstrations through collaborative writing in which students create a thesis statement, take notes, construct an introduction, and write a support section and conclusion.

Before each subsequent minilesson, I invite students to tell me what they have learned about writing a critical essay. The amount of recall I receive helps me evaluate what students remember. Continue collaborations until you feel students have internalized the process and are ready to apply independently what they know.

Developing a Thesis and an Introduction

A thesis takes a position about a character's actions, decisions, or motivations; a situation or an event in the book; or a theme in a book. An effective thesis can be supported with two to three pieces of evidence from the story. During the first minilesson, I show students how I create a thesis statement, and I take notes for ideas that I can develop to persuade the reader to agree with the thesis. I explain that I can find convincing arguments by evaluating literature circle discussion notes, selecting appropriate notebook entries, and skimming key parts of the text. As I model jotting down notes, I refer back to the book. "I want my details to be accurate and exact," I tell students. "That's why I reread parts."

I explain that the introduction opens with the thesis statement. The second sentence includes the title and author of the book and makes a transition from the thesis to the body of the essay. Here is the introduction I model for the short story "Amanda and the Wounded Birds" by Colby Rodowsky (1987):

Thesis: Dealing with problems can be difficult for many teens, especially if they have absentee parents.

Transition Sentence: In the story "Amanda and the Wounded Birds," by Colby Rodowsky, Amanda learns to communicate with her mother by pretending to be a different person.

Writing Support Paragraphs

During the second minilesson, I point out that in an essay, supporting ideas open with a general statement followed by convincing evidence from the text that backs up the statement. The challenging part is to connect the support to the thesis statement. Here is what I write for one piece of support:

General Statement: Amanda's mom, a famous talk-radio psychologist, never had time for her daughter.

Support: Her mom worried constantly about the people who called and spent long hours preparing for her radio shows. Once Amanda's mom became famous, she traveled, lectured, and did guest shows all over the country. Amanda wanted to talk to her mom about her friend Terri, about colleges, and about her English teacher, Mrs. Spellman.

Connection to Thesis: However, Amanda's mom was so busy there was no time for her daughter. Amanda felt that her mom had time for everyone else's problems, but no time for her own daughter.

Creating the Conclusion and Evaluating the Work

On the third day, I think aloud and explain the purposes of a conclusion. I tell the class, "In my conclusion, I want to restate my position without repeating the thesis statement. It's also a place where I can emphasize an important point I've made in the essay."

Now I write the conclusion to this essay:

Restatement of Thesis: By calling her mom and pretending to be someone else, Amanda helped her mother realize that she had been neglecting her own daughter.

Important Point: Amanda's courage to reveal who she was during the second telephone call helped her mom reserve time to connect and listen to her daughter.

Once I sense that students are ready to work independently, I ask them to create guidelines for writing and evaluating their essays. The list that follows, composed after one teacher demonstration and two student-teacher collaborations, is from eighth graders. The list also includes two things to avoid.

Guidelines for Writing a Critical Essay

1. Develop a thesis statement for your story or book.
2. Take detailed notes for the support section. Look back in the book so notes are accurate and specific.
3. Open your introduction with the thesis statement. Write a second sentence that includes the title and author of the story and that offers general ideas about what will be discussed in the second paragraph. This sentence makes a transition from the introduction to the support paragraph.
4. Decide on your first piece of proof.
5. Start the second paragraph. Introduce your point in a general statement, then move to specific examples from the text.
6. Connect the example to the thesis.
7. Repeat numbers 4 to 6 for each additional piece of support.
8. Write a conclusion of one to three sentences. Restate the thesis in a different way. You might also want to include another key point you were trying to make.

Things to Avoid

1. Retelling the story.
2. Bringing in details that do not support your thesis.

Students receive a set of these guidelines to keep in their writing folders or literature response notebooks. These form content and organizational criteria that students use for self-evaluation and peer evaluation of first drafts. Criteria provide a set of standards students use as they self- or peer-edit to make sure their essay reflects the guidelines. They also offer me the criteria for evaluating essays and providing meaningful feedback.

Eighth grader Jaime Lockhart's first essay, written about "Shadows" by Richard Peck (1987), illustrates how these guidelines help students compose (see Figure 2.4). The guidelines also permit the teacher to make comments that celebrate strengths and suggest goals that can move students forward. My comments to Jaime appear on page 43.

FIGURE 2.4   *Jaime's First Essay*

Jaime Lockhart   Loneliness   October 19, 1998

The struggle to grow up often sends youngsters into a fantasy world. In "Shadows" by Richard Peck, the narrator creates a world of ghosts, of shadows, because she is so lonely.

Alone in the world, except for her two eccentric aunts, the narrator says, "I was a solitary child." With no parents, no friends at school or home, the narrator creates a world of haunts, shadow people she can manipulate and befriend. When Seth comes, the narrator waits for him every evening, teaches him to read, and talks to him. Seth is a ghostly shadow, but he also represents the narrator's inner self. Once the narrator has friends, her need for Seth lessens. The story closes with the narrator saying goodbye to Seth before she goes to college. She's grown up and is finding a place in the real world. She doesn't need her fantasy world now.

Crossing from childhood to being an adult changed the narrator. Real friendships replaced the haunts of her fantasies. Seth is like part of the narrator, growing up as she grew up and finally saying "Goodbye."

- You followed the guidelines in all three paragraphs.
- I like the way you pick up "lonely" from intro and start support with the same idea. Good transition.
- Great use of quote. Share so others can see what you did.
- Detailed evidence. You show why she doesn't need fantasies and bring us back to thesis.
- Solid conclusion. I like the way you bring in the idea that maybe Seth is part of the girl. What made you think this? Can you find support in the story?

It is easy to write detailed, meaningful comments when there are guidelines. I always celebrate what works well in the piece and pose a question that invites the students to rethink a statement.

When students' essays reveal that they are having great difficulty working independently, I work with them, providing the scaffolding they need as they think and compose. To scaffold, I can ask a student to review notes, reread parts of the text, pose questions, or discuss key points. Often, I will record students' oral text to show that they can transform notes and thoughts into writing. The more skill they gain with the process, the less support I provide.

Closing Reflections

Thinking about books on paper is a six-step process. Teachers evaluate students' progress along the way, and they revisit any steps that require additional practice. Modeling and inviting students to question and reflect on what happened during minilessons and think-alouds provides the scaffolding students require to internalize the model. Here is an outline of the six steps students follow:

1. Students create oral texts through discussions.
2. In notebooks, students jot down notes as they read and reread after discussions.
3. The teacher models how to move from notes to a critical essay. Students evaluate their notes and select those that will persuade readers to agree with their thesis.
4. Students collaborate with the teacher to construct original essays.
5. Students, based on these experiences, create guidelines for writing a critical essay.
6. Students compose essays on their own.

REFERENCES

Harste, J.C., & Short, K.G. (with Burke, C.). (1988). *Creating classrooms for authors: The reading-writing connection.* Portsmouth, NH: Heinemann.

Paterson, K. (1981). *Gates of excellence: On reading and writing books for children.* New York: Elsevier-Dutton.

Robb, L. (1994). *Whole language, whole learners: Creating a literature-centered classroom.* New York: Morrow.

Robb, L. (2000). *Teaching reading in middle school: A strategic approach to teaching reading that improves comprehension and thinking.* New York: Scholastic.

Rosenblatt, L.M. (1978). *The reader, the text, the poem: The transactional theory of the literary work.* Carbondale, IL: Southern Illinois University Press.

Rosenblatt, L.M. (1983). *Literature as exploration* (4th ed.). New York: The Modern Language Association of America.

YOUNG ADULT LITERATURE CITED

Lee, H. (1960). *To kill a mockingbird.* New York: Warner.

Marshall, J. (1959). *Walkabout.* Boston: Sundance.

Peck, R. (1987). Shadows. In D. Gallo (Ed.), *Visions: 19 short stories* (pp. 2–9). New York: Bantam Doubleday Dell.

Rodowsky, C. (1987). Amanda and the wounded birds. In D. Gallo (Ed.), *Visions: 19 short stories* (pp. 78–85). New York: Bantam Doubleday Dell.

Soto, G. (1990). LaBamba. In *Baseball in April: And other stories* (pp. 101–111). New York: Harcourt Brace.

CHAPTER 3

Somewhere Over the Rainbow: Celebrating Diverse Voices in Young Adult Literature

Barbara G. Samuels

esterday I walked through the largest mall in Houston, Texas, looking at the faces around me. I watched the skaters whirl around the ice rink in the center of the mall. Once again I was struck by the diversity of our urban population. Groups of African American, Hispanic, Anglo, Korean, Vietnamese, and Chinese young people glided across the ice or giggled and chatted as they peered into store windows, obviously enjoying the weekend freedom from school.

Of course, our classrooms remind us again and again of the multicultural nature of the U.S. population. The United States is a pluralistic society. Overall, the 11 million immigrants age 10 or over who came to the United States during the 1990s accounted for more than one third of the nation's population growth. Nearly one of every eight U.S. residents between the ages of 10 and 19—more than 4 million people—was born in another country. Demographers estimate that when the full 2000 census is released it will indicate over 4 million foreign-born children under age 10 as well (C. Rodriguez, 2001). In California, 51% of school-age children belong to ethnic minority groups (Olson, 1996).

The Census Bureau projects that the nation's population will more than double in the next 100 years, from 274 million to 571 million, fueled largely by the gain of as many as 1 million immigrants a year. "One of the most robust elements, although it's not new, is that we are becoming more diverse, racially and ethnically," according to Frederick W. Hollmann, a Census Bureau demographer (Wrolstad, 2000). Steve Murdock, chief demographer of the Texas State Data Center at Texas A&M University, makes a similar observation: "We need to see this as an internationalization of the U.S. population, much like our economy has been internationalized" (Wrolstad, 2000).

The United States's black population continues to grow quickly as well. Census Bureau data note that about 33% of the nation's 35 million African Americans are age 18 or younger, compared with 24% of the United States's 193 million whites. According to the Census Bureau, the African American share of the total population is expected to increase from 13% to 15% in the first half of the 21st century. By 2059, according to the projections, minority groups will outnumber whites, whose share of the total population is now 72% ("U.S. Population," 2000). U.S. classrooms will continue to become more and more diverse as well.

In addition to these shifts in population, giant leaps in communication technology make us a more global society. We telephone, fax, or e-mail people on the other side of the world in seconds by pushing a few buttons. More than ever before, U.S. students are growing up in a world in which they will need skills and knowledge to cooperate and communicate with other ethnic and cultural populations.

Diversity in daily life provides an enormous opportunity for teachers and students to learn about the variety of backgrounds that make up the American and international quilt. Although learning English is essential for students who grow up in the United States, Americans who speak two or more languages will be important partners in the global economy of the future. As we struggle to touch the minds and hearts of all students, we realize the importance of helping

TEACHER IDEA

TOP 10 LIST

Using the idea of a late-night television show, have students create their own Top 10 list of clever reasons why they like a book they read. Remind students to list their reasons in order of importance, with the least important being Number 10:

10. Character description is true to life.

9. Words make you envision scenes in your mind.

...

1. Action-packed fun and adventure!

Collect and compile the lists into a booklet for students to review.

Joan B. Elliott is a professor at Indiana University of Pennsylvania, Indiana, Pennsylvania, USA.

them connect with their own cultures. At the same time, it is equally important to help them develop understanding and compassion by exposing them to the cultures of their fellow students. We need to honor and celebrate the pluralism of the contemporary United States. We need not only to recognize other cultures around us but also to incorporate them into the classroom every day. Non-European cultures must be presented as part of the total curriculum.

Literature provides one important resource for all students to learn about themselves and others. Students feel affirmed when they study books that reflect their cultures because such books make it easier for students to identify with characters and to connect with situations. African American students, for example, derive pleasure and pride from reading books by Walter Dean Myers, Virginia Hamilton, Jacqueline Woodson, or Angela Johnson. Mexican American students identify with the characters in books by Rudolfo Anaya, Gary Soto, Sandra Cisneros, or Diane Gonzales Bertrand.

Of course, students do not have to be black to relate to books by Myers, nor Latino to identify with the teens in Soto's books. These authors convey universal needs—love, health, and identity—as well as the particular background of the African American and Latino cultures. What better way to immerse ourselves in the lives and emotions of those whose cultural, economic, or ethnic backgrounds are different, but whose needs are the same as ours? We can lose ourselves in their world through the pages of a book and learn about the values, beliefs, and lifestyles of other people. Much of what we know about cultural and ethnic groups other than our own comes from a representation of these groups in books.

Teachers often feel unsure of themselves when selecting literature about other cultures. Concerns about the authenticity of the material are often valid. Rudine Sims Bishop (1992), citing her own survey and analysis (Sims, 1982) of 150 fictional pictures books published between 1965 and 1979, reports that "a substantial portion of children's books about people of color are created by Euro-American writers" (p. 41). Although some of these books have been recognized for their contributions to literature for children, others misrepresent the cultures they describe. Bishop also quotes playwright August Wilson, who said "Someone who does not share the specifics of a culture remains an outsider, no matter how astute a student or how well-meaning their intentions" (p. 42).

However, the discussion about authenticity of books by writers outside a culture is not totally one-sided. For instance, Bishop (1992) quotes African American studies expert Henry Lewis Gates, Jr., who rejects the idea that only an African American can write about the African American experience: "No human culture is inaccessible to someone who makes the effort to understand, to learn, to inhabit another world" (p. 42). There are, in fact, some excellent books written by people who are not part of the ethnic group the books feature.

Although there are differences of opinion about authenticity, all those concerned with literature for young people agree about the importance of reading about people like ourselves to help us develop self-esteem, enlightenment, and understanding. At the same time, literature also helps free us from the stereotypes that we have about those whose backgrounds are different from our own. As Frances Ann Day (1997) notes, "Without a complete vision of all that it means to be human, we live impoverished and isolated lives. Fortunately, the world of literature for children and teenagers is gradually being transformed to embrace the wondrous complexity, diversity, and depth of the human experience" (p. 3).

Selecting Multicultural Books to Use in Your Classroom

If you feel insecure about selecting authentic multicultural books for your classroom, start your own reading by becoming familiar with the writings of a few of the authors whose work is most recognized by others. Bishop (1992) suggests that "teachers who have read widely in the literature by members of the group will be able to recognize differences between 'typical' insider and outsider perspectives" (p. 47). When you have read a number of these books, you will be able to feel more confident in your own selections. A book should not be chosen simply because its protagonists are people of color, but rather because it is well written and has something of significance to say to young people. The books mentioned in this chapter are a beginning, a place to start reading. They are by no means an exhaustive list of multicultural titles or authors. In addition, the titles mentioned are primarily novels or personal memoirs. Many excellent nonfiction titles are available and should be included in every classroom library. Teachers should supplement classroom libraries with titles suggested in books such as *Your Reading: A Booklist for Junior High and Middle School* or *Books for You: An Annotated Booklist for Senior High*, each published every 3 years by the National Council of Teachers of English.

Other resources are available to help teachers select the best quality, authentic multicultural books for their classrooms. Violet Harris's text, *Teaching Multicultural Literature in Grades K–8* (1992), is an excellent resource that contains essays on literature by African American, Mexican American, Puerto Rican American, Caribbean American, Native American, and Asian Pacific American writers. These essays also discuss issues in book selection and analysis.

Reading, Thinking, and Writing About Multicultural Literature (Olson, 1996) suggests a variety of lessons that provide support to linguistic and ethnic minority students while challenging and empowering all students to think and write. Activities in the book are based on authors ranging from William Shakespeare and Alfred, Lord Tennyson to Amy Tan and Eloise Greenfield.

Both *United in Diversity: Using Multicultural Young Adult Literature in the Classroom*, edited by Jean E. Brown and Elaine C. Stephens (1998), and *Teaching and Using Multicultural Literature in Grades 9–12: Moving Beyond the Canon*, edited by Arlette Willis (1998), offer suggestions for book selections, highlight teaching strategies, and examine issues that teachers may face when using books that focus on the cultural themes of various populations. An excellent resource for teachers seeking books about the growing Hispanic population in the United States is Frances Ann Day's *Latina and Latino Voices in Literature for Children and Teenagers* (1997). Day's book celebrates the writing of 23 authors, discussing their lives and the books they have written. Her earlier text, *Multicultural Voices in Contemporary Literature: A Resource for Teachers* (1994), introduces 39 multicultural authors and illustrators representing backgrounds ranging from African American and Navaho to Jewish American and Chinese Canadian. Reference books such as *Our Family, Our Friends, Our World: An Annotated Guide to Significant Multicultural Books for Children and Teenagers* (Miller-Lachman, 1992) can also be useful for choosing effective materials.

Folk tales provide an excellent bridge across cultures, especially because versions of some folk tales are told in many cultures. Middle school students enjoy comparing the stories. Often the tales provide opportunities to discuss universal themes. Consider, for example, the many variants of the Cinderella story that exist: *Yeh Shen* is a Chinese version, *Little Burnt Face* is a Native American tale, *Tam and Cam* is a Vietnamese tale, *Tattercoat* is a British tale, and *Cinderella* is a French or German tale. Many folk tales from different cultures are available in beautifully illustrated versions that convey significant cultural information in the pictures. Collections of folk tales from various countries— such as Lynette Dyer Vuong's two collections of Vietnamese tales, *The Brocaded Slipper and Other Vietnamese Tales* (1982) and *Sky Legends of Vietnam* (1993)— provide an excellent window into the values of the culture.

Collections of short stories also can provide insight into contemporary teens from different cultural groups. Some editors have attempted to gather stories by authors from different cultural and ethnic groups. Joyce Carol Thomas's *A Gathering of Flowers: Stories About Being Young in America* (1990), Hazel Rochman and Darlene McCampbell's *Leaving Home: 15 Distinguished Authors*

Explore Personal Journeys (1997), Marilyn Singer's *I Believe in Water: Twelve Brushes With Religion* (2000), and Don Gallo's *Join In: Multiethnic Short Stories by Outstanding Writers for Young Adults* (1993) are examples.

Books About African American Youth

Among the most recognized African American authors for young adults are Virginia Hamilton and Walter Dean Myers. Using Bishop's terms, both authors write as "insiders," and both have works that have been recognized with Newbery Medals and other honors. Hamilton has written more than 30 books of different genres ranging from mysteries to historical fiction, romances to fantasy, realistic fiction to science fiction. In 1992 she received the Hans Christian Andersen Award, an international medal of recognition for the entire body of her work. Her language is musical and full of beautiful imagery, with dialogue that often reads like poetry.

Virginia Hamilton's books focus primarily on issues of self-identity, a major theme for young adults. Her characters are African Americans who are trying to find themselves. Often, situations in society make it difficult for these characters to be themselves. In *The House of Dies Drear* (1968), for example, Pluto is the caretaker for a house that was once a stop on the Underground Railroad. Pluto wants the treasure that is hidden under the house because it is a clue to his background. Like the children who have just moved to the house, he is searching for his identity.

Stories within stories are often a part of Hamilton's books. In *Zeely* (1967), Geeder Perry is fascinated with Zeely Thomas, who lives in the area. She becomes convinced that the beautiful 6-foot girl is a Watusi queen and spreads the story throughout the neighborhood. Finally, Zeely herself tells Geeder the story of her life and, in particular, a story her mother had once told her about the origin of the Watusi people. Geeder discovers from Zeely's stories that it is not whether you are a king or queen that matters, but rather what is in your heart.

While Virginia Hamilton grew up in the Midwest United States and sets many of her stories in the Midwest or South, Walter Dean Myers grew up in New York City and writes mostly about his Harlem neighborhood. *Bad Boy: A Memoir* (2001) is Myers's autobiography, describing his youth in Harlem. A tall, physically aggressive kid who often got into trouble in school for fighting, Myers was also a secretly voracious reader. His interest in language and words sometimes drove a wedge between his foster parents and him.

Like Hamilton, Walter Dean Myers is a prolific author. He has published nearly 70 books, including novels, picture books, short stories, poetry, and nonfiction. He has a strong sense of his own heritage and has written about it for young people. In *Bad Boy*, Myers says he writes best about the things he has experienced: "I began to rethink my first ventures into reading, trying to interpret those first books as a pathway into later writing" (p. 58). *Fallen Angels* (1991) grew out of his own Vietnam War experiences. To write *Monster* (1999), Myers spent hours interviewing prison inmates.

Some of Myers's earlier novels, such as *Fast Sam, Cool Clyde, and Stuff* (1975) and *The Mouse Rap* (1990), recall growing up in Harlem with groups of young people who somehow eventually do the right thing. However, others reflect the tougher realities and hopelessness of urban life today. For instance, *Somewhere in the Darkness* (1992)—a Newbery, Coretta Scott King, and Boston Globe-Horn Book Honor Book—describes the relationship between a teen and his father. Jimmy's father suddenly appears at his foster home, says he has been paroled from prison, and takes Jimmy away from what has been a loving environment. Jimmy would like to have a real father-son relationship, but as he and his father get to know each other, Jimmy realizes that some things are not what they seem. In *145th Street: Short Stories* (2000), a collection of short stories set in Harlem, Myers depicts injustice, heroism, and pain with a variety of characters who live on the same street.

Scorpions (1988), another Newbery Honor Book, tells the story of 12-year-old Jamal, who is African American, and his best friend, Tito, who is Puerto Rican. Jamal's older brother, Randy, is in jail for a robbery. Even though Tito tries to discourage him, Jamal is persuaded by Randy's friends to take a gun and join the Scorpions, Randy's gang. The gun helps Jamal feel powerful when stronger kids in school tease him. Ultimately, having a gun leads to a tragedy. In spite of the depressing concerns of gangs, poverty, guns, and crime, Myers leaves readers with the sense that survival in urban environments is possible, if not simple. Family loyalty in both the African American and Puerto Rican families is a major theme in this novel.

Monster, winner of the Coretta Scott King Author Honor Award, the Michael L. Prinz Award of the American Library Association, and a finalist for the National Book Award, uses both diary and play format to put the reader inside the head of a young man on trial for murder. Powerful and chilling in its impact, the courtroom drama raises important issues about the way in which U.S. society often condemns young black men to prisons. Taking the issue of identity beyond Myers's previous novels, Steve, the reflective protagonist, screams for self-understanding. "That is why I take the films of myself," he says. "I want to know who I am" (p. 281). Throughout the book Steve struggles to reconcile the image

POSTCARDS

- Pretend you are one of the characters from a book. Decide what picture you will draw on the front of your postcard. This picture should show a scene from the book.
- On the back of the card on the upper left-hand side, write briefly about your picture.
- On the back of the card on the lower left-hand side, write a message as if you are the character in your book.
- Write an address on the right-hand side of the back of the card.
- Draw a stamp in the space where the stamp should go.

Adapted from Moen, C.B. (1992). *Better than book reports*. New York: Scholastic.

of himself as a monster who participated in a robbery that ends with a murder and his own image of himself as a moral being.

Other contemporary African American writers for young adults include Angela Johnson and Jacqueline Woodson. Johnson's *Toning the Sweep* (1993) was a Newbery Honor Book in 1994. The tender story of a teen's relationship with a dying grandmother, this novel is a very different look at a search for identity. When Emmie and her mother go to the desert to help Grandmother Ola move back to Cleveland with them, Emmie decides to videotape interviews with Ola's friends and neighbors as a record of her grandmother's life. As she learns about her grandfather's tragic death in Alabama in 1964 and about the people who make up Ola's life now, Emmie begins to better understand her own place in the world.

Jacqueline Woodson's other short novels and short stories are also packed with tough issues of contemporary life. Writing in poetic prose, she explores issues of race, prejudice, abuse, homosexuality, and family relationships. Presenting characters who are sometimes mixed-race African American and Puerto Rican, several of her books have been Coretta Scott King Honor or Award books. In *From the Notebooks of Melanin Sun* (1995), a 13-year-old boy learns that his mother is gay. In addition, her partner is a white woman. Woodson's prose powerfully captures Mel's confusion, anxiety, and resentment as he tries to cope with his new knowledge. *Miracle's Boys* (2000), like the popular young adult title *The Outsiders* (Hinton, 1997), tells the story of three brothers coping with the pressures of living without parents. If their parents had not died, Ty'ree, the oldest brother, would have gone to MIT instead of working full-time to keep the family together. When Charlie, the middle brother, is released from Rahway, a correctional institution, his anger and hate threaten to dissolve the family bonds.

Rita Williams-Garcia's *Every Time a Rainbow Dies* (2001) is a tender love story set in a framework of violence in the West Indian community of Brooklyn, New York. The book opens with Thulani, the 16-year-old Jamaican protagonist, as he witnesses a rape. When he rushes to the aid of the young victim, he becomes obsessed with her beauty and with the rainbow colors of the clothing she wears. After months of dreaming about her and of following her through the neighborhood, Thulani finally establishes a relationship with the girl. Explicit in its sexual material, the book captures both adolescent innocence and tough urban life.

Rudine Sims (1982) terms books like these "culturally conscious" literature because they have African American characters, are set in African American homes or communities, and include African American customs and history. All of the books just described meet these characteristics. *Toning the Sweep* (Johnson, 1993), for example, focuses on an African American family. The title refers to an African American tradition in South Carolina in which family members notify others of a death by hammering on a sweep, a kind of plow. According to this tradition, "it's better if someone knows you're dying; then people are around to tone the sweep" (p. 65). Emmie's activities at her grandmother's house—including making a videotape of her grandmother's friends and life—is like toning the sweep.

Teachers looking for other "culturally conscious" books with African American protagonists might also consider titles by Mildred Taylor, Eleanora Tate, or Joyce Carol Thomas. Considering the large percentage of African American youth in U.S. schools, the numbers of books like these are extremely limited. Bishop (1992) suggests that one reason more are not published is the misconception that these books do not have a wide enough market. In truth, readers of all backgrounds find literature by these writers meaningful, universal, and important.

Books About Hispanic American Youth

Although there are not nearly enough books with African American protagonists available for young adults, there are even fewer books with Mexican American or other Latino/Latina protagonists. Population figures tell us that the number of Hispanics in the United States under age 18 increased 59% between 1990 and 2000 (L. Rodriguez, 2001). Given the recent growth and projected future growth of this ethnic group, concerned U.S. teachers are struggling to find works of literature that reflect the culture of their Hispanic students. One problem is that apparently there has not been support for Mexican American authors writing for children (Barrera, Liguori, & Salas, 1992). Another is that few Chicano authors have written in English for children until recently. Further, of the 40,000 books for children published from 1983 to 1991, only 19 books with a Puerto Rican presence were found (Nieto, 1992). In *Writers for Young Adults*, a three-volume work edited by Ted Hipple (1997), only 3 of the 129 authors write books with Latino/Latina protagonists. Many Hispanic authors write for small presses with limited circulation and marketing, so it is difficult for teachers to become familiar with their work.

Teens need to recognize that there are differences as well as similarities among the people who have a Latino/Latina background. Many of the Hispanic students in our schools come from Mexico, but others come from other countries in Central or South America or the islands off the coast of the Americas. When looking for literature to reflect the different cultures in the United States, teachers should try to include materials from a variety of Latino/Latina cultures.

A variety of texts by some of the authors whose books are available for young adults is discussed in the following pages.

Perhaps the best known book for young people by a Latino author is *Bless Me Ultima* (1972), by Rudolfo Anaya. Infused with cultural information about growing up in the traditions of Mexico, *Bless Me, Ultima* is the story of the maturation of Antonio Marez, a boy growing up in a small New Mexico farm village. Antonio's parents have different ideas about his future. His mother wants him to be a priest or farmer like the men in her family. Antonio's father wants him to be a *vaquero* (cowboy). Antonio struggles with his identity and his relationship to the Catholic Church, as his real guide is Ultima, a *curandera*, or spiritual healer.

Anaya has written and edited a number of other novels, stories, and essays. *The Anaya Reader* (1995) includes fiction, short stories, essays, and plays. Some of these stories explore mature themes, but they would help teachers become more familiar with Mexican culture. Others could be read with students. In one essay, Anaya urges educators to incorporate more multicultural material in the curriculum. He writes, "What we seek now, in our relationship to the broader society, is to eliminate the mindless prejudices that hamper our evolution, and to encourage people of goodwill who do not fear a pluralistic society…" (p. 302).

Gary Soto's writings have become perhaps the best known in school settings. Soto, a former National Book Award and Pulitzer Prize nominee who grew up in the barrios, or Mexican American neighborhoods, of Fresno, California, explores his own youth in autobiographical vignettes, fiction, picture books, and poetry. Soto's stories lend themselves to class discussions and expressive writings. Students find many parallels in their own lives to the events in the readings. For example, *Living Up the Street: Narrative Recollections* (1985) is a collection of 21 short essays. In "The Beauty Contest," Gary's brother competes against "blond and fair skinned kids in good clothes" (p. 43). In "One Last Time," he describes picking grapes. *Baseball in April* (1990) includes stories about Veronica, who longs for a real Barbie doll; Maria, who thinks she is old enough to stay home alone while her family goes on vacation; and Alfonso, who hates his crooked teeth and puny muscles. Alfonso's lack of confidence around girls is universal and reflects the same feelings of insecurity all teens have, whether they live in upper-middle-class, mostly white neighborhoods or in the barrios of an inner city. Soto's universality is part of his strength. While he shares stories of the particular children who made up his neighborhood, he also is telling stories familiar to all teens.

Soto's novels also speak to many adolescents. *Jesse* (1994), like most of Soto's writing, is also set in Fresno. Against the backdrop of the Vietnam War era, Jesse and his brother Abel struggle to live on Social Security checks while attending a community college. *Crazy Weekend* (1994) is the humorous adventure tale of two seventh graders, Hector and Mando, who spend a weekend in Fresno visiting Hector's Uncle Julio.

Parrot in the Oven: Mi Vida (1996), a first novel by Victor Martinez, received considerable attention when it appeared. A coming-of-age story about a Mexican American teen, Manuel Hernandez, it too reflects universal feelings while projecting the particular story of a boy growing up. In one of the episodic chapters, a tough guy at Manny's school, Lencho, tries to prove himself to the Berets, a gang that believes that

> white people were our worst enemy; and if they had one purpose in mind, it was to keep brown people down. We, on the other hand, were descendants of Indians blessed with a color that was as necessary as the sun to all the trees. We had treasures buried deep inside our blood, hidden treasures we hardly knew existed. (p. 119)

Lencho entices "two suckers," Albert and Chico, to participate with him in a school boxing tournament. As the crowd cheers for Chico, Lencho tells him, "That's for you! That's so you can show this guy who the real man is. Now don't let your Raza down" (p. 131). But the fighters in Coach Rogers's regular team defeat all of them. Embarrassed by the losses in the boxing match, the Berets kick Lencho out of the gang. An episodic novel, *Parrot in the Oven* is written with tender compassion and appreciation for the lives of those who grow up in the barrios of U.S. cities.

Sandra Cisneros's short stories also lend themselves to classroom discussion and a variety of writing activities. The 44 short, interrelated vignettes in *The House on Mango Street* (1984) tell the story of a young girl growing up in the Latino/Latina section of Chicago. These stories, like Soto's, are universal experiences of life in a neighborhood. We meet the people who walk the streets, as well as Marin, Rafaela, and Alicia, and we inhabit Esperanza's world. For example, after reading "My Name," in which Esperanza reflects on her name and on the great-grandmother whose name she inherited, students often examine their own feelings about their names. Sometimes they speculate about the ways in which their names reflect their personalities. Other times they think metaphorically about their names. Students' writings in response to this piece are personal and meaningful because of the emotions connected with names.

A Puerto Rican New Jersey neighborhood is the focus of Judith Ortiz Cofer's *An Island Like You: Stories of the Barrio* (1995). In "Bad Influence," Rita's parents send her to her grandmother's house in Puerto Rico for the summer, hoping to get her away from her boyfriend for a while. Rita expects to hate being in Puerto Rico, but finds she's having a wonderful time. Other stories in the collection focus on gangs, shoplifting, homosexuality, death, and peer pressures. Cofer's *The Year of Our Revolution: New and Selected Stories and Poems* (1998) is a collection of poems, stories, myths, and essays that explores the bicultural experiences of the author, particularly about growing up Puerto Rican in a New Jersey Hispanic neighborhood in the 1960s.

Older and sophisticated teens will appreciate the immigrant novel by Dominican American Julia Alvarez, *How the Garcia Girls Lost Their Accents* (1991). Loosely based on the experiences Alvarez had as an immigrant to New York, the novel begins with the girls as adults and then looks back on their experiences fleeing the Dominican Republic and starting school in New York. The girls are humiliated by schoolmates, a policeman, and the indignities of being different. Like many immigrants, the girls never feel they totally belong in the United States, but they are strangers in the Dominican Republic as well. The novel lends itself to serious discussion about racism, immigration, and privilege, as well as issues of anorexia, mental illness, drugs, and sexuality.

The immigrant experience is a familiar one in books with Hispanic protagonists. A character named Esperanza, the Spanish word for *hope*, is the protagonist in Pam Munoz Ryan's novel *Esperanza Rising* (2000). Set in the Depression era, Esperanza is forced to immigrate to the United States when her wealthy Mexican rancher father is killed by *bandidos* (bandits). As Esperanza is transformed from an aristocrat to a farm worker picking grapes, her story offers readers a glimpse of the pain of emigration and poverty and the injustices born of hunger and the Dustbowl Depression.

An immigrant story that grabs young readers with a mystery is *The Girl From Playa Blanca* by Ofelia Dumas Lachtman (1995). Seventeen-year-old Elena and her brother Carlos travel from their village in Mexico to Los Angeles to search for their father, who has not contacted them for 5 months. While she works for a wealthy Malibu couple, Elena begins to unravel a strange tangle of clues and to meet a variety of people who begin to shed some light on her father's disappearance. Because teens regularly select mysteries as a favorite genre, this one is sure to appeal.

Teenagers will enjoy learning about the tradition of a *quinceañera* celebration, which marks a 15-year-old girl's birthday, in Diane Gonzales Bertrand's *Sweet Fifteen* (1995). When her father dies, Stephanie Bonilla is even more reluctant to have a *quinceañera* party, a celebration she considers old-fashioned. But Rita, the seamstress who is making her gown for the party, helps Stephanie to understand Latino traditions and appreciate traditional values. A gentle romance makes this story even more appealing.

Novels by Arturo Islas, Gabriel Garcia Marquez, Isabel Allende, and Victor Villasenor are rich in their depiction of Hispanic traditions and can be recommended to older, more sophisticated young adult readers. In recent years, more titles written by Latino authors have become available. One way to keep up to date with new books is to regularly check the catalog of Arte Publico, a small publishing house dedicated to publishing for the Hispanic American population.

Books About Native American Youth

Although materials to reflect the various Latino/Latina cultures in our schools are becoming a little more available, it is still a challenge for teachers to find materials that accurately and authentically portray various Native American cultures. In the United States today, there are approximately 2 million Native Americans and close to 200 diverse tribal groups. The term "Native American" refers to all peoples indigenous to the Western Hemisphere. The different tribal groups are unique, separate, and distinct cultures with different beliefs, languages, and traditions. Trying to encompass all of them is, of course, impossible, but teachers should avoid lumping indigenous groups around a single term of "Indian" and should be cautious of books that do so.

A major problem in becoming familiar with Native American cultures through literature is that there are many books, even popular and respected books, that trivialize, stereotype, or even vilify Native Americans. Consider, for example, the attitude found in the *Little House on the Prairie* books by Laura Ingalls Wilder (1953). The general approach in these books is that the land belongs to the white settlers because they are farming it. Wilder ignored the fact that the Native Americans who lived there previously harvested the land in a different way. Critics have attacked the use of the word "squaw" in Elizabeth George Speares's *Sign of the Beaver* (in Kaywell, 2000, p. 136). Lynne Reid Banks's popular children's books *Indian in the Cupboard* (1980) and *The Return of the Indian* (1999) present distorted views of Native Americans. In *Teaching Multicultural Literature in Grades K–8* (Harris, 1992), Donnarae MacCann talks about these books:

> The cultural content is rooted in the image of the Indian as presented in Hollywood westerns and dime novels. Little Bear is a plastic toy Indian who comes to life in the boy's magical cupboard…. He grunts and snarls his way through the story, attacking the child, Omri, with a hunting knife and later attacking a traditional enemy, a three-inch cowboy…. Native Americans are seen as the primary perpetrators of havoc, even as they defend their own borders. (p. 145)

Given the fact that many Americans grow up with stereotypical images like these, it is particularly important that teachers seek authentic images of Native Americans for young adults. In addition to criteria already introduced, teachers should consider some of the following issues raised by Kaywell (2000),

1. Is there an oversimplification or generalization of Native cultures?
2. How is the Euro-American conquest of Native homelands presented?
3. How is the conflict between Native Americans and Euro-Americans presented? (p. 136)

A few of the authors whose writings reflect accurate portrayals of indigenous peoples are introduced next in this chapter. Teachers also are encouraged to search collections of Native American writings to find examples of song texts and oral narratives. Many of the Native American myths and folk tales have been beautifully illustrated in picture books that make wonderful classroom read-aloud material.

Author Joseph Bruchac's grandfather was an Abenaki who lived in the Adirondack foothills. He taught Bruchac how to walk quietly in the woods and how to fish, but was quiet about his heritage because he feared bigotry. When Bruchac became an adult, he sought information about his Native American background, writing down the Native American stories he had heard so that his own children would learn them. He searched out many stories from Native American elders. In recent years, Bruchac has become known as a master storyteller and writer. His extensive writings, heavily based on folk tales, appeal to all ages. *Keepers of the Earth: Native American Stories and Environmental Activities for Children* (Caduto & Bruchac, 1988) presents a collection of Native American stories that nurture an appreciation for nature and the Earth. The book is filled with interdisciplinary activities to help young people combine Native American and scientific understanding. Another Bruchac collection of Native American stories that deal with reverence for nature as well as rites of passage is *Flying With the Eagle, Racing the Great Bear: Stories from Native North America* (1993).

Bruchac's *The Heart of a Chief* (1998) is the story of an 11-year-old Penacook who is trying to hold on to his traditions in the face of the problems with alcoholism and gambling that exist in his community. He begins attending a junior high school and questions many of the issues facing contemporary Native Americans. Bruchac is also the author of one of the *My Name Is America* series books, *The Journal of Jesse Smoke* (2001), about a young Cherokee on the Trail of Tears.

An article by Jim Charles in *The ALAN Review* (2001) suggests that the novels of Virginia Driving Hawk Sneve are particularly appropriate for young adults. Charles quotes Sneve:

> I try to present an accurate portrayal of American Indian life as I have known it. I also try to interpret history from the viewpoint of the American Indian. In doing so, I hope to correct the many misconceptions and untruths which have been too long perpetuated by non-Indian authors who have written about us. (p. 60)

Sneve's novels include *Jimmy Yellow Hawk* (1972), *When Thunders Spoke* (1974), and *High Elk's Treasure* (1972). Fourth- and fifth-grade readers will identify with Little Jimmy's embarrassment about his childish name and enjoy the excitement of Jimmy's adventure in a dangerous storm, learning how to trap animals and being sprayed by a skunk in *Jimmy Yellow Hawk*. Sneve has also written a nonfiction series of books about various Native American tribes.

In Jamake Highwater's Newbery Honor Book, *Anpao: An American Indian Odyssey* (1977), Anpao sets out to find his father, the Sun, to ask his permission

WHIP AROUND

After reading a story, ask students to think of words to describe a certain character or event in the story. (See the character analysis vocabulary list below for words that might be used to describe characters.) Instruct students that you will "whip around" the room, or a row, and give each student a quick turn to give his or her thoughts or to say "I pass." Follow this with a discussion about why students feel such words are appropriate to describe the character or event.

Whip Around can be used with the whole class, small groups, or part of the class for each issue to be discussed. The activity gives all students a chance to participate and voice ideas while raising the interest level of the class.

Character Analysis Vocabulary

At a loss for words to describe a character in a story? Try selecting dynamic, descriptive words from this list of character traits:

active	confused	fearless	innocent	self-reliant
adventurous	considerate	fierce	intelligent	sincere
affectionate	cooperative	foolish	jealous	slovenly
afraid	courageous	frank	kind	snobbish
angry	cowardly	friendly	lazy	sociable
animated	cross	frustrated	lively	steady
annoyed	cruel	funny	lonely	stolid
anxious	curious	gentle	loquacious	strict
argumentative	dangerous	giddy	loving	suave
arrogant	daring	glamorous	loyal	sullen
astonished	dependable	gloomy	lucky	supercilious
attentive	determined	glum	mean	surly
blasé	diligent	grateful	mischievous	tactful
bored	discouraged	greedy	nervous	tolerant
bossy	disgusted	grumpy	noisy	uncouth
brave	dishonest	happy	obedient	unkind
brilliant	dismayed	harried	obnoxious	unruly
busy	dissatisfied	hateful	pessimistic	unscrupulous
capable	distressed	honest	precise	unselfish
careful	doubtful	hopeful	prodigal	unset
careless	dreamy	hopeless	punctilious	useful
caring	eager	hospitable	rash	vivacious
cautious	effervescent	humble	refined	vulgar
charming	embarrassed	humorous	remiss	weak
cheerful	energetic	ignorant	resolute	wealthy
childish	excited	imaginative	respected	witty
clever	exuberant	impatient	respectful	worried
clumsy	expert	impolite	retiring	
comical	fair	inactive	rowdy	
concerned	faithful	independent	sarcastic	
confident	fanciful	industrious	saucy	

Adapted from Harmin, M. (1994). *Inspiring active learning.* Alexandria, VA: Association for Supervision and Curriculum Development.

TEACHER IDEA

to marry. Anpao's journey becomes a rite of passage. He learns the secret of his birth and becomes a man as he learns how to see that good and evil exist in everything, including himself. Highwater's book reflects the oral tradition that is so much a part of Native American writing. He skillfully incorporates myths, legends, and stories from the Northern Plains culture as well as elements of the Southwest indigenous culture in Anpao's adventures.

Michael Dorris's two short novels convey important messages about Native American culture. *Sees Behind Trees* (1996), a coming-of-age story, is about a young Powhattan boy who is nearly blind. Although Walnut cannot see well physically, he uses his other senses to see things that others in his tribe are unable to see. Although he cannot pass the typical test for his rite of passage, Walnut helps his tribe and proves himself. In *Morning Girl* (1992), Dorris writes about Native Americans' initial encounter with Columbus and his men. Told in alternating chapters by 12-year-old Morning Girl and her younger brother, Star Boy, the book evokes an idyllic existence of the two young people on an unknown island. Not until the end does the reader realize that the two children are Taino Indians and the strange visitors they encounter are not as harmless as they seem. An excerpt from Christopher Columbus's diary forebodes future problems for these Native Americans.

Books About Asian American Youth

Another diverse group in the United States today is Asian Americans, who represent about 2.9% of the total U.S. population. In 1990, the largest Asian minority was Chinese, with Philippine, Japanese, Indian, Korean, and Vietnamese making up other large groups. Asian American students make up a large population in U.S. schools, but not nearly enough books represent these students. Although the situation has improved significantly since a 1976 committee of Asian American book reviewers found that only 66 books had at least one central character who was Asian American, there is still a paucity of such books (Aoki, 1992). With so few books accurately portraying Asian Americans, non-Asian children grow up stereotyping these citizens, many of whom have ancestry in the United States for up to 150 years.

Some of the Asian American authors for young adults write about these issues of bigotry and stereotyping. Perhaps the best-known Asian American author for young adults is Laurence Yep, a Chinese American. All of Yep's books focus on the role of the outsider, although they span historical fiction, realistic fiction, and fantasy. He says,

I was the Chinese American raised in a black neighborhood, a child who had been too American to fit into Chinatown and too Chinese to fit in elsewhere. I was the clumsy son of an athletic family. The grandson of a Chinese grandmother who spoke more of West Virginia than of China. (in Day, 1994, p. 206)

Yep's *Child of the Owl* (1977), a Boston Globe-Horn Book Award winner, is the story of a 12-year-old girl who is sent to live with her grandmother in Chinatown. At first, Casey feels lost. She does not speak Chinese, is unaccustomed to the crowds of Chinatown, and has not felt connected to her roots. In the sequel, *Thief of Hearts* (1995), Casey's daughter, Stacy, learns about her Chinese roots when a trip into San Francisco's Chinatown with her mother and grandmother forces her to face her Chinese heritage. Stacy has always felt totally American, but one day she is asked to show Hong Ch'un, a new immigrant, around school. Suddenly Stacy finds that her friends see her as connected to this new girl, whose attitude, clothing, and Disney barrettes look so foreign. Like the Thief of Hearts in a Chinese folk tale her grandmother tells her, Stacy begins to wonder where she belongs.

Yep's autobiography, *The Lost Garden* (1991), explores his own experiences of coming to appreciate his Chinese heritage. Yep describes how he is now able to translate his own painful experiences of being an outsider into stories that may help young people to cope with their own feelings. Whether the outsider is a dragon in *Dragon of the Lost Sea* (1982) or a teen feeling as different as Casey Young in *Child of the Owl*, Yep examines what it means to feel alienated. A collection of short stories edited by Yep, *American Dragons: Twenty-Five Asian American Voices* (1993), attempts to represent "just a portion of the diversity of theme and talent among Asian American writers" (p. xi). All teens feel like outsiders, whether they are immigrants or born in America. This collection has many universal stories.

Yoshiko Uchida, a Japanese American, is best known for her accounts of historical events that involve Japanese Americans. *Journey to Topaz* (1971) puts a face on the terrible time in American history when 120,000 people of Japanese ancestry were put in internment camps in the United States during World War II. After the FBI takes her father, 11-year-old Yuki and her family are forced to leave their home and go to a crowded desert camp. In *Journey Home* (1978), the sequel, Yuki and her family are released to face prejudice and hostility.

Other novelists have written about the adolescent immigrant's feeling of being different. In Lensey Namioka's *April and the Dragon Lady* (1994), April Chen's relationship with tall, redheaded Steve Daniels is threatened by her grandmother's old-fashioned Chinese beliefs. Grandma believes that good Chinese women serve their men. "The kind of man who doesn't expect a woman to wait on him will turn out to be unreliable," she says (p. 111). Grandma even makes April question Steve's motives in dating her. "White men," she says, "prefer Asian women because they find them submissive" (p. 111). April struggles with the problem of belonging neither to Steve's world nor to her grandmother's world.

Sherry Garland's *Shadow of the Dragon* (1993) focuses on the tension between a Vietnamese teen and his family. Sixteen-year-old Danny Vo is torn between the traditional Vietnamese world of his grandmother and his home and the American life he has in a Houston, Texas, high school. When Danny's newly arrived cousin Sang Le comes to live with them, Danny finds himself constantly struggling. Sang Le does not really fit in with Danny's friends. More than anything, Danny wants to build his relationship with Tiffany Schultz, but Sang Le seems to keep getting in the way. Frustrated by the difficulty of learning English, Sang Le gets involved with a Vietnamese gang.

Linda Crew's *Children of the River* (1989) addresses similar issues of identity in a Cambodian family. Sundara was one of the boat people who left her parents, brother, and sister, and a boy she had loved behind in Cambodia when she escaped the Khmer Rouge with her aunt's family. Four years later, a 16-year-old in a U.S. high school, Sundara feels torn when another student, Jonathan, asks her to go to the movies. She responds, "I'd like to go with you, but—in my country, we don't go out on a date at all" (p. 70). When she goes out sailing with Jonathan's family without telling her aunt, she feels very guilty. Is she betraying her past by dating a white American boy?

Kyoko Mori's two novels and memoir center on a young Japanese teen's loss of her mother and consequent struggle with an emotionless father. The novels are set in Japan and address the role of women in Japanese society. They help American teens understand some of the differences between Japanese and American cultures. In *Shizuko's Daughter* (1993), Yuki's mother kills herself because her husband has another woman. Divorce is not seen as an acceptable practice in Japan. After her mother's death, Shizuko is forced to live with a mean stepmother who resents her presence in the house. Similarly, in *One Bird* (1995), Megumi is a young girl living without her mother. When her mother leaves her father to go back to her own parents, Megumi lives with her father's mother, gruff Grandmother Shimizu. Finding understanding and confidence in her work as a part-time helper for Dr. Mizutani, a veterinarian who treats sick birds, Megumi also learns about independence. Although Japanese culture dictates the actions of the protagonists and their mothers, both Yuki and Megumi are free thinkers.

Kyoko Mori writes from her experience. After her mother's suicide and her father's remarriage, Mori left Japan and moved to the United States. Her memoir, *Polite Lies: On Being a Woman Caught Between Cultures* (1997), describes how the polite lies that are expected in Japanese culture mask true feelings. Throughout her essays, Kyoko Mori compares the codes of behavior for American women and Japanese women.

Perhaps the best-known Asian American writer is Amy Tan, author of *The Joy Luck Club* (1989), *The Kitchen God's Wife* (1991), and recently *The Bonesetter's Daughter* (2001). Although these books may be too great a challenge for some younger readers, older young adult readers often enjoy them. Tan's recurrent theme is the relationship between mothers and daughters, certainly a universal theme for teens. As with many popular books, Tan uses the specifics of a Chinese American immigrant background to address the more general issues of conflicts between generations.

Final Thoughts

This chapter has presented authors and titles of books for some of the major ethnic groups that make up the United States. By no means is this an exhaustive list. Other authors and titles are available for each of the groups described: African American, Hispanic American, Native American, and Asian American. In addition, teachers should continually search for books that reflect other populations in the United States as well as books set all over the world. The task is not easy; most young adult books are set in the continental United States and feature European American protagonists.

Introducing literature of diversity in the classroom is a challenge. Teachers must be prepared to read, read, read, and read some more. In addition, opening up classroom discussions about these books will inevitably raise difficult questions about the attitudes and guilt of white European Americans. Bigotry may emerge. Teachers must be willing to discuss the feelings in an atmosphere of respect and openness.

In this era of pluralism, international business, and openness, it is essential that our classrooms respond to the challenge. We must help our students become part of the diverse, interconnected world in which they will function as adults. Literature is one window into that world. Students must understand that underneath our differences there is a common humanity that binds us together as human beings. In addition, all young people deserve the right to see their own life experiences and cultures reflected in the books they read in school. Using multicultural literature is a way of empowering all students by building their self-esteem and expanding their ability to make contact with those whose experiences are different from their own.

REFERENCES

Aoki, E. (1992). Turning the page: Asian Pacific American children's literature. In V.J. Harris (Ed.), *Teaching multicultural literature in grades K–8* (pp. 109–135). Norwood, MA: Christopher-Gordon.

Barrera, R.B., Liguori, O., & Salas, L. (1992). Ideas a literature can grow on: Key insights for enriching and expanding children's literature about the Mexican-American experience. In V.J. Harris (Ed.), *Teaching multicultural literature in grades K–8* (pp. 203–241). Norwood, MA: Christopher-Gordon.

Bishop, R.S. (1992). Multicultural literature for children: Making informed choices. In V.J. Harris (Ed.), *Teaching multicultural literature in grades K–8* (pp. 37–53). Norwood, MA: Christopher-Gordon.

Brown, J.E., & Stephens, E.C. (Eds.). (1998). *United in diversity: Using multicultural young adult literature in the classroom.* Urbana, IL: National Council of Teachers of English.

Charles, J. (2001, Winter). Interrelated themes in the young adolescent novels of Virginia Driving Hawk Sneve. *The ALAN Review, 28*(2), 60–62.

Day, F.A. (1994). *Multicultural voices in contemporary literature: A resource for teachers.* Portsmouth, NH: Heinemann.

Day, F.A. (1997). *Latina and Latino voices in literature for children and teenagers.* Portsmouth, NH: Heinemann.

Harris, V.J. (Ed.). (1992). *Teaching multicultural literature in grades K–8.* Norwood, MA: Christopher-Gordon.

Hipple, T. (Ed.). (1997). *Writers for young adults.* New York: Scribner.

Kaywell, J.F. (Ed.). (2000). *Adolescent literature as a complement to the classics* (Vol. 4). Norwood, MA: Christopher-Gordon.

Miller-Lachman, L. (Ed.). (1992). *Our family, our friends, our world: An annotated guide to significant multicultural books for children and teenagers.* New York: Bowker.

Nieto, S. (1992). We have stories to tell: A case study of Puerto Ricans in children's books. In V.J. Harris (Ed.), *Teaching multicultural literature in grades K–8* (pp. 171–201). Norwood, MA: Christopher-Gordon.

Olson, C.B. (1996). *Reading, thinking, and writing about multicultural literature.* Glenview, IL: Scott, Foresman.

Rodriguez, C. (2001, May 15). Immigrants rejuvenate population. *Boston Globe*, p. 13.

Rodriguez, L. (2001, May 23). Latino mix becomes more diverse. *Houston Chronicle*, p. 1.

Sims, R. (1982). *Shadow and substance: Afro-American experience in contemporary children's fiction.* Urbana, IL: National Council of Teachers of English.

U.S. population is younger, growing faster, Census Bureau reports. (2000, February 28). *Jet.*

Willis, A. (Ed.). (1998). *Teaching and using multicultural literature in grades 9–12: Moving beyond the canon.* Norwood, MA: Christopher-Gordon.

Wrolstad, M. (2000, January 13). U.S. populations projected to double in next century. *Dallas Morning News*, p. 1A.

YOUNG ADULT LITERATURE CITED

Alvarez, J. (1991). *How the Garcia girls lost their accents.* New York: Algonquin.

Anaya, R. (1972). *Bless me, Ultima.* Berkeley, CA: Tonatiuh-Quinto Sol International.

Anaya, R. (1995). *The Anaya reader.* New York: Warner.

Banks, L.R. (1980). *Indian in the cupboard.* New York: Avon.

Banks, L.R. (1999). *The return of the Indian.* New York: Avon.

Bertrand, D.G. (1995). *Sweet fifteen.* Houston: Arte Publico.

Bruchac, J. (1993). *Flying with the eagle, racing the great bear: Stories from Native North America.* Mahwah, NJ: Bridgewater.

Bruchac, J. (1998). *The heart of a chief.* New York: Dial.

Bruchac, J. (2001). *The journal of Jesse Smoke.* New York: Scholastic.

Caduto, M.J., & Bruchac, J. (1988). *Keepers of the Earth: Native American stories and environmental activities for children.* Golden, CO: Fulcrum.

Cisneros, S. (1984). *The house on Mango Street.* Houston: Arte Publico.

Cofer, J.O. (1995). *An island like you: Stories of the Barrio.* New York: Orchard.

Cofer, J.O. (1998). *The year of our revolution: New and selected stories and poems.* New York: Delacorte.

Crew, L. (1989). *Children of the river.* New York: Dell.

Dorris, M. (1992) *Morning Girl.* New York: Hyperion.

Dorris, M. (1996). *Sees behind trees.* New York: Hyperion.

Gallo, D.R. (Ed.) (1993). *Join in: Multiethnic short stories by outstanding writers for young adults.* New York: Delacorte.

Garland, S. (1993). *Shadow of the dragon.* San Diego: Harcourt Brace.

Hamilton, V. (1967). *Zeely.* New York: Macmillan.

Hamilton, V. (1968). *The house of Dies Drear.* New York: Macmillan.

Highwater, J. (1977). *Anpao: An American Indian odyssey.* Philadelphia: Lippincott.

Hinton, S.E. (1997). *The outsiders.* Englewood Cliffs, NJ: Prentice Hall.

Johnson, A. (1993). *Toning the sweep.* Danbury, CT: Orchard Books.

Lachtman, O.D. (1995). *The girl from Playa Blanca.* Houston: Arte Publico.

Martinez, V. (1996). *Parrot in the oven: mi vida.* New York: HarperCollins.

Mori, K. (1993). *Shizuko's daughter.* New York: Fawcett Juniper.

Mori, K. (1995). *One bird.* New York: Fawcett Juniper.

Mori, K. (1997). *Polite lies: On being a woman caught between cultures.* New York: Henry Holt.

Myers, W.D. (1975). *Fast Sam, cool Clyde, and stuff.* New York: Viking.

Myers, W.D. (1988). *Scorpions.* New York: HarperCollins.

Myers, W.D. (1990). *The mouse rap.* New York: HarperCollins.

Myers, W.D. (1991). *Fallen angels.* New York: Scholastic.

Myers, W.D. (1992). *Somewhere in the darkness.* New York: Scholastic.

Myers, W.D. (1999). *Monster.* New York: HarperCollins.

Myers, W.D. (2000). *145th Street: Short stories.* New York: Delacorte.

Myers, W.D. (2001). *Bad boy: A memoir.* New York: HarperCollins.

Namioka, L. (1994). *April and the dragon lady.* San Diego: Harcourt Brace.

Rochman, H., & McCampbell, D.Z. (Eds.). (1997). *Leaving home: 15 distinguished authors explore personal journeys.* New York: HarperCollins.

Ryan, P.M. (2000). *Esperanza rising.* New York: Scholastic.

Singer, M. (Ed.). (2000). *I believe in water: Twelve brushes with religion.* New York: HarperCollins.

Sneve, V.D.H. (1972). *High Elk's treasure.* Lincoln, NE: Bison Books.

Sneve, V.D.H. (1972). *Jimmy Yellow Hawk.* New York: Holiday House.

Sneve, V.D.H. (1974). *When thunders spoke.* Lincoln, NE: Bison Books.

Soto, G. (1985). *Living up the street: Narrative recollections.* San Francisco: Strawberry Hill.

Soto, G. (1990). *Baseball in April.* San Diego: Harcourt Brace.

Soto, G. (1994). *Crazy weekend.* New York: Scholastic.

Soto, G. (1994). *Jesse.* San Diego: Harcourt Brace.

Tan, A. (1989). *The joy luck club.* New York: Putnam.

Tan, A. (1991). *The kitchen god's wife.* New York: Putnam.

Tan, A. (2001). *The bonesetter's daughter.* New York: Putnam.

Thomas, J.C. (Ed.). (1990). *A gathering of flowers: Stories about being young in America.* New York: HarperCollins.

Uchida, Y. (1971). *Journey to Topaz.* New York: Atheneum.

Uchida, Y. (1978). *Journey home.* New York: Atheneum.

Vuong, L.D. (1982). *The brocaded slipper and other Vietnamese tales.* Reading, MA: Addison-Wesley.

Vuong, L.D. (1993). *Sky legends of Vietnam.* New York: HarperCollins.

Wilder, L.I. (1953). *Little house on the prairie.* New York: HarperCollins.

Williams-Garcia, R. (2001). *Every time a rainbow dies.* New York: HarperCollins.

Woodson, J. (1995). *From the notebooks of Melanin Sun.* New York: Scholastic.

Woodson, J. (2000). *Miracle's boys.* New York: Putnam.

Yep, L. (1977). *Child of the owl.* New York: Harper & Row.

Yep, L. (1982). *Dragon of the Lost Sea.* New York: Harper & Row.

Yep, L. (1991). *The lost garden.* New York: William Morrow.

Yep, L. (Ed.). (1993). *American dragons: Twenty-five Asian American voices.* New York: HarperCollins.

Yep, L. (1995). *Thief of hearts.* New York: HarperCollins.

WEBSITES

http://factfinder.census.gov

http://www.census.gov/population/estimates/nation

SECTION ‖

Exploring
Genres

The goal of this section is to broaden the range of genres that teachers and students can use to enhance reading skills and advance knowledge. This focus is necessary because many YA readers have limited attention spans and lose interest quickly when the reading does not match their interests. The following chapters explore the use of historical fiction, nonfiction including biography and autobiography, poetry, and picture books in the YA classroom. Again, teacher-tested ideas are included in these chapters to demonstrate realistic ways to use the books discussed.

CHAPTER 4

Great Moments in History: Engaging Young Adults Through Historical Fiction

Barbara A. Illig-Avilés

Those of us who work with young adults know that an important part of their development involves exploring, questioning, critiquing, and testing as they struggle to discover the world and their own identities. As educators we are always looking for ways to meet the needs of adolescents and at the same time fulfill curriculum requirements that seem to grow in yearly spurts like the students we teach. Historical fiction, because of its unique characteristics, is a powerful genre to use as a bridge between content curriculum and the social and emotional needs of young adults.

Historical Fiction as a Bridge

The major task of adolescence, from a psychological point of view, is the establishment of a stable and resilient sense of personal identity. This sense of personal identity is not inborn. Young adults actively construct their personal identities as a result of their ongoing effort to integrate and make sense of their experiences (Elkind, 1994). Historical fiction, like excellent contemporary YA fiction, is the story of humankind, yet is removed from many of the problems and struggles of adolescents' everyday lives. As students vicariously engage in the dramatic and often vivid struggles of the characters, they confront feelings and behaviors that provide insight into their own quest for identity, recognize and validate viewpoints different from their own, and may even begin to consider alternative ways to handle their own problems (Norton, 1995).

Readers of historical fiction gain an understanding of their own heritage (Lynch-Brown & Tomlinson, 1993). When we as educators reflect on our own reading of historical fiction, as well as biography and autobiography, we often can pinpoint those pieces of literature that helped us appreciate the struggles and acts of personal courage required by people who, although they lived at a different time, were essentially the same as we are. As our admiration and empathy grew for the characters, so did the pride of our own national, ethnic, or racial connections. It was then that we came to understand that our lives were influenced by those who lived before us, and that our actions or inactions will influence the lives of those yet to come. One aspect of the intellectual development of young adults is their desire to reinvent society and to envision the possibilities of what might be, to find the ideal (Caissy, 1994). Historical fiction can provide a springboard for those critical and usually lively discussions.

Finally, historical fiction makes history come alive. As readers are immersed in the culture of the time, historical fiction provides a dramatic departure from the sterile world of the textbook. Historical fiction, because it focuses on history as story, is more accessible to students as they work to reconstruct and reinterpret the past, analyze multiple viewpoints, and identify and describe patterns of change. Without realizing it, readers begin to construct a clearer understanding of the values, beliefs, activities, events, and social issues that characterize a particular period of history, and they begin to build a schema for assimilating and accommodating factual information (Anderson, 1984). As a result, students gain more than a cursory knowledge of history; they gain a clearer understanding of history (Levstik, 1990).

According to Nawrot (1996), historical fiction may not be the most efficient means to teach history, but it is the most effective:

> It gives children a background for historical events, allowing them to relive the past, to internalize it, and thereby remember it far better than they remember information from a textbook. It encourages them to consider the cause of historical events and the consequences of those events on human lives.... At the same time, historical fiction exposes students to the power of literature. They see ordinary people doing extraordinary things. Those people, they learn, faced the same struggles and weaknesses that people do today. (p. 345)

Thus, historical fiction is an invaluable resource for meeting state and national standards for social studies that require learners to reconstruct and reinterpret the past, analyze multiple viewpoints, and identify and describe patterns of change.

BREAKER BY N.A. PEREZ

This is a story that takes place in hard coal country in a northern Pennsylvania town called Scatter Patch during the Industrial Revolution. It is told through the eyes of Pat. It begins with a tragedy that sends Pat abruptly into the world of labor in the mines at age 14. He works in the breaker separating the stones from coal coming through the building on chutes. Working under the conditions of the cold, flying dust, and other health hazards, he learns about the hardships of labor and the animosity that exists among the different ethnic groups in this coal town. Dreams of better working conditions and better pay are enough encouragement for Pat and his coworkers to organize a union.

Suggested Activities

- This activity is a group writing project that will help students see a familiar object in a different way by focusing on specific aspects. First, bring in objects for students to select from that are found in the book (baseball, lump of coal, lunch bucket, clothesline, etc.). Divide the class into groups of six, then subdivide each group into groups A–F. Ask all the A's to sit together, and so on for each letter. Vote on the object to be described, and then place it in the center of the room (or have one for each group). Give each child in the lettered group the following task (see Tompkins, 1998):

  A. Describe the object, its shapes, textures, colors, etc.

  B. Compare the object, explaining how it is like and unlike other objects.

  C. Apply the object, explaining all of its uses.

  D. Analyze the object, breaking it down into its constituent parts.

  E. Evaluate the object, describing its good and not-so-good attributes.

  F. Synthesize the object, describing how it was made, or describing how you could change it or improve it or have it perform different functions.

  Then, each student is responsible for writing a paragraph in the group to take back to the original group and share their writing (jigsaw strategy). Students then construct a cube and paste the six descriptions on the faces of the cube. This can be done with several objects and shared at a science fair as a "Guess Which Object" game.

- Create a timeline of Pat's life depicting six ways the character changed as he matured. Include specific parts from the book to support your timeline. Illustrate the six parts you have selected for the timeline, then write a brief description of the illustration below the picture.

- Select one photo from the scenes of life in coal-mining towns and complete one of the following:

  1. Write a diary entry from the viewpoint of one of the people in the photograph.

  2. Describe what you think is taking place in the photo.

  3. Look at the faces in the photos and describe the mood you sense, feelings they must have had, and possible dreams that would have kept them going.

Tracey Beard is a sixth-grade teacher in the Indiana Area School District, Indiana, Pennsylvania, USA.

Choosing the Best Historical Fiction

It is the story that counts! Good historical fiction, like any genre of literature, must be evaluated based on the strengths of the story itself. The plot must be engaging and of interest to young adults. No two people progress through adolescence at the same pace or with the same needs (Reed, 1994), so interest is of particular importance. Teachers who know the students they teach will be better able to choose just the right book.

One way to gain insight into the unique interests of our students is to develop a short interest inventory. Requesting information regarding the movies our students enjoy, the magazines they read, and their favorite television shows will help us select the most effective book for a particular class or group of students. Teachers might also consider sharing two or three books in a book talk and then allowing students to choose the one of most interest. The purpose of the book talk is to stimulate students' interest in the books and increase their motivation to read through a 2- to 3-minute, oral presentation on each book. Teachers usually show the book itself as they share information about the content, but they are careful not to tell too much about the plot. Some teachers read a short, exciting excerpt from the text; others introduce the main characters and allude to the conflict. What is important in the book talk is the teacher's authentic recommendation of the text as a good book.

The setting in historical fiction is of prime importance and must be integral to the story. Writers of good historical fiction re-create both time and place with rich, authentic details woven tightly into the fabric of the story. The details add color and texture but must never overwhelm the story itself. For example, in Avi's 1994 novel, *The Barn*, 9-year-old Ben; his brother, Harrison; and his sister, Nettie, are faced with two tragedies. First, their mother dies from diphtheria, and then their father suffers complete paralysis after a fit of palsy, which we now recognize as a stroke. In the following passage, the reader is quickly transported back to 1855 and to a land claim in the Willamette Valley, Oregon Territory:

> When Father first built it, the house had been sweet and clean, but hearth smoke had turned the walls all gray and streaked.... There were two windows, each stretched over with scraped elk hide to allow in pale light. There was a loft where Harrison and I slept and—between the windows—a shelf that held our Bible, Mother's copy of Pilgrim's Progress, and a book of sewing patterns. Father's big bed had a straw mattress that crinkled like a kindling fire when he moved about on it. Nettie's place was at the other end of the room. Because she was a girl, it was curtained with canvas from our old wagon. (pp. 12–13)

The authentic details continue to be an integral part of the tale as we watch Ben care for his father and then work alongside his brother and sister to build the barn, a gift to his father so he will want to live.

Susannah (Hickman, 1998) is another historical novel with an integral setting that is complemented with vivid and historically accurate details. The setting of Hickman's novel is a Shaker community near Lebanon, Ohio, in the year 1810. Through the eyes of 14-year-old Susannah, readers are introduced to the organization and utopian philosophy of this religious community. We empathize as Susannah struggles with rules she cannot abide and her unhappiness at living apart from her father in a house of children. Readers also come to understand the power of prejudice as this small community struggles with the feelings of its neighbors, who are suspicious of the Shakers' agrarian success. In this novel, as in other pieces of good historical fiction, the setting guides readers into the plot by creating visual images that capture their attention, foster their acceptance of the characters' experiences, and nurture their interest in the time period (Norton, 1995).

Like contemporary YA literature, outstanding historical fiction must also have characters with whom young adults can identify. In addition, the characters must exemplify the values, beliefs, and behaviors of the time period. According to MacLeod (1998), historical revisionism makes its way into historical fiction when writers "evade the common realities of the societies they write about" in order to align the novel with the social and political preferences in today's changing social climate (p. 31). She contends, for example, that it is preposterous to believe that 13-year-old Charlotte, the heroine in *True Confessions of Charlotte Doyle* (Avi, 1990), realistically portrays a young woman of the early 1800s. In the novel, Charlotte joins a ship's crew. On board, she not only performs the difficult duties of a seaman on a journey to America, but eventually becomes captain of the ship—quite a feat for *any* 13-year-old adolescent in 1832, but probably impossible when gender is considered. Although Charlotte is certainly a strong female character, an important characteristic to consider in YA literature, she does not provide students with accurate insights into the lives of the majority of females in the early 19th century.

It is important for teachers to encourage and stimulate critical discourse regarding historical authenticity as they help students understand characters within the social mores of the time. Teachers can provide a more balanced view of gender roles by also integrating contemporary YA novels or biographies with strong female characters in their curriculum. (See Chapter 7 in this volume for a good start in choosing biographies with strong characters.)

Balance is also important to consider with regard to viewpoint. Although some novels offer multiple viewpoints within the story, others deal with history from only one perspective. It is always a good idea to ensure that students view history from multiple perspectives by providing text sets on a particular time period. For example, *The Journal of James Edmond Pease: A Civil War Union Soldier* (Murphy, 1998), *With Every Drop of Blood* (Collier & Collier, 1994), *Be Ever Hopeful, Hannalee* (Beatty, 1988), *Run the Blockade* (Wisler, 2000), and *Bull Run* (Fleischman, 1993) are five novels on the American Civil War that teachers might consider to provide an engaging yet balanced view of that time period.

In her chapter in this volume, "Nonfiction Trade Books for Young Adults: A Complement to the Canon and Content Area Texts," Barbara Moss reminds us that adolescent students often prefer nonfiction as a genre (see Chapter 5). Consider, therefore, nonfiction texts like *Those Courageous Women of the Civil War* (Zeinert, 1998), *A Separate Battle: Women and the Civil War* (Chang, 1991), *Between Two Fires: Black Soldiers in the Civil War* (Hansen, 1993), *The Boys' War: Confederate and Union Soldiers Talk About the Civil War* (Murphy, 1990), and *North Star to Freedom: The Story of the Underground Railroad* (Gorrell, 2000) when developing a text set that encourages students to examine history from multiple perspectives.

The Scott O'Dell Historical Fiction Award is presented each year to an exemplary work of historical fiction set in the New World and published by a U.S. publisher. Figure 4.1 lists recent Scott O'Dell Award winners. The Annotated Bibliography of Historical Fiction at the end of this chapter includes an additional 13 recent YA titles recommended for use in the classroom.

FIGURE 4.1   Award-Winning Historical Fiction

2001	*The Art of Keeping Cool* (Janet Taylor Lisle)
2000	*Two Suns in the Sky* (Miriam Bat-Ami)
1999	*Forty Acres and Maybe a Mule* (Harriette G. Robinet)
1998	*Out of the Dust* (Karen Hesse)
1997	*Jip, His Story* (Katherine Paterson)
1996	*The Bomb* (Theodore Taylor)
1995	*Under the Blood-Red Sun* (Graham Salisbury)
1994	*Bull Run* (Paul Fleischman)
1993	*Morning Girl* (Michael Dorris)
1992	*Stepping on the Cracks* (Mary Downing Hahn)

Curricular Connections: Literature at the Crossroads

Social studies relies on making linkages and connections as students integrate knowledge, skills, and attitudes within and across disciplines. To support such a process, the National Council for the Social Studies (NCSS) identified five key principles that should undergird all social studies programs of excellence (1994). They explain that social studies teaching and learning are powerful when they are (1) meaningful, (2) integrative, (3) value-based, (4) challenging, and (5) accessible for active involvement. These principles are powerful and can be the framework for curriculum that includes literature-based instruction. In fact, after a review of the research regarding literature-based instruction and its effects on social studies learning, McGowan, Erickson, and Neufeld (1996) recommended that teachers "adopt this potentially productive instructional approach" (p. 206).

Using the text set in the American Civil War described earlier, we can examine one effective approach developed by a middle school humanities team. *Bull Run* (Fleischman, 1993) was selected as the core book that all students would read. The social studies teachers took responsibility for exploring the sociopolitical climate in the North and the South as the Civil War exploded. Fleischman's novel is well suited to such an analysis because it describes this volatile time through the eyes and experiences of 16 different characters: 8 from the North and another 8 from the South. The English teachers also provided students with a choice for a second novel from several fiction and nonfiction texts and engaged the students in heterogeneous literature discussion groups. The art

TEACHER IDEA

COMMEMORATIVE COIN

Most characters in a story have many unique characteristics. Choose a character from a story who is "one-of-a-kind" and create a commemorative coin in that person's honor. Following the format on a common quarter, penny, dime, or nickel, illustrate the front of the coin with the character's portrait. On the back of the coin, list 5 to 10 traits reflecting that character. Then, write a summary of the story incorporating some of the character's traits listed. Include details from the story to support the traits.

Tracey Beard is a sixth-grade teacher in the Indiana Area School District, Indiana, Pennsylvania, USA.

and music teachers collaborated as they guided students in the creation of a video montage that included both original artwork and lyrics as well as authentic music and photographs from the period. Toward the middle of the unit, as students began to ask for more in-depth information regarding medical and technological information of the time, the science teacher also became involved.

Making History Come Alive

In the journal *Middle Level Learning*, Dan Rea (1999) presents a "serious-fun" model for teaching social studies based on Dewey's belief that "the ideal learning condition is one that is playful and serious at the same time" (Dewey, 1933, p. 286). Rea emphasizes the need to stimulate student curiosity, provide for student choice, challenge students with thought-provoking dilemmas, and tap into students' creative abilities by establishing opportunities for young adults to explore and play with information. This last item often gets too little attention. What follows, therefore, are some suggestions for activities that stimulate student interest, tap into the theory of multiple intelligences, and promote an in-depth construction of knowledge.

The Open-Mind Portrait in Context

The Open-Mind Portrait in Context is an adaptation based on a technique developed by Tompkins (1998). The purpose is to visually represent story events from a character's perspective. In the Open-Mind Portrait in Context, students visually depict the inner feelings and struggles of a character using words and pictures within the outline of the portrait, the foreground of the drawing. The area around the portrait becomes the context, the historical setting in which the story takes place. Factual details surround the portrait so the viewer/reader understands how the story is related to time and place (see Figure 4.2). As with Tompkins's Open-Mind Portrait, students can elaborate by drawing the face of the character on one page, then attaching the "mind" and context as a second page.

Because good writers of historical fiction creatively weave details into a story, they often go unnoticed by the adolescent reader who is intent on following the plot line. Thus it may be a good idea to have students create a data chart as they analyze the novel for historic details (see Figure 4.3). Headings such as *historical character, events, documented places*, and *artifacts* will help students list important information for developing the context portion of the portrait. Ask students to verify historic details and to add new information to their lists using nonfiction

FIGURE 4.2   Open-Mind Portrait by Student Denise J. Frederick

"Inside and Outside" based on *Out of the Dust* (Hesse, 1997)

FIGURE 4.3   Data Chart

Historical Character	Events	Documented Places	Artifacts	Reference Source

trade books and other reference materials. Challenge students to represent visually, in as creative a way as possible, the context information that had both an explicit and implicit influence on the feelings, beliefs, and actions of the character. The data chart, along with a story map, is also an excellent tool to support students' analysis of text.

Living Illustrations: A Miniseries

Many students may be familiar with living manger scenes performed by many church groups during the Christmas holiday season, so they should have little trouble visualizing this next activity. Facilitate a discussion with students to explore the value of illustrations from both an aesthetic and efferent stance. Ask students to analyze the text to determine which six to eight scenes in the book would be most valuable for retelling the novel in a miniseries of live illustrations.

Once the class has determined the specific scenes, organize the students into groups of three or four, each with the task of designing a specific scene to become part of the whole-class performance. To begin, ask each group to determine which characters should be portrayed in the living illustration. Then ask them to position themselves like statues to depict or evoke the essential mood of the scene. Remind students that the figures should be frozen in a position of action and that body language and facial expression are important to convey the appropriate mood. Next, groups consider the order in which the characters should come to life. They may wish to practice integrating their still-life position into a natural action or movement.

This kinesthetic activity is a good prewriting experience before groups begin to write the dialogue for the scene. I have actually seen students move back into the position of the scene to try out and revise lines of dialogue or particular monologues they have written. Give students a time limit for the scene. I have found that 3 or 4 minutes seems to be most effective. The shorter time forces the dialogue or monologue to focus on the most important points, and it necessitates the use of just the right phrase or word to capture the moment. The short scripts can easily be memorized or presented as Readers Theatre. Caution students that they may need to do more revision in order to make smooth transitions with the scenes before and after theirs.

Students can set up their scenes in sequence around the classroom, in an auditorium, or down a hallway. All actors should remain motionless and "in position" until the spotlight shines on them. An audience of parents and community members or other classmates can move from one scene to another as they might move through a museum.

Historical Diaries: Writing Historical Fiction

Every young writer should have the opportunity to write a piece in each genre he or she studies, including historical fiction. Writing several entries for a diary is not an overwhelming task for even the most reluctant writer, and with the proper support, most students can be successful.

Begin by asking students to choose a specific time or incident in history to research. You might center the research on a particular topic or theme of study, or provide a list such as the following:

- A Chinese immigrant working on the Union Pacific Railroad
- A Welsh or Irish immigrant laboring in the coal mines or living in a mining community in western Pennsylvania in the 1850s
- A young woman in New York City drawn into the campaign for women's rights in the early 1900s

- An army medic in the ambulance corps in France during World War I
- A member of the Sons of Liberty living in Massachusetts prior to the outbreak of the Revolutionary War
- A Quaker girl in Pennsylvania involved in political justice issues concerning Native Americans or slaves
- A seaman on the *Amistad*, a slave ship

Have students create a data chart of factual details specific to that time period (see Figure 4.3, page 79). I usually require students to work with a number of different references, including videotapes and photographs. I often suggest that they work in teams of two or three to complete the research.

Once students have completed their research, ask them to describe and name the fictional character whose diary they will write by developing a character profile or sketch. This could be in writing, but many students prefer to develop their character by creating a character web (see Figure 4.4). Details such as appearance, age, family, education, and living conditions are part of the web development.

FIGURE 4.4   *Character Web*

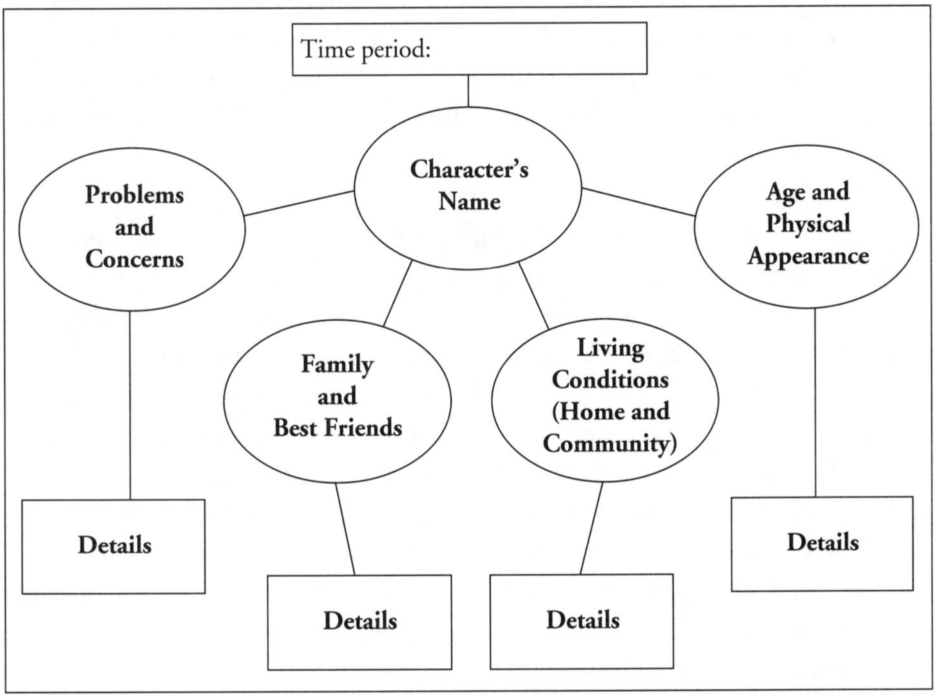

Now students are ready to begin their historical diary entries. Share a variety of trade books for students to refer to as models for their own writing. Four of my favorites are *Diary of a Drummer Boy* by Marlene Targ Brill (1998); *Hannah's Journal: The Story of an Immigrant Girl* by Marissa Moss (2000); *Standing in the Light: The Captive Diary of Catharine Carey Logan* (1998), one of the Dear America series authored by Mary Pope Osborne; and Osborne's recent book, *My Brother's Keeper: Virginia's Diary* (2000). I always remind students that each entry must be written in the first person, reveal the feelings or beliefs of the character, and contain at least four or five factual details from the research. Students who choose the same time period or incident can organize their diary entries into a book modeled after *Bull Run* (Fleischman, 1993). Single character entries can also be bound into a diary or journal to be shared with classmates, friends, and family.

Extra, Extra, Read All About It: Creating a Period Newspaper

Historical fiction is a particularly effective genre for developing efferent and persuasive writing skills when students analyze and reflect on a historic time and place in order to create a period newspaper. The classroom can be organized like a city newspaper staff with an editor-in-chief, reporters, section editors, copy editors, and so forth, with the goal of producing period newspapers. Because I want my students directly engaged in all parts of the writing process and expect them to develop writing skills in a variety of forms, I usually organize my class into heterogeneous cooperative groups of four or five. Each group's final product is, of necessity, a smaller paper, but the students seem to enjoy the variety of tasks and appreciate the creativity and diversity of the published products.

A number of minilessons may be required to develop the knowledge and skills necessary for students to be successful. Acquainting students with the parts of a newspaper and with analyzing headlines, major news stories, local items, and editorials for style and form are crucial. We should also help students note the subtle—and sometimes not so subtle—differences in the way news is reported from paper to paper. Classrooms with Internet capabilities can easily examine a variety of national and even international papers. Local historical societies often have artifacts, files of photographs, and newspaper accounts of local events that provide flavor as well as insight into the political mood, economic conditions, and social mores of a particular period. Community libraries and the Internet are also excellent sources for obtaining old newspaper stories and other valuable reference material.

Although the newspapers themselves provide models for writing, I am particularly fond of a series of trade books with text in a newspaper format published by Candlewick Press. Sharing trade books such as *The Roman News* (Langley, Desouza, Powell, & Steele, 1996) seems to give students permission to use their creativity and research skills to write engaging pieces.

Period newspapers can be developed based on nearly all historical fiction. In the past, I have worked with young adults to create newspapers after reading *Across Five Aprils* (Hunt, 1964), *The Slave Dancer* (Fox, 1973), *The Slopes of War* (Perez, 1984), and *Bull Run* (Fleischman, 1993). Figure 4.5 is an example of a news story one student developed after reading *Bull Run*.

FIGURE 4.5   Student News Story

The Southern Gazette

| July 22, 1861 | Monday | 5cents | Section 1 | Page 1 |

The Day that the Battle Began

Sunday, July 21, on the muddy creeksides of Bull Run, a place located right above the Manassas Gap in Richmond, Virginia, is where it all began. The morning was hot and muggy and our soldiers were ready to fight for our beliefs.

The brave young volunteers of the South met the Union army yesterday. Northerners came as spectators to watch the show. Everyone was surprised at the violence. The smoke, dirt, and death of the battle was too much for any

bystander to watch. The Union soldiers and sightseers from Washington stampeded back home after General Beauregard and his men showed the power of right over wrong.

The battle went on all day until just after 4:00 p.m. At the day's end, close to 900 young men had died. The day was long and rang bitter in the mouths of the Northern troops. McDowell's men were tired and discouraged as they withdrew.

Final Thoughts

Historical fiction entertainingly enlivens history. It invites adolescents to think more critically about the world's past. It helps them gain a deeper understanding of the effect historical events have on the social, political, and economic issues of the times. Teachers who integrate historical fiction into their curriculum capitalize on a genre that can help their students "make sense" of their historical past, present, and, by extension, their future. Today's wide range of historical fiction titles written specifically for young adults makes it easier to find literature that will engage adolescents on a personal level and entice them to journey more widely into the world of books.

REFERENCES

Anderson, R.C. (1984). Role of the reader's schema in comprehension, learning and memory. In R.C. Anderson, J. Osborn, & R.J. Tierney (Eds.), *Learning to read in American schools: Basal readers and context texts* (pp. 243–258). Hillsdale, NJ: Erlbaum.

Caissy, G.A. (1994). *Early adolescence: Understanding the 10 to 15 year old.* New York: Plenum Press.

Dewey, J. (1933). *How we think.* Boston: D.C. Heath.

Elkind, D. (1994). *A sympathetic understanding of the child* (3rd ed.). Boston: Allyn & Bacon.

Levstik, L.S. (1990). Research directions: Mediating content through literary texts. *Language Arts, 67*(8), 848–853.

Lynch-Brown, C., & Tomlinson, C. (1993). *Essentials of children's literature.* Boston: Allyn & Bacon.

MacLeod, A.C. (1998, January/February). Writing backward: Modern models in historical fiction. *The Horn Book,* 26–33.

McGowan, T.M., Erickson, L., & Neufeld, J.A. (1996). With reason and rhetoric: Building the case for the literature-social studies connection. *Social Education, 60*(4), 203–207.

National Council for the Social Studies (NCSS). (1994). *Curriculum standards for social studies: Expectations of excellence.* Washington, DC: Author.

Nawrot, K. (1996). Making connections with historical fiction. *The Clearing House, 69*(6), 343–345.

Norton, D. (1995). *Through the eyes of a child: An introduction to children's literature.* Englewood Cliffs, NJ: Merrill.

Rea, D. (1999). Serious fun in social studies for middle schoolers. *Middle Level Learning, 6,* 2–5.

Reed, A.J. (1994). *Reaching adolescents: The young adult book and the school.* New York: Macmillan.

Tompkins, G.E. (1998). *Language arts: Content and teaching strategies* (4th ed.). Upper Saddle River, NJ: Merrill.

YOUNG ADULT LITERATURE CITED

Avi. (1990). *True confessions of Charlotte Doyle*. New York: Avon.

Avi. (1994). *The barn*. New York: Avon.

Beatty, P. (1988). *Be ever hopeful, Hannalee*. New York: Morrow.

Brill, M.T. (1998). *Diary of a drummer boy*. Brookfield, CT: Millbrook.

Chang, I. (1991). *A separate battle: Women and the Civil War*. New York: Lodestar/Dutton.

Collier, J., & Collier, C. (1994). *With every drop of blood*. New York: Delacorte.

Fleischman, P. (1993). *Bull Run*. New York: Harper Trophy.

Fox, P. (1973). *The slave dancer*. New York: Bantam Doubleday Dell.

Gorrell, G. (2000). *North Star to freedom: The story of the Underground Railroad*. New York: Delacorte.

Hansen, J. (1993). *Between two fires: Black soldiers in the Civil War*. Danbury, CT: Watts.

Hesse, K. (1997). *Out of the dust*. New York: Scholastic.

Hickman, J. (1998). *Susannah*. New York: Harper Trophy.

Hunt, I. (1964). *Across five Aprils*. Prairie Grove, AR: Follett.

Langley, A., Desouza, P., Powell, A., & Steele, P. (Eds.). (1996). *The Roman news*. Cambridge, MA: Candlewick.

Moss, M. (2000). *Hannah's journal: The story of an immigrant girl*. San Diego, CA: Silver Whistle.

Murphy, J. (1990). *The boys' war: Confederate and Union soldiers talk about the Civil War*. New York: Clarion.

Murphy, J. (1998). *The journal of James Edmond Pease: A Civil War Union soldier*. New York: Scholastic.

Osborne, M.P. (1998). *Standing in the light: The captive diary of Catharine Carey Logan*. New York: Scholastic.

Osborne, M.P. (2000). *My brother's keeper: Virginia's diary*. New York: Scholastic.

Perez, N. (1984). *The slopes of war*. Boston: Houghton Mifflin.

Rappaport, D. (1991). *Escape from slavery: Five journeys to freedom*. New York: HarperCollins.

Salisbury, G. (1995). *Under the blood-red sun*. New York: Dell Yearling.

Wisler, G.C. (2000). *Run the blockade*. New York: HarperCollins.

Zeinert, K. (1998). *Those courageous women of the Civil War*. Brookfield, CT: Millbrook.

ANNOTATED BIBLIOGRAPHY OF HISTORICAL FICTION

Avi. (1996). Beyond the Western Sea [series]. New York: Avon.

The Escape from Home and *Lord Kirkle's Money* are the first two books in this series that develops the Irish immigrant story. During the potato famine in 1851, 11-year-old Sir Laurence Kirkle, fleeing a privileged life, meets Maura O'Connel, 15, and her brother, Patrick, 12. The siblings are also fleeing Ireland. Their hovel has been destroyed, and they have been evicted by Lord Kirkle's overseer.

Ayres, K. (1998). *North by night: A story of the Underground Railroad.* New York: Delacorte.
Readers learn about the Underground Railroad through the fictionalized letters of a 16-year-old girl. Set in Ohio in 1851, this provocative and compelling novel is based on solid research. Teachers might pair this novel with Doreen Rappaport's *Escape From Slavery: Five Journeys to Freedom* (1991).

Bat-Ami, M. (1999). *Two suns in the sky.* Chicago: Cricket.
To many residents of Oswego, New York, the 1,000 refugees housed by the U.S. government at Fort Ontario in 1944 were a problem to be solved. In this thought-provoking novel, readers come to a clearer understanding of what it means to be a refugee. The story is told through the voices of Adam Bornstein, a 15-year-old from Zagreb, Yugoslavia, and Christine Cook, an adolescent resident of the town.

Bruchac, J. (1998). *The arrow over the door.* New York: Dial.
Set in Saratoga, New York, in 1777, this piece of historical fiction is based on the encounter of the Algonquin Indians and the Quakers at the Friends' meetinghouse.

Bruchac, J. (2000). *Sacajawea: The story of Bird Woman and the Lewis and Clark expedition.* San Diego, CA: Silver Whistle.
The story of Clark's journey is told from the alternating viewpoints of Sacajawea and William Clark. Clark's voice is often based on authentic excerpts from his journals, and Bruchac, a Native American author, uses many research sources to accurately portray Sacajawea. The result is a wonderful story that blends historical fact and fiction.

Cushman, K. (1996). *The ballad of Lucy Whipple.* New York: Clarion.
Lucky Diggings, California, the setting for this novel, portrays the less romantic side of the gold rush through Lucy's letters. Helping her widowed mother run a boarding house for miners is no easy task, and Lucy longs to return to her grandparents' house in Massachusetts. (Also consider *Catherine, Called Birdy* [Cushman, 1994], which is the story of a daughter of an English country knight who is not ready to become a quiet, obedient wife—especially to old Shaggy Beard. Her story, told through humorous diary entries, gives us a good picture of life during the Middle Ages.)

Durrant, L. (1998). *The beaded moccasins: The story of Mary Campbell.* New York: Clarion.
The year is 1759 when Mary Campbell is captured by the Delaware Indians and forced to walk miles to their new home in the Ohio wilderness. This engaging novel, based on an actual event, contains both a bibliography and a glossary.

Hunter, M. (1998). *The king's swift rider: A novel on Robert the Bruce.* New York: HarperCollins.
The story of Robert the Bruce's 7-year fight for independence from the English is told through the eyes of Martin, a young man offered into service by his widowed mother. Martin's only interest is to be a scholar, but he soon becomes a key figure in Scotland's fight for freedom. He risks his life again and again as a spy and courier in this gripping tale set in the 14th century.

Karr, K. (1998). *The great turkey walk.* New York: Farrar, Straus & Giroux.
A humorous tale that centers on driving a thousand turkeys from Missouri to Denver in 1860 before the advent of railroads. Simon, whom some consider simple-minded, is not interested in what others say about him. He seeks the aid of a recovering alcoholic mule-

skinner, befriends a runaway slave, and confronts his long-lost father in this fast-paced, fun-filled novel.

Paulsen, G. (1998). *Soldier's heart: A novel of the Civil War.* New York: Delacorte.

This story is based on the true story of Charley Goddard, a 15-year-old who lies about his age and joins the First Minnesota Volunteers. Readers follow Charlie as he first meets the Confederate forces of war at Manassas, until he is wounded at Gettysburg. At age 19, this veteran returns home, a victim of "soldier's heart," which is now known as traumatic stress syndrome. The novel is well researched and describes in a powerful and dramatic style the reality of war. (Pair this text with *My Brother's Keeper: Virginia's Diary* [Osborne, 2000], which follows the experiences of Virginia and her family as they live through the Battle of Gettysburg.)

Reeder, C. (1998). *Foster's war.* New York: Scholastic.

Pearl Harbor has been bombed and the mortal storm of World War II has begun. This powerful piece of historical fiction describes the devastating effects of war, including racism and internment, on a young soldier's family. (Consider pairing the novel with Graham Salisbury's 1995 novel, *Under the Blood-Red Sun.*)

Rinaldi, A. (1997). *An acquaintance with darkness.* Orlando, FL: Harcourt Brace.

The Civil War has ended, and President Lincoln has just been assassinated. Fourteen-year-old Emily's mother dies, and she must decide where to live. Will it be with her uncle, a doctor who could be involved in body snatching? On top of everything else, Emily fears that one member of her best friend's family may be one of John Wilkes Booth's accomplices.

Rinaldi, A. (1999). *Amelia's war.* New York: Scholastic.

Folks are taking sides in Hagerstown, Maryland, a town split in two by the Civil War. Amelia, after a painful incident, vows that she will not take sides, but an opportunity to make a small difference in the course of the war leads to a compelling and suspenseful tale.

CHAPTER 5

Nonfiction Trade Books for Young Adults: A Complement to the Canon and Content Area Texts

Barbara Moss

Most adolescents in the United States choose not to read. Interest in reading begins to decline in the middle grades and continues its descent through the high school years. According to Thomas and Moorman (1983), "The student who can read, but chooses not to, is probably the most crucial concern confronting our educational institutions today. It is not illiteracy we are combating, but aliteracy" (p. 137). Findings of the 1994 National Assessment of Educational Progress (NAEP) confirm this point: More than one fourth of eighth and twelfth graders reported never or hardly ever reading for pleasure outside of school (Campbell, Donahue, Reese, & Phillips, 1996). Results of the 1998 NAEP data are equally discouraging: 34% of eighth graders and 21% of twelfth graders reported never or hardly ever talking about their reading with family or friends (Donahue, Voelkl, Campbell, & Mazzeo, 1999).

Studies dating from the 1950s show that when adolescents do read, they often prefer nonfiction (Carter, 1987; Norvell, 1950; Purves & Beach, 1972). This genre, which includes biography and information books, can be the catalyst that turns teenagers into lifetime readers (Abrahamson & Carter, 1991).

Despite its popularity, nonfiction seldom makes its way into middle or high school classrooms. In fact, most adolescents get little exposure to information books in school. Teachers are often unfamiliar with this genre and uncertain about how to incorporate it into their curriculum. In a recent study, even teachers who provided time for sustained silent reading insisted that students read fiction instead of information books (Worthy, 1998).

Nonfiction trade books are an untapped resource with great potential for motivating the many reluctant adolescent readers in our middle and high school classrooms. Whether provided for free-choice reading or used instructionally, nonfiction may turn adolescents who do not read much into those who read even after the final school bell rings. Evidence for this point comes from the voices of students themselves. In interviews with Kylene Beers (1990), several unmotivated seventh-grade readers identified six activities that would motivate them to read on their own:

1. Choosing their own books.
2. Having teachers read entire books aloud.
3. Comparing movies to books.
4. Reading illustrated books.
5. Doing art activities related to books.
6. Reading nonfiction materials, including sports handbooks and magazines.

Today's nonfiction can enhance adolescents' understanding of an array of topics and may even cultivate interests that last a lifetime. Nonfiction can complement fictional novels used in the English classroom by providing different, true-to-life perspectives of events encountered in fiction. It can enrich the study of every content area, including history, mathematics, science, art, and music. It can deepen students' knowledge of real people, places, and phenomena of the present and the past.

This chapter discusses ways teachers can introduce and incorporate nonfiction in both English language arts and content area classrooms. The first section of the chapter offers a rationale for using nonfiction and guidelines for its selection. The second recommends ways to introduce nonfiction through sustained silent reading and teacher read-alouds. The third section suggests ways to organize the classroom for student reading of nonfiction. The final section explores response to nonfiction through discussion and writing.

Why Use Nonfiction Young Adult Trade Books?

As mentioned earlier, nonfiction is the literature of choice for many adolescents' out-of-school reading. In a study of high school students who dropped out, 65% reported "a consistent interest, even a love of reading" (Altenbaugh,

Engel, & Martin, 1995). On their own, they read books by a range of authors, including Nelson Mandela and Malcolm X, but none reported reading biographies or information literature in school. Sadly, all lost interest in academic reading because their in-school reading diet consisted mainly of assignments in sterile, lifeless textbooks.

In another study, several successful students diagnosed as having dyslexia described the importance of voluntary reading to their growth as readers. They read widely in areas of passionate personal interest, including biography, science, history, physics, math, religion, and business (Fink, 1995/1996). According to Allington (1994), this kind of reading is "the most potent factor in the development of reading processes" (p. 21).

By using nonfiction in classrooms, teachers can bridge the gap between students' in-school and out-of-school reading and capitalize on their interest in this genre. They can link books that engage reluctant readers with classroom content in ways that promote critical thinking and, at the same time, encourage reading both in and out of school. In this way, they can promote student engagement with a variety of text types, a practice found to improve reading achievement.

As Egan (1992) notes, adolescents are captivated by

> the most courageous or the cruelest acts, the strangest and the most bizarre natural phenomena, the most terrible or the most wonderful events. These are staples of the TV shows, books, and films that exploit this prominent characteristic of students' imaginations.... Students are interested in limits and extremes because such exotica provide the context within which their daily lives and experiences are meaningful. (pp. 72–73)

Many nonfiction books address the types of extremes Egan describes. Recent titles like *Into Thin Air: A Personal Account of the Mount Everest Disaster* (Krakauer, 1998) clearly fall into this category. This book describes in excruciating detail the May 1996 Mount Everest expedition in which 12 people were killed. It could provide a powerful complement to a survival unit incorporating novels like *Call of the Wild* (London, 1990) or the popular *Hatchet* (Paulsen, 1996).

Other books, such as *Rocket Boys: A Memoir* (Hickam, 1998), explore extremes in circumstances and determination. This memoir by Homer Hickam, a NASA engineer who trained astronauts for space walks, became a movie titled *October Sky* in 1999. It describes the author's determination as a teenager to build rockets and ultimately escape his home—a dying West Virginia coal mining town. This title could be an important addition to a middle or high school science classroom.

Teachers can easily locate other nonfiction books that explore these extremes. For instance, Karen Grindall, a middle-grade teacher in Akron, Ohio, used Robert Ballard's *Exploring the Titanic* (1993) to involve her students in a theme study of life at the turn of the 20th century. Students read and discussed the book in small and large groups. Through simulations, they experienced life aboard the *Titanic* in first-, second-, and third-class berths. They conducted research about the ship's passengers. Then each assumed the identity of an actual Titanic passenger and wrote about their experiences from that passenger's point of view.

Nonfiction books can do more than motivate, though; they can also improve student comprehension of expository text. This ability to understand exposition is essential to success in the Information Age—an age when information is doubling every 5 years (Wurman, 1989). Many adolescents have trouble understanding expository text, possibly because students most often meet exposition in poorly organized, badly written, and user-unfriendly textbooks (Anderson, Armbruster, & Kantor, 1980). Today's nonfiction trade books are well written, clearly organized, and attractive. Their authors are skilled in the art of molding facts into clear, enticing language that moves these books well beyond being baskets of facts to being works of literature.

In addition, nonfiction can complement textbook content and enliven every area of study. It can provide in-depth, up-to-date information about an array of subjects ranging from diverse topics such as art museums to zoology. By exploring topics through trade books, adolescents see how knowledge in different domains is organized, used, and related; they become familiar with the language and vocabulary of the discipline. The range of topics available, the variety of formats, and the varying levels of difficulty make these books an indispensable resource for content area classrooms. For example, books such as *Leon's Story* (Roth & Tillage, 1997) and *Through My Eyes* (Bridges, 1999) explore 20th-century racism and could enhance a social studies unit about the U.S. Civil Rights movement. *Leon's Story*, the life story of a southern sharecropper's son, details the author's painful childhood and his youth as a Civil Rights activist. *Through My Eyes* is a personal recollection of how the author, Ruby Bridges, at 6 years of age became the first black student at an all-white Louisiana school in 1960. Both books put a face on the Civil Rights struggle in ways no textbook can.

Furthermore, nonfiction can provide insights into contemporary issues of interest to today's teens that get little attention in textbooks. Consider *New Kids in Town: Oral Histories of Immigrant Teens* (Bode, 1991), which presents voices of adolescent immigrants from places like Afghanistan, El Salvador, India, Cuba, and China. Other topics—such as AIDS, global warming, the environment, and technology—are easy to find among today's nonfiction titles.

Finally, nonfiction trade books can help teachers individualize instruction in ways that exclusive use of a textbook cannot. Brian Factor, a teacher of American

ANTICIPATION GUIDE

Sample Book: *The Faithful Elephants* by Yukio Tsuchiya

	Before Reading	After Reading
1. An elephant can be trained to blow a trumpet.	_____	_____
2. Americans bombed Tokyo in World War II.	_____	_____
3. Elephants are able to tell if there's poison in their food.	_____	_____
4. Lions and tigers are able to tell if there's poison in their food.	_____	_____
5. It is easy to give an elephant an injection.	_____	_____
6. If not fed, elephants will starve to death in one week.	_____	_____
7. Elephants will not eat potatoes.	_____	_____
8. It's all right to kill zoo animals in war time.	_____	_____

Although anticipation guides are used as a prereading activity, their importance is primarily as a postreading activity enhanced by class discussion. When constructing an anticipation guide, teachers should keep the following points in mind: (1) Determine the main ideas of the passage. (2) Write 7 to 10 clear declarative statements. (3) Present each statement to elicit prediction. (4) Discuss all predictions before reading takes place. (5) Assign the reading and evaluation of statements. (6) Compare and contrast the predictions the readers make with the intentions of the author's meaning.

Suzanne Mateer is a sixth-grade teacher in the Homer-Center School District, Homer City, Pennsylvania, USA.

history, engages students in small-group inquiry projects on a wide range of topics. When his 10th graders explored a unit on the Labor Movement, Factor suggested a range of titles at varying reading levels, including *Kids at Work: Lewis Hine and the Crusade Against Child Labor* (Freedman, 1998a), *Growing Up in Coal Country* (Bartoletti, 1996), and *Big Annie of Calumet: A True Story of the Industrial Revolution* (Stanley, 1996a). In this way, all students had access to information regardless of their ability level.

Choosing Nonfiction Trade Books

For many teachers, the nonfiction genre represents unfamiliar territory. To effectively identify and select high-quality nonfiction, teachers need to be familiar with the possibilities this genre has to offer. Fortunately, a number of excellent resources can help. Reviews of adolescent nonfiction appear in journals such as *School Library Journal, Booklist, Journal of Adolescent & Adult Literacy, The ALAN Review,* and many others. An outstanding source for all teachers is *Booklinks,* which features books clustered by themes from all genres.

How can teachers select excellent nonfiction books from the thousands of available choices? Naturally, teachers will select books on the basis of the books' appeal to their students and their relevance to the curriculum. However, book selection should extend beyond these two considerations.

Quality is of primary concern when selecting nonfiction for classroom use. When evaluating nonfiction trade books, teachers should consider the five A's (Moss, 1995):

1. The *authority* of the author
2. The *accuracy* of the text content
3. The *appropriateness* of the book for an adolescent audience
4. The literary *artistry*
5. The *appearance* of the book (pp. 123–124)

Authority

When selecting nonfiction, it is important to consider the author's qualifications for writing the book. Some authors are experts on the subjects they write about, but most are not. The best authors consult authorities in a variety of fields to ensure accuracy and the credibility of their text.

Authors usually credit these experts on the preliminary pages of the book. For example, on the copyright page of *Volcano: The Eruption and Healing of Mount St.*

Helens, Patricia Lauber (1986) recognizes 13 different people, including geologists, naturalists, and foresters, who provided her with information used in this Newbery Honor Book.

Accuracy

Clear, correct, and up-to-date facts and concepts are the linchpin of good adolescent nonfiction. Visual matter—including maps, graphs, charts, and other information—should also be clear and correct. Jim Murphy, author of *The Great Fire* (1996) and *The Boys' War: Confederate and Union Soldiers Talk About the Civil War* (1990), takes great pains to ensure the accuracy of his books. He never writes anything in his books that cannot be verified for accuracy. For example, if he states that it rained on a particular date, he checks historical records to ensure that it actually did rain (Murphy, 1999).

How can teachers know if the information in a book is accurate? One way is to check a book's copyright date for currency. Another is to compare text information with that in an encyclopedia. A third way is to consult expert teachers who can confirm or deny the accuracy of information in a given book.

Accuracy is more than getting the facts straight. The best authors distinguish between facts, theories, and opinions. They take great pains to provide both sides of an issue in order to ensure fair and thorough treatment of a topic. In *Spill! The Story of the Exxon Valdez*, for example, Terry Carr (1991) uses qualifying words such as *about, estimated,* and *probably* when discussing how many birds perished during the spill:

> By the end of the first summer after the spill, rescue workers had counted *about* 30,000 dead birds. Wildlife biologists *estimated*, though, that this number is only 10 to 30 percent of the toll, meaning that between 90,000 and 270,000 birds have *probably* died and disappeared in the waters of the Sound. (p. 53; italics added)

These words alert the reader to information that may not be verified at the time of the book's publication.

Appropriateness

Informational books must be suitable for an adolescent audience. It may not have the depth and scope of an adult treatment of the same subject, but well-written nonfiction does not talk down to the adolescent reader. Instead, it conveys information in ways appropriate to their level of maturity. Albert Marrin's (1997) biography of Lincoln, *Commander in Chief: Abraham Lincoln and the Civil War*, for example, is not as comprehensive as adult biographies of Lincoln, but it still provides important information about his presidency during the Civil War.

Literary Artistry

Although giving information is a major purpose of nonfiction, the best books of this genre go beyond facts. Exemplary nonfiction is literature; it uses a range of literary devices that make information come alive. The author's approach to the material, along with the use of narrative devices like metaphors, similes, and visual imagery, moves these books beyond lists of facts to carefully crafted works of literature.

Jim Murphy (1999) uses a range of narrative devices to enliven his writing. He likes to use humor or include odd details. He sets up scenes in much the way a fiction author does. He inserts quotations to replicate dialogue. He tries to build the drama in his books. Chapters end with an emotional moment or leave the reader wanting to know more.

Appearance

Appearance or attractiveness is essential to nonfiction in this age of visual media. As Beverly Kobrin (1995) points out, most of us do judge books by their covers. Modern teens, conditioned by the visual images bombarding them on the television and computer screen, expect materials with dramatic visual impact. Today's nonfiction does not disappoint; it is more visually oriented than ever before. Interesting cover designs, attractive graphics, and effective illustrations entice today's adolescents in ways that textbooks cannot. Photos are increasingly common, lending a sense of immediacy. Primary source documents are increasingly important, as are interesting layouts. The popular Dorling Kindersley Eyewitness books are an example of this trend. They combine elegant design with engaging text and arresting photos. Titles like *Cars* (Sutton, 1990), for example, contain compelling photographs that may capture the interest of reluctant adolescent readers.

Bringing Nonfiction Into the Classroom

This section explores two easy ways to begin using nonfiction in the classroom: (1) incorporating nonfiction during sustained silent reading, and (2) reading nonfiction aloud. Each of these strategies can be implemented in middle or high school English language arts or content area classrooms.

Sustained Silent Reading

In an effort to make reading a more meaningful part of students' lives, more and more schools are involving students in uninterrupted sustained silent reading. Sustained silent reading involves all students (and their teachers) in reading books of their own choice for a specified period each day. Nonfiction trade books represent a natural choice for students during sustained silent reading. Biographies such as *Martha Graham: A Dancer's Life* (Freedman, 1998b) may capture the imagination of aspiring young dancers. First-person accounts of teenagers' own lives include *Seen and Heard: Teenagers Talk About Their Lives* (Kalergis, 1998) and *Hard Time: A Real Life Look at Juvenile Crime and Violence* (Bode & Mack, 1996). These books connect adolescents to their peers and let them measure their own lives against the lives of others. Titles such as *The New Way Things Work* (Macaulay & Ardley, 1998) fuel the curiosity of teens who stay up at night wondering how their CD players—and thousands of other inventions—work.

If students are to make nonfiction choices during sustained silent reading, however, nonfiction trade books must become part of the classroom library. Most of these libraries are dominated by what Aiden Chambers (1996) calls the "Holy Three": fiction, poetry, and drama. Although more and more teachers incorporate adolescent literature into their classroom libraries, their choices are typically confined to these three genres.

By including nonfiction in classroom libraries, teachers give students the opportunity to select nonfiction titles during sustained silent reading. These books can help students make links between novels and the outside world. Recent titles such as *Jack London: A Biography* (Dyer, 1997) can deepen student understanding of London's work through appreciation for his life. Other nonfiction titles like *An Album of the Vietnam War* (Lawson, 1986) or *Always to Remember: The Story of the Vietnam Veterans Memorial* (Ashabranner, 1988) can complement fiction books like Walter Dean Myers's *Fallen Angels* (1991).

Teacher Read-Alouds

Read-alouds can bring nonfiction into the classroom in an informal way. They can spark interest in a topic, enrich literature study, or provide tie-ins to many curricular areas. Most important of all, read-alouds may whet students' appetites for information, leading to silent, independent reading.

Nonfiction read-alouds can introduce, culminate, or provide new information about a cross-curricular unit. For example, *Kennedy Assassinated! The World Mourns* (Hampton, 1997) might introduce a unit on the 1960s. Patricia

COMIC STRIPS

Nonfiction books lend themselves well to constructing comic strips. Students can incorporate new information about a topic into a brief three- or four-segment comic strip. They will need to create a character that will deliver facts through illustrations and dialogue, as in the following example:

Beth Shellenbarger is an art education major at Indiana University of Pennsylvania, Indiana, Pennsylvania, USA.

Lauber's *Hurricanes: Earth's Mightiest Storms* (1996) could culminate a science unit study of weather and its effects. Excerpts from books like *Lives of the Artists* (Krull, 1995), *Lives of the Musicians* (Krull, 1993), or *Lives of the Athletes* (Krull, 1997) make excellent read-alouds for art, music, and physical education classes, respectively. These breezy thumbnail sketches of the lives of prominent artists, musicians, and athletes teach today's students about outstanding achievers from the past and the present.

Some nonfiction books, such as these "Lives of" books, are best read in bits and pieces, which might include a single chapter or section of a given book. Yet another read-aloud strategy involves reading picture captions only, providing a sneak preview for a book. The lengthy captions for the pictures and documents in *Anne Frank: Beyond the Diary* (Van der Rol & Verhoeven, 1993) connect artifacts back to the diary itself. For example, beneath a photo of Otto Frank glued inside Anne's diary, the caption reads,

> Anne stuck this photograph of Otto Frank in her diary. Anne was very attached
> to her father. Otto defended her when the others criticized her, consoled her
> when she was sad, and helped her with her studies. He was her support and her
> refuge. Otto understood how difficult it must be for the lively, active Anne to
> live in hiding, always having to whisper and sit still during the day, never able to
> go outside. He tried to help her whenever he could. Anne wrote: "I adore
> Daddy, he is the one I look up to. I don't love anyone in the world but him"
> (November 7, 1942). (p. 65)

Moving Ahead With Nonfiction: Organizing the Classroom

After incorporating nonfiction into the classroom through sustained silent reading time and teacher read-alouds, the next step is to involve students in reading nonfiction as part of class assignments. Teachers' purposes for using nonfiction will determine classroom grouping patterns, whether whole-group, small-group, or individual. With whole-group reading, all students read the same book at the same time. A modification of this pattern involves all students reading two complementary titles—one fiction and one nonfiction. Following the second pattern, small groups of students read different nonfiction books related to the same theme. Following the third pattern, students select individual books, either for inquiry projects, for reading/writing workshop, or for voluntary reading. The following examples illustrate ways nonfiction can be used and grouping patterns appropriate to those uses.

Whole-Group/Single Book

When using nonfiction for the first time, seventh-grade science teacher Alan Detwiler used the whole-group/single book model to extend his science unit on environmental issues. With district funds, he purchased 25 copies of *Come Back, Salmon: How a Group of Dedicated Kids Adopted Pigeon Creek and Brought it Back to Life* (Cone, 1992). This is an inspiring title about how students in Everett, Washington, worked with their teachers to clean up Pigeon Creek and reclaim it as a salmon-spawning ground. Every student read the book and participated in large-group discussions about the book and its relationship to a host of environmental issues.

Whole-Group/Complementary Books

Nonfiction books can be coupled with other literary genres on the same or related topics. Jody Hallum's seventh-grade language arts class read and discussed Gary Paulsen's *Nightjohn* (1993), a powerful historical novel about a man who risks torture by sneaking into slave camps to teach slaves to read. This book affirms the power of literacy and portrays the horrors of slavery. Students then read Julius Lester's *To Be A Slave* (1968). This Newbery Honor Book contains former slaves' oral accounts of slavery, collected as part of the Federal Writers' Project in the 1930s. After reading both titles, students explored the similarities and differences in the two genres. In this way, they extended their understanding and appreciation of each. They discussed the research required for writing each type of book and identified ways in which the authors' creative processes would differ depending on the genre.

Each year, Bonnie Pratt's eighth graders read an excerpt from *Anne Frank: The Diary of a Young Girl* (Frank, 1967) in their literature anthology. Then they follow that reading with *Anne Frank: Beyond the Diary* (Van der Rol & Verhoeven, 1993). This book is full of primary-source documents and visuals that extend the reader's understanding of Anne Frank's experience; the photographs of the diary, the Nazis' list of the names of the Frank family members, and the maps of the Secret Annex make the words of Anne's diary even more meaningful. Large-group discussions of the text focused on the ways in which the second book informed student understanding of the first.

Small-Group/Multiple Books

World history teacher Alan Trent uses nonfiction to enrich students' study of medieval times. To supplement textbook content and give students glimpses of everyday life, Trent assigned the students to literature circles based on their selection of four different titles related to that era: *Castle* (Macaulay, 1977), *The Viking News* (Wright, 1998), *When Plague Strikes: The Black Death, Smallpox, AIDS* (Giblin, 1995), and *A Proud Taste for Scarlet and Miniver* (Konigsburg, 1973). Students read and discussed each title in small groups over a 2-week period. Then they shared the information obtained through creative extensions, including projects, dramatic presentations, and debates.

Individual Inquiry

Individual or group inquiry is an increasingly popular way to involve students in research. The purpose of inquiry is to let students explore issues of interest to them. Through these research projects, students select a topic to investigate. Then they collect, analyze, and organize information to be presented through a project or report. By using several sources about the same topic, students can examine multiple points of view and evaluate the accuracy of information.

Joan Kaywell (1994) engaged her high school students in an inquiry project that combined young adult problem novels with nonfiction. Students first generated a list of problems affecting adolescents, such as anorexia nervosa, stress, suicide, pregnancy, and sexual abuse. Then they formed inquiry groups by topic. Each student in the group then selected and read a novel related to the identified problem.

After reading their novels, each student used nonfiction trade books to conduct research. After locating 10 facts related to the topic, students reconvened in small groups, where they pooled these facts. At this point they selected the best 25 facts to be included in an information sheet. They discussed source credibility, timeliness, and relevancy of information as they narrowed down their lists. Finally, they presented these to the larger group.

Responding to Nonfiction

Response to literature has become a staple in many American classrooms. The importance of allowing students to react and respond to text individually heightens the impact of the literary experience. Opportunities to discuss and write about their reading provide students the chance to reflect upon and refine their feelings as they compare their reactions to those of their peers.

Discussing Nonfiction

Discussion is an essential activity in promoting response to literature, whether fiction or nonfiction. Discussion deepens student thinking about text and leads to critical thinking. It links listening and speaking as students exchange ideas and react to text and the ideas of others. It has the potential to increase student curiosity, broaden interests, and influence what students choose to read.
As teachers incorporate discussion of nonfiction for the first time, they soon find that many of the usual questions used to prompt fiction discussions will not work. For example, questions about character motivation, plot development, and

TEACHER IDEA

CAN IT!

After reading a book, students should choose 5 to 10 artifacts that represent important events of the story (e.g., a feather, sea shells, rope, pictures from the Internet, figurines). These objects can be placed in a coffee can or a can of similar size with the lid securely on top. Have students illustrate a scene from the book and use the illustration to cover the outside of the can. Each student then tells about the story using the objects in the can. This is a great way for the speaker and the audience to enjoy a book report.

Suzanne Mateer is a sixth-grade teacher in the Homer-Center School District, Homer City, Pennsylvania, USA.

setting are inappropriate to nonfiction. However, process-centered questions work well for nonfiction, giving teachers glimpses into students' reading habits and promoting metacognitive reflection. The following questions have been adapted from Aiden Chamber's *Tell Me: Children, Reading, and Talk* (1996):

1. Why did you select this book?

2. How did you read this book? At one sitting? A little at a time?

3. Was it a fast read for you? A slow one? Why?

4. Which parts of the book were most interesting to you and why?

5. Which parts seemed to drag for you?

6. Did this book remind you of any other books you have read?

7. How did reading this book compare to reading a fiction book on the same subject? Which would you rather read and why?

Still other questions, like these from Carter and Abrahamson (1990), can be used for large- or small-group discussion:

1. How would this book be different if it had been written 10 years earlier? Later?

2. Compare this book with another you have read: How do they differ? How are they alike? Which do you like best?

3. How would this book be different if written for an older child? Younger one?

4. How is this book different from an encyclopedia article on the same topic?

5. If you could interview the author, what would you ask him?

6. Tell me three facts, theories, or incidents you thought were interesting.

7. Analyze the title and cover. Do they accurately reflect the content? Why or why not? (pp. 185–187)

These questions prompt reflection on nonfiction titles and help students focus on the characteristics of this genre.

Literature circles provide another way to engage students in discussion of nonfiction. Although many teachers use literature circles with fiction, literature circles work equally well with nonfiction. With literature circles, students form groups based on common book selection and meet regularly to determine how many pages they will read. Harvey Daniels (1994) recommends assigning students specific roles for discussion and rotating those roles as students work their way through the book. These roles include Literary Luminary, Discussion

Director, Vocabulary Enricher, Connector, and Artful Artist. The Literary Luminary identifies sections of the text to be read aloud, and the Discussion Director identifies questions to be asked about the text. The Vocabulary Enricher locates words to be discussed and explored, and the Connector draws connections between the text and other literary works or people, places, or events. The Artful Artist sketches a significant scene from the book.

The teacher introduces each of these roles over a period of time, modeling the responsibilities for each role. Students are taught, for example, how to create effective discussion questions and select interesting and meaningful excerpts for read-alouds.

In Judy Hendershot's middle-grade classroom, students formed literature circles around five nonfiction books: *I Am An American: A True Story of Japanese Internment* (Stanley, 1996b), *The Lost Wreck of the Isis* (Ballard, 1990), *Buried in Ice* (Beattie, Geiger, & Tanaka, 1993), *The Wright Brothers: How They Invented the Airplane* (Freedman, 1991), and *On Board the Titanic: What It Was Like When the Great Liner Sank* (Tanaka, 1996). They assumed their assigned roles and rotated roles over time as they completed the books.

One Discussion Director's questions, which were based on *I Am An American,* revealed her understanding of the ways in which effective questions can promote personal response to literature, as well as her ability to connect information in this book to the previously read *Children of the Dust Bowl: The True Story of the School at Weedpatch Camp* (Stanley, 1992):

1. How did you feel when they said the Japanese were refused admittance to movies and cafes?

2. Do you think the Okies (*Children of the Dust Bowl*) were like the Japanese? Why? Why not?

3. Did anything surprise you while reading this chapter? Why? Why not?

4. What do you think of this book so far?

Ryan, a Connector, listed the following connections between *On Board the Titanic* (Tanaka, 1996) and other people, places, and events. Through these responses, Ryan revealed other books he had read, as well as tragic national events that formed part of his own experience:

1. The ship *Lusitania,* its sister

2. The Oklahoma City bombing

3. Harriet Tubman helping free slaves

4. The loss of the spaceship *Challenger*

Writing in Response to Nonfiction

Researchers have long emphasized the important connections between reading and writing text. By linking reading and writing, students deepen their engagement, improve their recall of key ideas, and extend their thinking. Writing about expository text helps learners elaborate on and manipulate ideas while gaining insight into the writer's craft. These experiences sensitize them to the organization of nonfiction text. In time, they begin to see ways to use those patterns in their own writing. Written responses to nonfiction may take a variety of forms, including journals, letters to the author, and many others.

Journals provide a natural means for students to express their thoughts and feelings about their reading. A variety of traditional types of journals will work, but the two-column journal is especially useful for response to this genre. With two-column journals, students record "What the author says" on the left side and "What I thought" on the right. In this way, students record the author's message along with their personal feelings about that message. Figure 5.1 provides a sample of a two-column journal written by a middle grader in response to *The Boys' War* (Murphy, 1990).

FIGURE 5.1 Student's Two-Column Journal Entry About The Boys' War

What they said	*What I think*
Boys didn't go to war. They talked against slavery.	I think boys shouldn't have to worry about slavery.
Boys joined war just to get out of work	I think boys should do work until the age of 18.
A boy said "I reather die than becom a slave in the north.	I disagree. I think boys under 18 should not die or be a slave.
Later rules stated that boys under 18 could not join the war.	I agree with that. I disagree w/ that if you a tall 14 yr. old. You could be in the war.
Boys could enter war at any age if only a musician.	I always thought that if a rule was stated you would have to follow that.
A boy could enter if the parents wanted them to under age.	I think that it would be the parents fault if the boy dies.

Other writing activities might include response to specific prompts. For example, after a whole-class reading of *Exploring the Titanic* (Ballard, 1993), eighth-grade teacher Toni Stevens asked students to select someone on the ship and write about the topic "If Only" from that person's point of view. For example, a student might write from the point of view of the radio operator explaining that "if only" he had not ignored the ice warnings he received, the disaster might have been averted. Other prompted responses might involve comparing and contrasting different titles or writing poems about the literature being studied. (See Chapters 8 and 9 in this volume for information about incorporating poetry in classrooms.) Many of the suggested discussion questions listed earlier would also make good written responses to nonfiction. Still other activities might involve students in writing letters to nonfiction authors. Such letters allow students to act as critics of the books they read, noting the strengths and weaknesses of an author's work.

Final Thoughts

By linking adolescents with the many superb nonfiction books available today, teachers not only can capitalize on student enthusiasm for this genre, but also can deepen their students' understanding of course content. Today's nonfiction has the potential to engage even the most reluctant adolescent readers while it increases their knowledge about people, places, and events of the past and present. By linking such literature with other genres, as well as textbooks, teachers help students to prepare for the literacy demands of the 21st century. Perhaps even more important, they expose students to a genre that could be the catalyst that transforms a reluctant reader into an avid one.

REFERENCES

Abrahamson, R.F., & Carter, B. (1991). Nonfiction: The missing piece in the middle. *English Journal, 80*, 52–58.

Allington, R. (1994). The schools we have. The schools we need. *The Reading Teacher, 48*, 14–29.

Altenbaugh, R.J., Engel, D.E., & Martin, D.T. (1995). *Caring for kids: A critical study of urban school leavers.* London: Falmer Press.

Anderson, T., Armbruster, B., & Kantor, R. (1980). How clearly written are children's textbooks? Or of bladderworts and alfalfa. *Reading Education Report*, #15F. Champaign, IL: Center for the Study of Reading.

Beers, K. (1990). Choosing not to read: An ethnographic study of seventh-grade aliterate students. *Dissertation Abstracts International, 51*(06), 1965. (UMI No. 9029833)

Campbell, J.R., Donahue, P.L., Reese, C.M, & Phillips, G.W. (1996). *NAEP 1994 reading report card for the nation and the states.* Washington, DC: U.S. Department of Education.

Carter, B. (1987). *A content analysis of the most frequently circulated information books in three junior high libraries.* Unpublished doctoral dissertation. Houston, TX: University of Houston.

Carter, B., & Abrahamson, B. (1990). *Nonfiction for young adults: From delight to wisdom.* Phoenix, AZ: Oryx Press.

Chambers, A. (1996). *Tell me: Children, reading, and talk.* York, ME: Stenhouse.

Daniels, H. (1994). *Literature circles: Voice and choice in the student-centered classroom.* York, ME: Stenhouse.

Donahue, P.L., Voelkl, K.E., Campbell, J.R., & Mazzeo, J. (1999). *NAEP 1998 reading report card for the nation and the states.* Washington, DC: U.S. Department of Education.

Egan, K. (1992). *Imagination in teaching and learning: The middle school years.* Chicago: University of Chicago Press.

Fink, R.P. (1995/1996). Successful dyslexics: A constructivist study of passionate interest reading. *Journal of Adolescent & Adult Literacy, 39,* 268–280.

Kaywell, J. (1994). Using young adult problem fiction and nonfiction to produce critical readers. *The ALAN Review, 21,* 1–6.

Kobrin, B. (1995). *EyeOpeners II.* New York: Scholastic.

Moss, B. (1995). Using children's nonfiction tradebooks as read-alouds. *Language Arts, 72*(2), 122–126.

Murphy, J. (1999, February). *Meet the author.* Presentation at The Ohio State University Children's Literature Conference, Columbus, Ohio.

Norvell, G. (1950). *The reading interests of young people.* East Lansing, MI: Michigan State University Press.

Purves, A.C., & Beach, R. (1972). *Literature and the reader: Research in response to literature, reading interests, and the teaching of literature.* Urbana, IL: National Council of Teachers of English.

Thomas, K., & Moorman, G. (1983). *Designing reading programs.* Dubuque, IA: Kendall Hunt.

Worthy, J. (1998). Removing barriers to voluntary reading for reluctant readers: The role of school and classroom libraries. *Language Arts, 73*(7), 483–492.

Wurman, R.S. (1989). *Information anxiety: What to do when information doesn't tell you what you need to know.* New York: Bantam.

YOUNG ADULT LITERATURE CITED

Ashabranner, B. (1988). *Always to remember: The story of the Vietnam Veterans Memorial.* New York: Putnam.

Ballard, R. (1990). *The lost wreck of the Isis.* New York: Scholastic.

Ballard, R. (1993). *Exploring the Titanic.* New York: Scholastic.

Bartoletti, S.C. (1996). *Growing up in coal country.* Boston: Houghton Mifflin.

Beattie, O., Geiger, J., & Tanaka, S. (1993). *Buried in ice.* New York: Scholastic.

Bode, J. (1991). *New kids in town: Oral histories of immigrant teens.* New York: Scholastic.

Bode, J., & Mack, S. (1996). *Hard time: A real life look at juvenile crime and violence.* New York: Delacorte.

Bridges, R. (1999). *Through my eyes.* New York: Scholastic.

Carr, T. (1991). *Spill! The story of the Exxon Valdez.* New York: Franklin Watts.

Cone, M. (1992). *Come back, salmon: How a group of dedicated kids adopted Pigeon Creek and brought it back to life.* San Francisco: Sierra Club Books.

Dyer, D. (1997). *Jack London: A biography.* New York: Scholastic.

Franco, L.J., & Gordon, C. (Producers). (1999). *October Sky* [film]. Universal Pictures.

Frank, A. (1967). *Anne Frank: The diary of a young girl.* New York: Doubleday.

Freedman, R. (1991). *The Wright brothers: How they invented the airplane.* New York: Holiday.

Freedman, R. (1998a). *Kids at work: Lewis Hine and the crusade against child labor.* New York: Clarion.

Freedman, R. (1998b). *Martha Graham: A dancer's life.* New York: Clarion.

Giblin, J.C. (1995). *When plague strikes: The Black Death, smallpox, AIDS.* New York: HarperCollins.

Hampton, W. (1997). *Kennedy assassinated! The world mourns.* Cambridge, MA: Candlewick.

Hesse, K. (1997). *Out of the dust.* New York: Scholastic.

Hickam, H. (1998). *Rocket boys: A memoir.* New York: Delacorte.

Kalergis, M.M. (1998). *Seen and heard: Teenagers talk about their lives.* New York: Stewart, Tabori, & Chang.

Konigsburg, E.L. (1973). *A proud taste for Scarlet and Miniver.* New York: Atheneum.

Krakauer, J. (1998). *Into thin air: A personal account of the Mount Everest disaster.* New York: Anchor Books.

Krull, K. (1993). *Lives of the musicians: Good times, bad times (and what the neighbors thought).* San Diego, CA: Harcourt Brace.

Krull, K. (1995). *Lives of the artists: Masterpieces, messes (and what the neighbors thought).* San Diego, CA: Harcourt Brace.

Krull, K. (1997). *Lives of the athletes: Thrills, spills (and what the neighbors thought).* San Diego, CA: Harcourt Brace.

Lauber, P. (1986). *Volcano: The eruption and healing of Mount St. Helens.* New York: Bradbury.

Lauber, P. (1996). *Hurricanes: Earth's mightiest storms.* New York: Scholastic.

Lawson, D. (1986). *An album of the Vietnam War.* New York: Franklin Watts.

Lester, J. (1968). *To be a slave.* New York: Dial.

London, J. (1990). *Call of the wild.* New York: Tor Books.

Macaulay, D. (1977). *Castle.* Boston: Houghton Mifflin.

Macaulay, D., & Ardley, N. (1998). *The new way things work.* Boston: Houghton Mifflin.

Marrin, A. (1997). *Commander in chief: Abraham Lincoln and the Civil War.* New York: Dutton.

Murphy, J. (1990). *The boys' war: Confederate and Union soldiers talk about the Civil War.* New York: Clarion.

Murphy, J. (1996). *The great fire.* New York: Scholastic.

Myers, W.D. (1991). *Fallen angels.* New York: Scholastic.

Paulsen, G. (1993). *Nightjohn.* New York: Delacorte.

Paulsen, G. (1996). *Hatchet.* New York: Aladdin.

Ray, D. (1990). *A nation torn: A story of how the Civil War began.* New York: Lodestar.

Ride, S., & Okie, S. (1986). *To space and back.* New York: Lothrop, Lee & Shephard.

Roth, S.L., & Tillage, L.W. (1997). *Leon's story.* New York: Farrar, Straus & Giroux.

Stanley, J. (1992). *Children of the Dust Bowl: The true story of the school at Weedpatch Camp.* New York: Crown.

Stanley, J. (1996a). *Big Annie of Calumet: A true story of the Industrial Revolution.* New York: Crown.

Stanley, J. (1996b). *I am an American: A true story of Japanese internment.* New York: Crown.

Sutton, R. (1990). *Cars.* London: Dorling Kindersley.

Tanaka, S. (1996). *On board the Titanic: What it was like when the great liner sank.* New York: Hyperion.

Van der Rol, R., & Verhoeven, R. (1993). *Anne Frank: Beyond the diary.* New York: Viking.

Wright, R. (1998). *The Viking news.* Cambridge, MA: Candlewick.

CHAPTER 6

Using Nonfiction Books to Launch a Successful Research Project

Christine Carlson

R
esearch papers. Students hate writing them. Teachers hate grading them. But when the curriculum demands that students produce them, and when it is sometimes the only opportunity students get to learn research skills and use multiple information sources, many teachers reluctantly fit research projects into their lesson plans. With all this negativity, making the process fun for everyone involved appears to be an insurmountable challenge.

With the right approach and planning, however, the entire research paper process can become a positive experience, as it has for students on Team 6-1 at Haines Middle School in St. Charles, Illinois, USA. This chapter details the successful I-search research unit implemented by Team 6-1. The reason for the success is clear: Nonfiction books were used to launch research into topics of each student's choosing. At the beginning of the unit, students were allowed to choose their own topic with guidance from the language arts teacher and the school librarian. Each student then read a nonfiction book on the topic he or she chose to research. Choosing and reading a nonfiction book is one of the critical pieces that makes this project so successful. In addition, sufficient time was allowed for instruction and the use of the resources available in the Learning Resource Center (LRC).

While serving as the school library media specialist (SLMS) at Haines Middle School, I was inspired by my reading of *Nonfiction Matters: Reading, Writing, and Research in Grades 3–8* (Harvey, 1998) to develop this research unit. Knowing that the Team 6-1 teachers were disappointed in the papers that resulted from previous student research experiences, I was particularly interested in Harvey's approach. She stresses that before any successful inquiry can be accomplished, students must have some background knowledge about the topic being researched. In planning the I-search unit, Team 6-1 language arts teachers and I cooperatively decided that reading a nonfiction book would satisfy this need for background information. In the sixth-grade unit, students got the chance to choose a book on a topic in which they were interested, an idea also advocated by Harvey.

While students chose their topics, they did so with guidance from their language arts teacher and the SLMS. Because the classroom teacher must read the final papers, he or she may choose to eliminate some topics from consideration. For example, one year at Haines Middle School, most of the students decided to write about pets. After reading six papers about dogs, the teacher opted to eliminate "pets" as a topic in future projects.

Selecting Nonfiction to Initiate Research

This sixth-grade research unit began when the students visited the school's LRC. As the SLMS, I greeted them with a cart full of nonfiction books on many different topics. In recent years, publishers have made great strides in producing nonfiction titles that not only grab the reader's interest but also appeal visually. As a result, choosing books that will capture the students' notice was an easy task.

As I began the introduction, I assured the students that the books I was sharing were just a sampling of a wide variety of books available on thousands of topics. The purpose of talking about the books was to pique students' interest and get them thinking about possible topics they would like to explore. Examples of books that have had great appeal are *Special Effects in Film and Television* by Jake Hamilton (1998), *The Story of Golf* by Dave Anderson (1998), *The Story of Figure Skating* by Michael Boo (1998), and Nick Cook's *Roller Coasters: Or I Had So Much Fun, I Almost Puked* (1998). The Eyewitness series by Dorling Kindersley and other books that place an emphasis on illustrations are good choices for students with lower reading skills.

I not only talked about the books on the cart, but I also made further suggestions for other topics related to the books that were displayed. After the book talks, students were given ample time to look over all the books and to ask about the availability of books on topics that were not displayed on the cart. The classroom teacher and I also assisted students in using the online catalog to find books on other subjects in which they had an interest. Students often were amazed at the variety of books available, and they literally pounced on the cart after the book talks, trying to secure one of the books before a fellow student could grab that topic.

RESEARCH MANIA

Try the following activities as an alternative to the research paper, or to launch a more involved research project.

- Ask students to read a nonfiction book on a "concern" (e.g., organ transplants, animal experimentation). Then have them write a fictional story using the concern as a major plotline, or write a public service announcement about the concern.

- Search books and animal encyclopedias to identify an endangered animal. Using three different sources, students must discover (1) the animal's habitat and where it is located in the world, (2) why the animal is endangered, and (3) what could be done to change the animal's endangered status.

- Have students research an occupation and use facts and graphics to create a trifold career brochure on a word processor. The brochure should entice people into choosing that career.

- Research a variety of sources to generate a bio-board—a poster that includes graphics and text on a person (Stonewall Jackson), event (Battle of Gettysburg), or topic (medical care) related to a certain historical period (the U.S. Civil War).

Christine Carlson is a school library consultant in St. Charles, Illinois, USA.

Reading an entire book on one topic gives students an opportunity to immerse themselves in details. They gain the background information necessary to form good questions about their topic for later inquiry. Further, allowing students to choose a book on a topic in which they are interested gives them a sense of ownership in the project. As well, teachers gain an opportunity to teach reading skills specific to nonfiction. This gives students some additional tools to add to their reading toolbox.

Conducting Research

Approximately 1 month later, students returned to the LRC to begin the second phase of the research unit. By this time, they had read their chosen nonfiction book. The classroom teachers had instructed them on how to take notes and how to use the notecard and bibliography sheets available in the LRC for organizing their data. As part of a lesson on how to take notes and use the notecard sheets, the classroom teacher had students practice by reading a short article and summarizing the information read. Therefore, before students returned to the

LRC to begin research, they knew how to summarize details or paraphrase to avoid plagiarism. The students also had compiled a list of 5 to 10 questions about their topic that they hoped to answer through their research. Some teachers used a K-W-L chart (Ogle, 1986) for this, whereas others simply asked students to jot down questions on a piece of paper for further inquiry while they read the nonfiction book.

The students also received a packet to guide them through the research unit. The packet included

- a timetable for the unit (see Figure 6.1 for a sample timetable),
- the rubric for how the project will be assessed (see Figure 6.2 on page 113),
- a Big6 worksheet (Eisenberg & Berkowitz, 1990) (a sample Big6 assignment organizer is available at http://www.standrews.austin.tx.us/library/Assignment%20organizer.htm),
- sample notecard and bibliography sheets (see Figures 6.3 and 6.4 on pages 114 and 115), and
- a model paper from a previous student.

The timetable and rubric help students determine the scope and format of the finished product, the Big6 worksheet helps students organize their research, and the sample paper helps students understand what the final paper will look like. These items were then kept in a folder that the student brought to the LRC during the research phase of the project.

At this point, although students had a general idea about their topic and a list of questions they wanted to answer, research did not begin immediately. It was important that students received research skills instruction first. As SLMS, my part of the research skills instruction began by teaching students how to formulate the essential keywords that would guide their research. Using examples, I modeled how this is done and allowed time for students to begin their own list of keywords. Students added to this list as their research led them down new paths of inquiry. My instruction also included guiding students through the requirements of the assignment, so all participants were aware of what needed to be done in the next few days.

The students were now ready to begin the actual research. They spent the next 5 to 8 days, in 105-minute blocks, in the LRC. They learned how to use sources, learned how to find information on their topic, and had ample time to take notes. Because time was allotted for the students to research during school hours, the need for parental help was eliminated, and students benefited from available assistance from the teacher and media specialist.

FIGURE 6.1   I-Search Timetable

NOVEMBER						
Sunday	**Monday**	**Tuesday**	**Wednesday**	**Thursday**	**Friday**	**Saturday**
1	2	3	4	5	6	7
8	9 KWL about topic	10 Develop list of questions about topic that you want answered	11 Create key-word list for topic	12 Packet discussion and respon-sibilities	13	14
15	16 **Proposal due** LRC to research—encyclopedia	17 LRC to research—periodical	18 LRC to research—nonfiction book	19 LRC to research	20 LRC to research—Internet	21 **Work on final drafts of exit slips**
22	23 Organize notes—determine three or four main areas (make topic sentences)	24 Work on draft of answers in paragraph form using transitions	25 Organize biblio-graphical information	26 No school	27 No school	28
29	30 Putting it all together				December 4 **Due date for the paper!!**	

FIGURE 6.2   I-Search Rubric

I-Search	Exceeds Expectations	Meets Expectations	Goal for Improvement
Proposal or Introduction	• paper has a good lead that states topic • describes what is known • describes search questions	• topic is stated • states what is known • states search questions	• topic is stated • few ideas stated • very few questions stated
My Search Process	• sequence of steps described clearly • details, feelings, and reactions described • problems, good sources, additional help described	• simple step-by-step format • some details, feelings, and reactions included • some problems, sources, and help stated	• steps to process are minimal • details, feelings, or reactions stated insufficiently • problems, sources, and help stated minimally
What Have I Learned?	• focused on three or four major areas • included details that answer questions stated in the proposal • organized in a logical manner using good transitions	• focused on one or two main areas • limited number of questions answered • evidence of transitions and order	• no clear focus • very few questions answered from the proposal • unorganized
What This Means to Me Conclusion	• described development as a researcher • described which things meant the most • described what effect this will have on you in the future	• stated development as a researcher • stated which things meant the most • stated what affect this will have on you in the future	• no evidence that reader developed as a researcher • meaningfulness not stated • no mention on what effect this will have on you in the future
Work Cited Bibliography	• use of at least five different sources • references in alphabetical order • correct format for each reference	• use of three or four different sources • one or two references out of order • some errors in format used for references	• two or less sources used • more than two references out of order • many errors in bibliographic format

FIGURE 6.3   I-Search Notecards

Name: _____	

Ref# _____ Page# _____	Ref# _____ Page# _____
quote ☐	quote ☐
Ref# _____ Page# _____	Ref# _____ Page# _____
quote ☐	quote ☐

To maximize instruction and make sure students had experience using all of the information sources, I began each day with the introduction of a new source for inquiry. On Day 1, the research skills instruction dealt with traditional print reference sources, such as general encyclopedias and subject-specific encyclopedias. On Day 2, I showed students how to use the online catalog, browse for books on the shelves, and search the bibliographies and Library of Congress cataloging-in-publication data in books to find additional sources. The third day, I introduced periodical indexes and online periodical databases. A few additional days were provided so students could become familiar with and use these more "traditional" information sources. Five to six days into the research part of the project, research skills instruction shifted to training students how to use the Internet and search engines for research.

Each day, students followed a similar format for time usage:

1. The SLMS began the period with instruction.

2. Students had time to locate information in the sources that had been discussed.

3. Students took notes from the sources on the notecard sheets and registered the source on their bibliography sheets.

FIGURE 6.4   I-Search Bibliography Sheet

Name _____ Team _____

#_____ (Check one source) Encyclopedia _____ Vol. # _____ Book _____
       Periodical _____   Internet _____   Videotape _____   CD-ROM _____
       Index _____   Other _____   (identify) _____

Title _____

Author _____ Pages Used _____

Title of Article _____

Publisher _____ Place Published _____

Date Published _____ URL _____

#_____ (Check one source) Encyclopedia _____ Vol. # _____ Book _____
       Periodical _____   Internet _____   Videotape _____   CD-ROM _____
       Index _____   Other _____   (identify) _____

Title _____

Author _____ Pages Used _____

Title of Article _____

Publisher _____ Place Published _____

Date Published _____ URL _____

#_____ (Check one source) Encyclopedia _____ Vol. # _____ Book _____
       Periodical _____   Internet _____   Videotape _____   CD-ROM _____
       Index _____   Other _____   (identify) _____

Title _____

Author _____ Pages Used _____

Title of Article _____

Publisher _____ Place Published _____

Date Published _____ URL _____

Ten minutes before the end of period, students recorded their activities on an exit slip. They described what they did during the period, summarized what they learned, noted what sources they located, and shared any successes or disappointments they incurred. This exit slip was then placed in the unit folder, and it eventually became part of the research paper submitted at the end of the project.

Writing the Research Paper

After the research phase was concluded, the classroom teacher led students through the construction and writing of the research paper. Unlike most research papers, which only include what the students have discovered about their topic, this research project gives equal weight to the process (doing the research), the evaluation (reflecting on what was learned by the assignment), and the information that students have discovered during the research. The final draft of the paper has five sections: (1) an introduction, (2) a description of the research process the student followed, (3) information that the student learned, (4) an evaluative essay, and (5) the bibliography of sources used. (A sample and discussion of the format of the I-search paper used in this unit can be found on the Internet at http://www.edc.org/FSC/MIH/mini-emily.html.)

Students worked first on good introductory paragraphs. Teachers emphasized that students should create something catchy that would entice the reader into the paper. This important paragraph introduces the topic and explains the motivation behind what led the student to choose it.

The next section of the paper deals with the research process itself. Using the exit slips that chronicled the use of their time in the LRC, students described the steps they took in researching their topic and any successes or difficulties they experienced.

The third section describes what the students learned. Students prepared to write this section by cutting up the notecard sheets and organizing their notes into categories. These categories became an outline for the section. Using the notes, the students wrote about what they discovered during their research.

The final section of the paper is an evaluative essay. Students may reflect on what they have learned about the research process and about their topic. This evaluative essay is often the most interesting part of the entire paper, as it gives students an opportunity to be honest about the activities of the previous few weeks, their successes, and their frustrations. It often helps the instructors to determine how the research unit can be improved in the future. The paper concludes with a list of sources the student used to get information for the paper.

Students consulted their bibliography sheets, organized the sources alphabetically, and used proper bibliography form for their final bibliography.

Most of the actual work on the paper is done in school; however, students may take their work home to polish it and retype it for the final draft. If the classroom instructor is lucky enough to reserve computer lab time for the class, the final paper can also be produced during school time. The final paper contains the four sections described here and a bibliography of sources. Students should also turn in their notecards.

Conclusion

The I-search assignment contributes to important learning. It allows students to learn how to form good questions for inquiry, how to separate out needed data, and how to organize their notes into a cohesive whole. The reflective section of the paper consistently reveals that most students enjoy the experience. Students often express the confidence they gained in learning and using different information sources. Many comment that before the project, they were unsure of how to find information and use things like the online catalog and periodical databases. Now they demonstrate an awareness of the strengths and weaknesses of each of the sources for different information needs. Most students will comment on the sources they used and explain which were the most helpful. Some students express a desire to use the skills again for other assignments. The views are honest and demonstrate that student learning has taken place. Amazingly, one common refrain is the students' surprise at discovering that everything on the Internet is not true.

The sixth-grade teachers at Haines Middle School are pleased by the results of the research project. Students gain valuable research skills that aid them in future assignments. Students learn how to complete a successful inquiry and evaluate the experience. The format of the unit allows every child to be successful. In addition, the teachers and media specialist gain valuable insights into how students think and how they research.

In evaluating the experience, the classroom teachers and I have determined that two factors make this assignment successful: sufficient time is allotted for instruction and guidance, and students know something about their topic before they begin.

This unit has paid dividends in other ways. Nonfiction books also help students discover other sources and organizations that will provide additional information. Because the unit is introduced early in the school year, students are familiar with the resources in the LRC and confident enough to use these resources successfully later in the year on other assignments that require research. Because the SLMS and language arts teachers collaborated successfully on this unit, a basis was laid for further successful collaborations. The SLMS and language arts teachers have used student experiences to continually revise units to facilitate learning. And, the success of this unit has encouraged other teachers in the school to plan units that involve the use of the resources in the LRC.

Using the nonfiction book to spark student interest has made a real difference in the quality of the research. Nonfiction books are also invaluable for helping students decide on keywords and questions for inquiry, which has been a problem in the past. The experience gained from reading nonfiction to form a basis for learning about topics before beginning research can improve any research inquiry. For example, when students read an entire book about photosynthesis and growing patterns before they begin a science project on plants, they are able to make better hypotheses and describe what happens in the experiment more knowledgeably. When students have the opportunity to immerse themselves in background information before they start their research, their projects—regardless of subject—do improve.

REFERENCES

Eisenberg, M.B., & Berkowitz, R.E. (1990). *The Big6 skills information problem-solving approach* [online]. Available: http://www.big6.com

Harvey, S. (1998). *Nonfiction matters: Reading, writing, and research in grades 3–8*. York, ME: Stenhouse.

Ogle, D. (1986). K-W-L: A teaching model that develops active reading of expository text. *The Reading Teacher, 39*, 564–570.

YOUNG ADULT LITERATURE CITED

Anderson, D. (1998). *The story of golf*. New York: Morrow.

Boo, M. (1998). *The story of figure skating*. New York: Morrow.

Cook, N. (1998). *Roller coasters: Or I had so much fun, I almost puked*. Minneapolis, MN: Carolrhoda.

Hamilton, J. (1998). *Special effects in film and television*. New York: Dorling Kindersley.

CHAPTER 7

Whose Life Is It, Anyway?
Biographies in the Classroom

Teri S. Lesesne

For many people, the scope of young adult literature includes only novels. Unfortunately, this limited definition prevents many young adult readers from experiencing the benefits of reading nonfiction materials. Biographies and autobiographies are two nonfiction genres that can be used successfully to motivate young adults to read. After all, look at the popular reading materials that flood the supermarkets and convenience stores. Teen magazines offer tantalizing glimpses into the lives and loves of musicians, actors, sports figures, and other cultural icons. A few years ago, my granddaughter Cali, who was 13 at the time, was enthralled with unauthorized biographies of the bands 'N Sync and the Backstreet Boys, which have led her to read biographies of other pop icons over the years. And before you readers feel inclined to sneer at this type of reading, be reminded that over the past few decades, numerous biographies of pop musicians and television stars have been driven up the bestseller lists by teen readers.

Of course, I am not suggesting that these drugstore biographies provide literary experiences for teens, but I am suggesting that the interest in reading biographies is present. As teachers, we need to tap into that attraction and extend teens' interest in the biography genre. Literary, reading, and writing skills can be incorporated into a classroom study of biographies. Moreover, biographies and autobiographies also can provide a successful transition from the English language arts classroom to other content area classes. After a study of these genres, students also might want to try their hands at writing their own autobiographies, or biographies of family, friends, and community members.

Why should we consider using biographies and autobiographies in the classroom? How can we begin using biographies in the classroom? How can we select biographies that reflect the very best the genre has to offer YA readers? What kinds of activities are logical extensions of the study of biographies in the classroom? These are the questions addressed in this chapter. The purpose of this chapter, then, is threefold: First, it examines the criteria for evaluating biographies for young adults. Then it discusses how to integrate biographies and autobiographies in the English language arts classroom, as well as across the curriculum. Finally, this chapter presents some thoughts on using biographies and autobiographies in writing scenarios, and highlights the works of several writers of biographies for teens. An annotated bibliography of biographies for young adult classrooms is included at the end of the chapter.

The Benefits of Biographies in the Classroom

Before we begin a discussion of the *how* and *what* of using biographies and autobiographies in the classroom, we need to talk about the *why*: Why should

TEACHER IDEA

BODY BIOGRAPHY

Direct students to choose a character from the story they have read. The next step is for the students to create a human silhouette for their character. Students will be relaying important aspects of this character's life through writing and illustrating. Students need to decide where specific information should be placed in relation to parts of the body. An example would be to place the character's loved ones in the heart area of the silhouette or the character's goals in the spinal area. Other ideas to help guide students are as follows:

- All writings and illustrations should be based on the text.

- Remember to include admirable traits or discouraging qualities.

- Choose colors to reflect the mood of the character in certain situations.

- Include symbols that could be associated with the character.

- Use poems as writings. Poems can reflect the character's outward actions, the character's inner self, or how others perceive the character.

Amy Jones is a teacher in the State College Area School District, State College, Pennsylvania, USA.

egocentric adolescents care to read about the lives of other people? Why is it important that we include this genre in the classroom? What benefits can result from a study of biographies?

The most important reason we have for sharing biographies and autobiographies with our students is this: This genre extends students' opportunities to identify with a diverse group of people. As Barbara Samuels notes in her chapter on multicultural literature, students feel affirmed when they read books that reflect their cultures (see Chapter 3 in this volume). To view the need for this diversity, walk into any classroom in any town and ask students to name for you famous women in U.S. history, or famous African American scientists of the 20th century, or famous Hispanic Americans who have contributed to U.S. society. Now wait through the silence and accept the handful of answers students offer. It becomes instantly clear that despite changes in our textbooks and continued commitment to multicultural education, students are still not exposed to as much diversity as we would like. Biographies can provide students the chance to meet a wide range of people—people whose accomplishments might not warrant a footnote in a history, math, or science textbook, but people who reflect the rich diverse heritage of the United States.

Biographies and autobiographies can also allow students to encounter a plethora of role models. Imagine reading about the heroic actions of Andrea Castanon Ramirez Candalaria, the nurse who ministered to the wounded at the siege of the Alamo (Munson, 1989). Or perhaps learning that the golf tee was invented in 1899 by Dr. George F. Grant, an African American, in a time when African Americans were not permitted to compete in golf tournaments (Miller, 1999). Maybe students will meet Sadako Sasaki, a young Japanese girl whose dream of peace after the bombing of Hiroshima in World War II did not die, although her young life ended due to leukemia; her friends collected money to erect a statue in Peace Park, which is engraved with this message: "This is our cry. This is our prayer. Peace in the world" (Coerr, 1979). Unless we pull biographies into the classroom, our students might miss these and the dozens of other opportunities to meet people who lived quiet, purposeful lives.

Biographies and autobiographies can be used in classrooms to supplement information that already appears in textbooks. No matter how current our texts may be in any content area, they become dated. Also, unless we wish to have 10-pound textbooks, some people and their contributions will be either omitted or given brief space. This does not refer only to content area classrooms; we need only look as far as the anthologies in our English and reading classrooms. Applebee's 1992 study of the classics most frequently covered in high school

English classrooms reflects a stunning paucity of works by people of color or authors from countries outside of the United States and Great Britain, so students might not know much about the lives and works of Zora Neale Hurston or Tomas Rivera. Biographies and autobiographies can supplement what is presently in the textbooks and allow students a wider window through which to view their world.

A fourth reason for incorporating biographies and autobiographies into the classroom is that this literature meets the stated reading needs and interests of some of our students. Surely, my granddaughter is not the only teen who loves reading about the stars of contemporary culture! This year, as I worked with a group of at-risk middle school students, I found that one of their favorite books was Gary Paulsen's *Guts* (2001), the true-life stories behind *Hatchet* (1987) and the other books about Brian Robeson. Paulsen's previous slice-of-life autobiography, *Woodsong* (1990), also remains popular with readers. As Moss notes in her chapter on nonfiction, genres such as biography and autobiography might be just the vehicle for transporting students from school-time to lifetime readers (see Chapter 5 in this volume).

The Good, the Bad, and the Silly: What Is the Difference?

So now that we know that bringing biographies and autobiographies into the classroom is important, we want to be certain that the books we include meet some standards. How can we ascertain the quality of works in this genre? Knowing the evaluative criteria for the genre will help us ensure that the reading experiences we provide are worthwhile for our students.

Does the Book Tell a Good Story?

First and foremost, we want to provide our students with reading materials that are both interesting and informative. Giving teens books that do not use the techniques of good fiction might be counterproductive. How can we expect students to become interested in reading biographies and autobiographies unless the books we ask them to read are fast-paced narratives that engage students as readers? Good biographies and autobiographies hook readers, so the first place to focus our examination is on the opening pages of a book. What is in the first paragraph to make teens want to read on? How long before readers are actually introduced to the subject of the book?

Involving students in the evaluation is critical. Begin by visiting the school or public library and checking out as many different biographies as permitted. Be sure to include books about contemporary cultural icons—that is, figures from the sports and entertainment industries—as well as figures from history. Bring the books to your classroom and do the following exercise, a quick activity called Pass It On: Place one biography at each seat. Tell students they will have 3 minutes (or more, depending on your particular students) to begin reading the book in front of them. Assure them that if the book is less than engaging, they only have to bear it for 3 minutes. Have them begin reading. At the end of 3 minutes, ask students to pass the book they are reading along to the person on the right (or the left, or in front, or behind, or whatever). Give them another 3 minutes and pass the books along again. Repeat this process at least 5 times (you have only taken 15 minutes at this point). After the students have had a chance to pass several books along, ask if anyone found a book that might be worth another 3 minutes or more. What did that book do to engage the reader?

By the end of the Pass It On activity, you and your students should have a good idea of the techniques authors use to engage readers as well as some titles that students would find interesting to read on their own. Make a list of these books, or simply allow students who found interesting books to begin reading them. You can then work individually with the students who have not found interesting reading material, or allow them to visit the library to find some suitable reading material. This activity gives students the chance to select books that appeal to them. If more than one student expresses an interest in the same book, teachers can either recommend other similar titles or allow students to form reading groups based on their similar interests. An alternative might be to have students drop out of the rotation in Pass It On once they have found a book of interest to them. This puts the book out of circulation at that point. By allowing for some selection, we increase the likelihood that students will actually read the books.

Are the Facts Accurate?

This just flat-out makes good sense: Of course we want the biographies and autobiographies we use in the classroom to get the facts right. But how can those of us who generally are not expert in the lives of many people tell whether or not the facts are accurate? There are several sources that can offer us assistance in guaranteeing high quality, accurate biographies and autobiographies. Journals that focus on book reviews are one such source. Ask the school media specialist for issues of *School Library Journal, Booklist,* or *Voice of Youth Advocates (VOYA),* which present careful reviews of contemporary works for teens. Your media specialist might even be willing to prepare a list of recent books he or she would suggest for your students.

At the same time, given decreased budgets, the cost of new books mentioned in these journals might be prohibitive. Therefore, retrospective collection development aids might be of more use. The National Council of Teachers of English (NCTE) publishes aids such as *Books for You* and *Your Reading* every 3 years. These volumes present annotations of books for high school and middle school, respectively. Your media specialist can also prepare a list of books already in the school collection that are accurate and authentic examples of quality biographies and autobiographies for teens. Professional organizations such as the National Council of Teachers of Mathematics (NCTM) and the National Council for the Social Studies (NCSS) generally have available lists of recommended books for the individual content areas. Rely on the work of those more expert in the field to help assess books using the accuracy criteria.

Is the Person Presented as a Round Character?

For too long, biographies created mythical characters, people with whom students could hardly be expected to identify. Remember the old chestnut about George Washington never telling a lie? Can we really expect our students to relate to a character who has no flaws, no real human foibles? What our students need is a complete picture of the subject of the book, a person who has strengths and weaknesses, a REAL person with whom to identify. Take, for example, Jean Fritz's

TEACHER IDEA

BIO-CUBE

- Cover a cube-shaped box with paper.
- Choose a character from a story to use for this activity.
- On one side of the cube, write the name of the character.
- On the other five sides, list traits of that particular character.
- Encourage the students to use words with different fonts, drawings, and color to make that character come to life through description.

Suzanne Mateer is a sixth-grade teacher in the Homer-Center School District, Homer City, Pennsylvania, USA.

biography of General Sam Houston in *Make Way for Sam Houston* (1986). Fritz presents the story of this larger-than-life Texas statesman in terms that today's readers can understand. Houston's childhood is not idyllic; his older brothers tease him. His adult life is plagued with challenges, as well, and although Houston meets some of these challenges, others defeat him. This realistic portrayal of someone who could easily be characterized as a legendary hero makes Sam Houston more accessible to today's teens. They can see some of their own strengths and weaknesses reflected in the life of this great leader. Presenting subjects with warts and all, so to speak, is paramount for a good biography for our students.

Easy as A-B-C: Autobiographies and Biographies Across the Curriculum

Now that we have determined that our selections are appropriate for the classroom and our students, how can we make connections across the curriculum? The simplest method of establishing the connection is by selecting biographies and autobiographies that present subjects from the pages of those content area textbooks. Subjects might include famous people from art, music, history, science, mathematics, sports, and the like. However, a more intensive cross-curricular unit might develop from a thematic unit of study. By selecting a broad theme, it is a fairly simple matter of bringing in the various disciplines. Examine, for instance, a theme such as "Making Decisions." In reading and English classes, students can read various pieces about people who are faced with tough decisions and, ultimately, have to live with the consequences of those decisions. Social studies classes might examine historical figures who have had to make difficult choices (such as the decision to use the atom bomb during WWII, decisions made to secede prior to the Civil War, or the decisions of the Civil Rights workers to disobey the Jim Crow Laws). Science classes can focus on topics such as scientific and medical ethics (such as euthanasia or animal experimentation), topics in which big decisions are crucial. Creative arts classes such as music, art, and dance can discuss the choices artists make during the creative process. By keeping the theme broad, the possibilities for connections across content areas are more numerous.

Write All About It!

Making the connections to other content areas is a wonderful way of getting students to see that the various disciplines are related. However, once students have completed discussions, we must find some way of taking their newfound knowledge and applying it in a new situation in order to assess the effectiveness of their learning. Developing quick and motivating assignments is as crucial as selecting the very best books to share with students. After all, if we kill their love of reading with overly dull and lengthy assignments, we have gained little in our battle to create lifelong learners. So, how can we hold students accountable for their learning in ways that might improve the chances for future connections to books? The following activities are a few that have worked in middle school and high school classrooms.

Writing a Reading Autobiography

This activity dates back many years to the college classroom of G. Robert Carlsen (1980). As Carlsen began each semester teaching courses in literature for young adults, he would ask his students to write about their own reading as children, as teens, and as adults. The tradition of writing a reading autobiography became part of the routine for some of Carlsen's students, including Dick Abrahamson, my college professor. At the beginning of each school year, I ask my students (at both the college and the secondary levels) to write their reading autobiographies. This activity helps me to see immediately which class members are already avid readers, which students might need a bit of extra motivation or guidance because they have become dormant readers, and which students have had such powerfully negative experiences with books and reading that I need to work closely with them to reestablish a connection to books early in the year.

I usually limit the reading autobiography requirement to three pages, typed and double-spaced. I ask students to address the following questions:

- What are your earliest memories of reading?
- What do you remember about reading outside of school?
- How do you think you learned to read?
- What are your reading experiences at school?
- What did you like to read as a child? as a teen? as an adult?

I ask students to complete these autobiographies by the end of the first week of class, and I allow one class period for students to begin to outline. You can share these autobiographies anonymously with the class and discuss what they have in common in terms of positive and negative reading experiences. I generally write comments in the margins as I read these pieces, noting surprise when a student mentions a book or author I love or noting dismay when a student relates a negative experience with books in a classroom.

I evaluate these papers with a basic check/minus system—either the student has completed the assignment or he or she needs to revise and resubmit. Assigning a numeric grade to someone's memories and experiences is too dicey, although that does not mean I cannot make comments about the quality of the writing. Often, this first piece of writing gives me direction for what writing, grammar, and usage issues I will cover early in the semester. More important, this assignment allows me the chance to see students as individuals who bring a variety of experiences to the classroom.

Coat of Arms

We have all seen the kiosks in our shopping malls that offer to locate our family's coat of arms (or perhaps to help us design one of our own). My husband's family has a coat of arms, one he proudly displays on our walls. He is descended from French Huguenots, and the family name has been part of the history of the southern United States since the 17th century. He can trace his family back to the original descendant who crossed from France more than 300 years ago. However, I am only a third-generation American, and one with a varied ancestry as well. There is no single coat of arms in existence that could represent my family fully. Whatever their situation, students might enjoy creating their own coat of arms, a family crest that is reflective of the lives of their parents and other relatives.

To create a coat of arms, students must first conduct some research into their families. Questions and procedures can be brainstormed as a class in order to ensure uniformity, or students can be left on their own to develop questions and interview procedures. Once students have completed the background research, they can prepare a coat of arms. You can provide the "shell" of the final product and even designate that each coat of arms be divided into a set number of pieces with specific information to be graphically represented in each piece (see Figure 7.1).

Again, some more choices can be allowed in completing this project. After the coats of arms have been finished, students can present brief oral explanations of the choices they made in their projects. This assignment can be combined with other activities such as "A Profile of Me" or "Writing Our Own Stories," two activities we will look at next.

FIGURE 7.1   *Coat of Arms Guide*

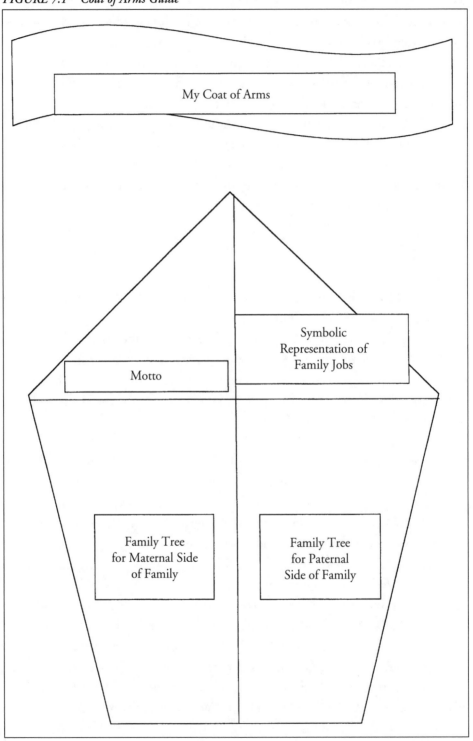

A Profile of Me

For this activity, you will need butcher paper (preferably white or neutral color), an overhead projector, markers, magazines that can be cut up, scissors, and paste. Put students into pairs. Their task is to trace the profile of their partner onto the butcher paper using the overhead projector to create the profile. Once the profiles have been drawn, students are given time to locate and cut out pictures and text in the magazines that reflect their interests, hobbies, likes, dislikes, and so forth. Then they create a collage, gluing the pictures and text onto the paper profiles. Students can also attach a paragraph or two at the bottom of each profile to explain the choices of words and photos included in the profile. If students omit their names, classmates might see if they can identify one another. Similarly, at Open House, parents could also try to locate their child's profile.

This activity takes little class time, but it provides us with rare glimpses behind the facades that so many of our students hide behind. There are many variations of this activity, as well, that can be used to teach skills. For example, instruct students to select only collective nouns or other parts of speech for various areas of the profile, and you have a quick and relatively painless grammar lesson.

Writing Our Own Stories

A logical follow-up to reading biographies and autobiographies is to ask students to write their own autobiographies. If we have carefully selected the models of this genre, students should be able to accomplish this task more readily. First, we must decide if we want students to write about their own lives or the lives of other people. Beginning with autobiographies or biographies of family members or classmates makes for the simplest approach. The research process will certainly be easier to complete.

For a brief writing project, students might emulate the biographical styles of authors who write for younger readers. Examine the resplendent picture book biographies of Diane Stanley. In 32- to 48-page picture books, Stanley provides an interesting and informative text. Though the picture books might run 48 pages, the actual text for these books is quite limited. Students could be instructed to design a picture book of a specific length (e.g., 48 pages) with "X" number of words per page (which teachers can adjust to meet the needs and abilities of the students and the curriculum) plus illustrations and/or other visuals. A PowerPoint or other multimedia presentation is one alternative to this picture book assignment. This rather simple approach to writing is best if used at the outset of a school year. However, as the days of the school year wind down and students need activities to distract them from the approaching days of summer vacation, a more involved writing project might be in order.

For a longer project, help students brainstorm a list of topics to cover in the biographies. Each topic can serve as an individual chapter. Each chapter might be one paragraph or one page in length. Teachers can, again, adjust the length of the writing to meet the needs and abilities of their students. Then ask students to select about five of those topics for their biographies. Such a list might include

- The night I had my worst scare
- The person I admire the most
- Wishes, hopes, and dreams
- The teacher from the Black Lagoon
- Treasures under my bed
- A perfect day for me
- TROUBLE!
- My first night out
- Adventures in babysitting
- What I would never do
- Take it from me
- A dark and stormy night
- Vacation blues
- I grew up here
- My best friend in the world
- Hide and seek
- When I am in charge
- My special place

Some Authors to Know

A handful of authors produce biographies and autobiographies that are consistently recognized as exemplary of the genre. These authors provide entertaining and informative books for teens. The subjects of their writing are diverse and include the famous, the infamous, and the everyday. As you begin to select those books that you will bring into the classroom, you may wish to begin with works by some of the following people.

Jean Fritz

Jean Fritz first came to prominence during the frenetic days of the U.S. Bicentennial. Her short illustrated biographies of the country's founding fathers proved immeasurably helpful in classrooms. Fritz soon branched out and began writing biographies for secondary students. *Bully for You, Teddy Roosevelt* (1991) is one example of the Fritz Formula for Biographical Success. In the opening pages, readers meet a young, sickly Teddy Roosevelt, who suffered from such severe asthma that doctors suggested he be driven around in a carriage at top speeds to try to force air into his lungs; some doctors even advised that he puff on cigars to toughen his lungs. From the opening chapter, readers will be captivated, eager to learn more about this figure from U.S. history.

Fritz does not disappoint. She makes each and every one of her subjects come to life by offering readers insights into their day-to-day lives. Her careful research includes numerous primary sources, which she notes in her bibliography. In addition, she shares with readers her notes for each chapter. It is easy to see, then, how she discovered that Sam Houston stood over 6 feet tall and wore only a size 7 shoe (Fritz, 1986). These bits and pieces of personal information deepen students' interest in the subject. More important, they make the subject come to life for today's readers.

Other Fritz biographical subjects include James Madison (1989), Pocahontas (1983), and Harriet Beecher Stowe (1994). Once students have read one of the outstanding biographies by Fritz, a great follow-up is to direct them to Fritz's autobiography, *Homesick: My Own Story* (1982), and have students discuss what traits and experiences Fritz shares with her subjects.

Russell Freedman

Seldom does nonfiction of any kind receive critical acclaim and awards. The exception to this rule seems to be the work of Russell Freedman, whose Newbery Medal and Newbery Honor books include biographies of Abraham Lincoln (1987) and the Wright brothers (1991). The defining characteristic of a biography by Freedman lies in the array of photographs, diagrams, and other artwork that accompany a lively text. It is difficult to turn a page of a Freedman book without encountering some illustration. For secondary students, this serves two purposes: First, it breaks up the text and makes it appear more manageable. Second, the illustrations elaborate and expand on the text, giving readers a concrete example of what is being discussed.

Freedman's research ethic is exemplary. As part of his research for the biography of the Wright brothers, he spent a night in the house that Orville and Wilbur designed. This interest in the day-to-day lives of his subjects is apparent in Freedman's writing as well. From Franklin Delano Roosevelt (1990) to Martha Graham (1998) to Louis Braille (1997) and Native American leaders (1988), from inventors to world leaders, Freedman's biographies are a sure bet for quality.

Students who have read a biography by Freedman might also investigate the research process of this incredible author. How, for example, does Freedman select a topic? How does he go about his research? What about the photos and other illustrative medium? Locating interviews with this author will give students a deeper insight into the writing process, especially as it pertains to nonfiction. Interviews with young adult authors appear regularly in journals such as *School Library Journal, The ALAN Review, Horn Book*, and *Teacher Librarian*. Interviews with authors are also available online. Check the publishers' websites as well as sites maintained by authors themselves.

Jim Haskins

Leaders in the African American community are frequently the subjects of biographies by Jim Haskins. From cultural icons such as Spike Lee (1997a) and Louis Farrakhan (1996) to military leaders like Colin Powell (1997b), Haskins provides readers with interesting and insightful biographies. Haskins's collective biographies are perfect for classroom use because they present quick glimpses into the lives of a wide assortment of prominent African Americans. The brief entries in collective biographies such as *African American Military Heroes* (1998a), *Black Eagles: African Americans in Aviation* (1997c), *Outward Dreams: Black Inventors and Their Inventions* (1992), and *African American Entrepreneurs* (1998b) will whet students' appetites for more information.

One interesting way to use Haskins's work is as a model for student writing. After students have completed reading a full-length biography, ask them to write about their subject as though he or she were to be included in a forthcoming collective biography. Students could work in groups with this assignment. Together, they could write the introductory and connecting text that would string together the various biographies and make the entire collection a coherent and cohesive whole.

BIOGRAPHY COLLAGE

Using magazines, scissors, and glue, have students create collages that have pictures to represent protagonist, antagonist, setting (time and place), conflict, plot, and theme of any biographical novel. The collage must be all cut and paste—no drawing or handwriting permitted. Students then explain their collages to the class in an informal oral report. This activity can also be used with any fiction book.

Audrey M. Quinlan is a doctoral candidate at Indiana University of Pennsylvania, Indiana, Pennsylvania, USA.

Kathleen Krull

Like Haskins, Kathleen Krull has written many collective biographies. Her work provides students not only with motivating reading material but also with excellent models for their own writing. In her various collections, Krull brings to life famous contributors to the fields of art (1995a), music (1993), politics (1998), sports (1997), and literature (1994). For example, in *Lives of the Musicians: Good Times, Bad Times (and What the Neighbors Thought)* (Krull, 1993), readers learn about famous composers such as Mozart and Bach as well as the lesser known contributions of Nadia Boulanger and Charles Ives. In a few short pages, Krull gives information sufficient to understand the contributions of the individual to the field. Additionally, she provides endnotes (cleverly labeled "Music Notes"), which serve as tantalizing teasers and invite readers to learn more about the subjects. The charming caricatures by Kathryn Hewitt add to the attraction of Krull's work.

Students could well use Krull's writing as models for their own work. Indeed, Krull has written a biography of another famous writer in the lives of our teens, Paula Danziger (1995b), which will be useful to aspiring writers in our classrooms.

Diane Stanley

Although Diane Stanley's books are classified as picture-book biographies, the intricate illustrations, the well-researched text, and the careful attention to detail make these books reach beyond an elementary audience. Secondary teachers might find her biographies of William Shakespeare (1992) and Charles Dickens (1993) useful when introducing the works of these famed authors. Stanley's biographies of leaders such as Cleopatra (1994), Shaka, King of the Zulus (1988), Peter the Great (1999), and Queen Elizabeth I (1990) make a natural connection to the social studies curriculum. Other Stanley biographies include the winner of the 1998 Orbis Pictus Award, *Leonardo da Vinci* (1996), and a biography of Joan of Arc (1998). Stanley's husband, Peter Vennema, served as her research assistant for several of her picture-book biographies and is listed as a coauthor on those titles.

Not only will the text of these biographies provide readers with excellent models for writing, the illustrations deserve close attention as well. Stanley's paintings reflect the style of the period when the subject lived and provide information about the subject, which elaborates the text. The cover of *Leonardo da Vinci*, for example, features a classically posed portrait of da Vinci on the front and a mirror image of the painting on the back cover. Within the text, readers discover that da Vinci was adept at producing mirror writing, hence the choice for the cover art. As a cross-curricular connection, the art teachers in the school could assist students in an examination of the art in Stanley's works.

Final Thoughts

Now, more than ever before perhaps, sharing biographies and autobiographies with adolescents is important. Too many surveys of teens indicate that the people they most admire are the rich and famous of our contemporary culture. Although there is nothing wrong with admiring the skill and talent of athletes and entertainers, today's students need to extend their identification to include the unsung heroes of our culture: political leaders and activists, researchers and scientists, historians and geographers, teachers and other professionals. In order to provide students the opportunity to explore career options, we need biographies that present an ever-growing range of choices. What are the possibilities of future vocations? Which people, living here and around the world, are shaping the events of today? What accomplishments need to be not only acknowledged but celebrated? Biographies give us the tools to enrich the lives of our students now and in the future.

REFERENCES

Applebee, A. (1992). Stability and change in the high-school canon. *English Journal, 81*(5), 27–32.

Carlsen, G.R. (1980). *Books and the teen age reader* (2nd ed.). New York: Harper & Row.

YOUNG ADULT LITERATURE CITED

Coerr, E. (1979). *Sadako and the thousand paper cranes.* New York: Dell Yearling.

Freedman, R. (1987). *Lincoln: A photobiography.* Boston: Houghton Mifflin.

Freedman, R. (1988). *Indian chiefs.* New York: Holiday House.

Freedman, R. (1990). *Franklin Delano Roosevelt.* New York: Clarion.

Freedman, R. (1991). *The Wright brothers: How they invented the airplane.* New York: Holiday House.

Freedman, R. (1997). *Out of darkness: The story of Louis Braille.* New York: Clarion.

Freedman, R. (1998). *Martha Graham: A dancer's life.* New York: Clarion.

Fritz, J. (1982). *Homesick: My own story.* New York: Putnam.

Fritz, J. (1983). *The double life of Pocahontas.* New York: Putnam.

Fritz, J. (1986). *Make way for Sam Houston.* New York: Putnam.

Fritz, J. (1989). *The great little Madison.* New York: Putnam.

Fritz, J. (1991). *Bully for you, Teddy Roosevelt*. New York: Putnam.

Fritz, J. (1994). *Harriet Beecher Stowe and the Beecher preachers*. New York: Putnam.

Haskins, J. (1992). *Outward dreams: Black inventors and their inventions*. New York: Bantam Starfire.

Haskins, J. (1996). *Louis Farrakhan and the nation of Islam*. New York: Walker and Company.

Haskins, J. (1997a). *Spike Lee: By any means necessary*. New York: Walker and Company.

Haskins, J. (1997b). *Colin Powell: A biography*. New York: Scholastic.

Haskins, J. (1997c). *Black eagles: African Americans in aviation*. New York: Scholastic.

Haskins, J. (1998a). *African American military heroes* (Black Star Series). Chichester, UK: John Wiley & Sons.

Haskins, J. (1998b). *African American entrepreneurs* (Black Star Series). Chichester, UK: John Wiley & Sons.

Krull, K. (1993). *Lives of the musicians: Good times, bad times (and what the neighbors thought)*. Orlando, FL: Harcourt Brace.

Krull, K. (1994). *Lives of the writers: Comedies, tragedies (and what the neighbors thought)*. Orlando, FL: Harcourt Brace.

Krull, K. (1995a). *Lives of the artists: Messes, masterpieces (and what the neighbors thought)*. Orlando, FL: Harcourt Brace.

Krull, K. (1995b). *Presenting Paula Danziger*. New York: Twayne.

Krull, K. (1997). *Lives of the athletes: Thrills, spills (and what the neighbors thought)*. Orlando, FL: Harcourt Brace.

Krull, K. (1998). *Lives of the presidents: Fame, shame (and what the neighbors thought)*. Orlando, FL: Harcourt Brace.

Miller, W. (1999). *Night golf*. New York: Lee & Low.

Munson, S. (1989). *Our Tejano heroes*. Holmes Beach, FL: Panda Books.

Paulsen, G. (1987). *Hatchet*. New York: Bradbury Press.

Paulsen, G. (1990). *Woodsong*. New York: Simon & Schuster.

Paulsen, G. (2001). *Guts, or how I lived the same as Brian Robeson*. New York: Delacorte.

Stanley, D. (1996). *Leonardo da Vinci*. New York: Morrow.

Stanley, D. (1998). *Joan of Arc*. New York: Morrow.

Stanley, D. (1999). *Peter the Great*. New York: Morrow.

Stanley, D., & Vennema, P. (1988). *Shaka: King of the Zulus*. New York: Morrow.

Stanley, D., & Vennema, P. (1990). *Good Queen Bess: The story of Elizabeth I of England*. New York: Morrow.

Stanley, D., & Vennema, P. (1992). *Bard of Avon: The story of William Shakespeare*. New York: Morrow.

Stanley, D., & Vennema, P. (1993). *Charles Dickens: The man who had great expectations*. New York: Morrow.

Stanley, D., & Vennema, P. (1994). *Cleopatra*. New York: Morrow.

ANNOTATED BIBLIOGRAPHY OF BIOGRAPHIES FOR YOUNG ADULT CLASSROOMS

Beals, M.P. (1995). *Warriors don't cry: A searing memoir of the battle to integrate Little Rock's Central High.* New York: Archway.

> Beals was one of the Little Rock Nine, nine teens selected to be the first African Americans at Central High School in Little Rock, Arkansas. What should have been the carefree times of high school were instead dark days of taunting and torture. Beals manages to relate the awful incidents of her ordeal with a total lack of bitterness, a real model for today's youth.

Coerr, E. (1979). *Sadako and the thousand paper cranes.* New York: Dell Yearling.

> Sadako Sasaki survived the bombing of her hometown of Hiroshima only to fall prey to the aftereffects of the atom bomb. Though she died of leukemia before reaching adolescence, her message of peace so touched her peers and people around the world that her story continues to resonate today.

Frank, A. (1993). *Anne Frank: The diary of a young girl.* New York: Bantam.

> This classic autobiography remains a favorite of teens who recognize in Anne so many of the emotions in their own lives. Reading this title along with other books recounting real-life experiences of the Holocaust, such as *No Pretty Pictures* by Anita Lobel, will allow students a chance to see that World War II affected the lives of countless youth.

Levine, E. (1995). *Freedom's children: Young Civil Rights activists tell their own stories.* New York: Avon.

> The title of this book is quite descriptive. Levine located and interviewed people who were children and teens during the days of the Civil Rights movement. She records their narratives about marching with Dr. Martin Luther King Jr., about the bus boycotts, and about the lunch room sit-ins. Most of all, readers will get a sense of the incredible courage of these youngsters, who stood up for their convictions even though it might have meant imprisonment or perhaps death.

Lobel, A. (1998). *No pretty pictures: A child of war.* New York: Greenwillow.

> Anita Lobel was only 5 years old when the Nazis began their occupation of her native Poland. In simple, objective detail she recounts the years spent hiding to save her life, including a stint in a concentration camp. Lobel, best known for her Caldecott award-winning picture books, has written a memoir sure to rivet readers.

Meltzer, M. (1998). *Ten queens: Portraits of women of power.* New York: Dutton.

> The large format of this collective biography makes it a feast for the eyes. Great illustrations add to the brief glimpses into the lives of 10 women who led their people in good times and bad. Included are well-known rulers such as Elizabeth I and Eleanor of Aquitaine, along with less familiar figures such as Queen Zenobia of Syria and Queen Christina of Sweden.

Morey, J., & Dunn, W. (1996). *Famous Hispanic Americans.* New York: Cobblehill.

> The lives of 14 Hispanics are detailed in this collective biography. All are contemporary figures who come from a variety of backgrounds. From athletes like Felipe Alou and Gigi Fernandez to stand-up comic Paul Rodriguez to fashion designer Caroline Herrera and

ballet dancer Lourdes Lopez, there are many opportunities within these pages for students to learn more about the contributions of these individuals.

Munson, S. (1989). *Our Tejano heroes*. Holmes Beach, FL: Panda Books.

This collective biography examines the lives of Hispanics living in Texas, from its early fight for independence from Mexico to contemporary times.

Paulsen, G. (1990). *Woodsong*. New York: Simon & Schuster.

This slice-of-life autobiography discusses how Paulsen's views on nature were changed by his experiences with his beloved sled dogs, his sole companions on the grueling Iditarod race in Alaska. Readers will be moved from tears to laughter as this master storyteller survives freezing temperatures, irate wildlife, and a host of other challenges.

White, R. (1992). *Ryan White: My own story*. New York: Signet.

White's unforgettable tale of living with AIDS is simple and honest. More important, it is a biography about someone close to the age of its readers, making it even more accessible. Pair this one with Susan Kuklin's *Fighting Back: What Some People Are Doing About AIDS* to give readers more information on the subject.

CHAPTER 8

Poetry Pathways for Teens

Rosemary Chance

Student:	Where's the love poetry?
Librarian:	Do you have a poetry assignment?
Student:	No, I just need love poetry.
Librarian:	Poems about love are scattered throughout collections of poetry.
Student:	You mean there isn't just one poetry book about love?

That is the way it used to be. If you were an eighth grader looking for a romantic poem to read to your girlfriend, you had to search through anthologies of classic poets to find the right love poem. A budding romantic in a hulking boy's body would grudgingly accept Lord Byron's "She Walks in Beauty" and Elizabeth Barrett Browning's "Sonnet #43," which begins, "How do I love thee? Let me count the ways." What he really wanted, though, was one book with modern poetry for teens. With the steady rise of poetry written especially for both younger and older teens, libraries today can offer both classic and modern poetry.

At this time, more poets are writing for teens and selecting poems for a teenage audience than in previous years. These collections make it easier and more pleasurable for teens to find paths to poetry for their constantly changing lives. Poetry published for teens explores teen interests, touches their emotions, and tells their stories. These collections offer three types of poetry: poetry with regular metrical pattern; free verse, which depends upon natural rhythms of spoken language; and writing that looks like poetry but has more in common with prose. No matter the form, poetry today explores love, death, loss, families, friends, identity, and growing up. The best of these poetry forms contain emotional intensity that speaks to teens about their interests.

As well as offering a wide range of topics, most poetry collections published recently for teens offer poetry for a wide range of ages. Preteens will identify with some poems in collections labeled for young adults. Other collections offer poems that appeal to older teens nearing high school graduation. Teens who may consider themselves too old for young adult novels will often read young adult poetry collections. The eclectic nature of the collections and the combination of classic and contemporary poems encourage readers to browse and find poems that speak to them on a personal level.

Poetry About Love

One of the interests of teens is love—from frivolous to sensuous, from friendship love to romantic love. Recently published poetry books should satisfy the need for poetry about different types of love.

Arnold Adoff takes readers solidly into adolescence with *Slow Dance Heart Break Blues* (1995). Written in Adoff's trademark free verse style, the title poem asks questions teens wrestle with: "what is like what is love what is lust" (p. 73). Two collections of Ralph Fletcher's poetry, *I Am Wings* (1994) and *Buried Alive: The Elements of Love* (1996), speak of the joys and sorrows of young love. A poem about the death of a loved one may appeal to some teens. In the title poem in *Buried Alive*, a student has a crush on her teacher, who dies. The poem ends with these words full of pain:

> At the cemetery
> I throw down
> one fistful of dirt,
> a million microbes
> onto his coffin
> though he never taught
> how to let your heart
> get buried
> alive. (p. 6)

Poems That Address Loss

Death is another emotionally intense experience, and thus, like love, is well suited for poetry. A few volumes specifically address death and loss. *Stopping for Death: Poems of Death and Loss* (1996), selected by Carol Ann Duffy and illustrated by Trisha Rafferty, includes classic poems from Emily Dickinson and Christina

Rosetti, but most poems in the collection were first published in the 1990s. Despite the topic, these poems are upbeat, treating death and loss as a matter-of-fact part of life. Teens of all ages can find at least one poem that speaks to them. The same can be said for two other collections: *Pierced by a Ray of Sun: Poems About the Times We Feel Alone* (1995), selected by Ruth Gordon, and *What Have You Lost?* (1999), selected by Naomi Shihab Nye, with photographs by Michael Nye.

Pierced by a Ray of Sun includes translations of poems from other countries, Paul Simon's "I Am a Rock," and poems by more recent writers, such as Cynthia Rylant, author of the poem "Forgotten":

> Mom came home one day
> and said my father had died.
> Her eyes all red.
> Crying for some stranger.
> Couldn't think of anything to do,
> so I walked around Beaver
> telling the kids and feeling important.
> Nobody else's dad had died.
> But then
> nobody else's dad had worn
> red-striped pajamas
> and nobody else's dad had made
> stuffed animals talk
> and nobody else's dad had gone away
> nine years ago.
> Nobody else's dad had been so loved
> by a 4-year-old.
> And so forgotten by one
> now
> thirteen. (p. 14)

What Have You Lost? raises a special possibility for involving teens in writing poetry. Nye says that she entered a room of students and said simply, "What have you lost? Write it down" (p. xiii). She suggests that students will write better and with more energy when they answer this question. Everyone has lost something: innocence, a favorite toy, a parent, a friend, a pet. Nye's collection provides excellent reading and excellent models for poems about loss.

Poetry About Teens' Varied Interests

Love and death are basics to life's journey, but there are other things that interest teens, and many collections address these important (and not-so-important) topics. *Step Lightly: Poems for the Journey* (1998), collected by Nancy Willard, includes classic and modern poems about topics such as writing, purple, big hips, cows, slugs, and more. The poems in *Behind the Wheel: Poems About Driving* (1999), by Janet S. Wong, reflect a clear interest of most teens. One such poem, "Restraint," provides a model for teens to compose their own car-related analogies:

> When the poet came
> to visit our school
> to make us write some poetry,
> people from our families
> turned into trees
> and owls and slugs.
> My sister was a hurricane.
>
> End of class,
> Jim raised his hand.
>
> *My parents are like seat belts.*
> *They're always around me—*
> *But I guess*
> *they help keep me safe.*
>
> The room was quiet.
> Then a hum spread all around.
> I wished I could have thought like Jim.
>
> Things are different at my home.
> Sometimes you wonder if they care.
> But when you mess up—WOOOMPH!—
> they're there, like air bags,
> in your face. (p. 33)

Another combination of modern and classic poetry, *Light-Gathering Poems* (2000), edited by Liz Rosenberg, intends to inspire readers through poems gathered from many peoples and traditions. Brief biographical sketches of the poets at the end of the book provide a gentle way to introduce literary criticism to students. A similar approach can be found in two volumes of Paul Janeczko's collections, *Poetspeak: In Their Work, About Their Work* (1983) and *The Place My Words Are Looking For: What Poets Say About and Through Their Work* (1990).

Both volumes contain poetry, photographs of the poets, and brief explanations in the poet's own words about how and why he or she writes.

Paul Janeczko's other collections of contemporary poetry provide a full range of topics for life's journey, such as *Looking for Your Name: A Collection of Contemporary Poems* (1993) and *Wherever Home Begins: 100 Contemporary Poems* (1995). What is delightful about Janeczko's selections is the variety, the humor, and the awareness of teen readers. From letters between Ann Landers and Frankenstein's wife to poems about wrestling, there really is something to which every teen can relate. Titles of the poems Janeczko selected to include in *Looking*

TEACHING FREE VERSE AND NONTRADITIONAL POETRY

Teaching poetry, particularly to middle school and high school students, is a difficult task. Free verse and nontraditional poetry present an even greater problem, because students struggle with the lack of a strict format and rhyme scheme. The following introduction to poetry not only exemplifies the literary elements of free verse, but also enhances students' reading of verse:

- Create a set of notecards (numbered for organization) with various questions or directions written on them (e.g., In three words, describe what a sneeze sounds like under water. Name three colors. Describe the sound a cricket makes in four or less words.). It is important to establish a consistent tone to the questions.

- As students enter the room, distribute the notecards and give students 3 to 5 minutes to complete the task on each card. Students are not permitted to confer with classmates. After the students are finished, collect the cards, reorganize them in numerical order, and edit them for appropriateness. Place them aside.

- The next day (or at the end of class), read a new poem directly from student responses on the notecards. With the right inflection and with the addition of some articles and conjunctions, the class has created an invaluable piece of poetry. After discussing and interpreting the poem, show students that it was constructed from their responses on the notecards. It is a great way for students to learn the benefits of effective oral reading, of writing poetry, and of taking ownership for their learning.

- Display the "poem" in the classroom or during parent conferences or board meetings to showcase the class efforts. Also be sure that each student receives a copy of the poem.

This activity can be used with students from grades 7–12.

Jessica A. Ocipa teaches in the Blacklick Valley School District, Nanty Glo, Pennsylvania, USA.

for Your Name hint at the pleasures within: "Why I Quit Dancing Lessons," "The Black Thumb," "Ineffable Beauty," "Conscientious Objector," and "Poem Ending With an Old Cliché," to name a few poems.

Other collections for teens also have unique characteristics. In *I Feel a Little Jumpy Around You: A Book of Her Poems & His Poems Collected in Pairs* (1996), Naomi Shihab Nye and Paul B. Janeczko pair male and female poets to offer separate views of the same topics. Teachers can immediately see the possibilities for poetry connections. For example, they can pair a boy and a girl to write separate poems on a topic, and then see how their viewpoints differ or how they are alike. Students can search poetry collections for poems on the same topic and discuss the differences and similarities in the poetry. Nye and Janeczko provide numerous examples of this pairing technique.

Teens express their emotions about topics and issues important to them in two recently published poetry collections: *Movin': Teen Poets Take Voice* (2000), edited by Dave Johnson, and *The Pain Tree and Other Teenage Angst-Ridden Poetry* (2000), collected and illustrated by Esther Pearl Watson and Mark Todd. Through workshops sponsored by the New York Public Library and Poets House, Orchard Books published 36 poems by teenagers from across the United States in *Movin'*. A glimpse at the titles of their poems provides clues to a range of subjects: "Ode to Eyebrows," "I Wish I Didn't Feel So Old," "If Peaches Had Arms," and "Jealousy." *The Pain Tree* includes 25 poems that express the raw emotions of teens ages 13 through 18. They write about "Hate," "Exasperation," and "Trust." Budding poets should enjoy reading these published poems written by their peers.

African American Poetry

Just as there has been a steady increase in poetry for teens, there has been an increase in poetry for teens written by African Americans. This poetry highlights emotions and experiences of African Americans and serves as a special pathway to poetry for African American teens. Some teens will be enticed by reading poetry written by favorite African American authors, such as Maya Angelou and Alice Walker. Other teens will be drawn to specific topics and to illustrated editions featuring a single poem or a collection of poems.

Maya Angelou, author of *I Know Why the Caged Bird Sings* (1997), has written poetry about being an African American woman. Her collection is titled *I Shall Not Be Moved* (1990). Poems about the African American experience come together in *I Am the Darker Brother: An Anthology of Modern Poems by African Americans* (Adoff, 1997). Included in the collection are poems by Langston

Hughes, Gwendolyn Brooks, Nikki Giovanni, Alice Walker, Paul Dunbar, and other well-known African American poets.

The illustrated format of recent poetry collections by African Americans may succeed in capturing the interest of teens. *The Dream Keeper and Other Poems* (1994) is a collection of Langston Hughes's poetry accompanied by Brian Pinkney's beautiful black-and-white scratchboard illustrations. The collection consists of 66 poems that will appeal to young readers, and the collection includes familiar poems such as "Dreams":

> Hold fast to dreams
> For if dreams die
> Life is a broken-winged bird
> That cannot fly.
>
> Hold fast to dreams
> For when dreams go
> Life is a barren field
> Frozen with snow. (p. 4)

A large-format picture book also features poems by Langston Hughes. *The Block* (1995) is illustrated with collages by Romare Bearden and celebrates life in Harlem through 13 poems. From "Theme for English" to "Juke Box Love Song" to the final poem, "Stars," this collection throbs with energy.

Perhaps these illustrated collections will provide incentives to teens who are reluctant to read a book of poetry. *I, Too, Sing America: Three Centuries of African American Poetry* (1998), selected and annotated by Catherine Clinton, presents 25 poets and their poetry in a large-format collection. Stunning full-page mixed media illustrations by Stephen Alcorn dramatically enhance each poem. Once again, this is a poetry collection that can ease students into literary criticism; a brief biography prefaces each poet's work and invites students to explore the lives of these talented poets.

Words With Wings: A Treasury of African-American Poetry and Art (2001), selected by Belinda Rochelle, pairs 20 poems with 20 works of art by African Americans. Alice Walker's "How Poems Are Made" is paired with Beauford Delaney's "Can Fire in the Park." Walker's words are especially appropriate to this chapter:

> I understand how poems are made.
> They are the tears
> that season the smile.

The stiff-neck laughter
that crowds the throat.
The leftover love. (p. 27)

Latino American Poetry

The Latino American experience is also present in recent collections of poetry for teens. Gary Soto, an author of fiction for teens, has written a book of poems based on his life growing up Mexican American in California. In *A Fire in My Hands: A Book of Poems* (1990), some of Soto's poems contain universal messages about love and friendship; other poems center on dancing in Kearney Park and being Catholic. A dozen questions and answers by Soto about his poetry complete this detailed and thoughtful volume of images.

Latino American teens and teens of other cultures who want to gain a better understanding of Latin America will enjoy two other collections: *Cool Salsa: Bilingual Poems on Growing Up Latino in the United States* (Carlson, 1994) and *My Own True Name: New and Selected Poems for Young Adults* (Mora, 2000). In *Cool Salsa*, most poems are printed in both English and Spanish, but the initial poem is a mix of both. "English con Salsa," by Gina Valdes, begins, "Welcome to ESL 100, English Surely Latinized" (p. 4). It continues in a charming mix of Spanish and English words and images. Pat Mora begins her collection of poetry, *My Own True Name*, by sharing her "secrets" of writing poetry. She divides her 62 poems into 3 sections: Blooms, Thorns, and Roots. Some poems directly reflect a Chicano experience; others will appeal universally. Mora aims almost all of her poems at teens, but one poem, "Teenagers," is more for adults and shows she understands what it is like to have a child become a teen:

One day they disappear
into their rooms.
Doors and lips shut
and we become strangers
in our own home.
I pace the hall, hear whispers,
a code I knew but can't remember,
mouthed by mouths I taught to speak.

Years later the door opens.
I see faces I once held,
open as sunflowers in my hands. I see
familiar skin now stretched on long bodies

that move past me
flowing
almost like pearls. (p. 24)

Narrative Poetry

Perhaps each poem tells a hidden story, no matter how brief—a glimpse of someone else's life. Narrative poems and certain collections of poems intend to tell someone's story as completely as a short story or a novel. Teens who enjoy reading fiction may be more easily persuaded to read and enjoy poetry in a familiar narrative form. Several authors and poets have written absorbing and intriguing stories in this form. The leader in this form is Mel Glenn. Until recently, Glenn was best known for his free verse spotlighting high school students in *Class Dismissed: High School Poems* (1982). In the last few years, he has written five novels in poetry form: *Who Killed Mr. Chippendale? A Mystery in Poems* (1996), *Jump Ball: A Basketball Season in Poems* (1997a), *The Taking of Room 114: A Hostage Drama in Poems* (1997b), *Foreign Exchange: A Mystery in Poems* (1999), and *Split Image: A Story in Poems* (2000). As their titles suggest, mystery, sports, romance, family, friends, and enemies are present in these unusual stories. Glenn's story poems could be paired with conventional novels for a unique reading experience and for a way to get students to think about writing form. For example, *Jump Ball* could be paired with another story about basketball, such as *On the Devil's Court* by Carl Deuker (1991). *Who Killed Mr. Chippendale?* could be paired with *Killing Mr. Griffin* by Lois Duncan (1993).

Other narrative collections will intrigue readers with their imagery, characters, and action. Two recent novels accomplish satisfying stories through poetry. Karen Hesse's *Out of the Dust: A Novel* (1997) won the 1998 Newbery Medal for its portrayal of a disfigured young girl living in the Oklahoma Dust Bowl during the Great Depression. Sonya Sones's *Stop Pretending: What Happened When My Big Sister Went Crazy* (1999) chronicles the life of a young girl trying to deal with her older sister's hospitalization and the subsequent loss of her confidante. One poem reveals,

Sister's in the psycho ward
and when I visit, I glance toward
the other patients' twisted faces,
quaking fingers,
frightened eyes,
wishing I could somehow break her out of here…. (p. 9)

CLERIHEWS

Clerihews are poems about famous people or celebrities. They are rhymes that are biographical in nature. Following are some items to keep in mind when you are developing a clerihew:

- Brainstorm ideas. Gather a lot of names that you think you might want to write about.
- Jot down all the facts and interesting details you learned about them.
- Choose the one that you would like to write about.
- Write four lines with two couplets in the following format:
  - Line 1 is a proper name.
  - Lines 2, 3, and 4 describe the person.
  - Be sure lines 1 and 2 rhyme and lines 3 and 4 rhyme.
- It should be humorous in a nice way.
- Include details about your well-known person.

Examples by students of the Homer-Center School District, Homer City, Pennsylvania, USA:

Beverly Cleary…
I hold her books dearly
because they're very good.
I would read them all if I could.

Darren Shan
Is a man.
He writes good books.
But I'm not real sure about his looks.

Golden Gate Bridge
was built by a ridge.
Built at San Francisco Bay.
Good thing it wasn't built in a day.

Dr. Seuss
Drew a moose
He couldn't think of a name
So the moose just wasn't the same.

Adapted from Janeczko, P.B. (1999). *Favorite poetry lessons (Grades 4–8)*. New York: Scholastic.

Stop Pretending could be paired effectively with *I Never Promised You a Rose Garden* by Joanne Greenberg (1984).

For those teens wanting a romantic story, brief poems about the joy and agony of love and dating can be found in Ann Turner's *A Lion's Hunger: Poems of First Love* (1998), illustrated by Maria Jimenez. This slender illustrated volume in diary form features the ups and downs of teen love. Some pieces could be quoted or recited to express romantic feelings: "Your hand reaches/out/mine stretches to meet,/the space ignites—/flame/on/flame" (p. 14).

For preteens and young teens, *Love That Dog: A Novel* (2001), by Sharon Creech, chronicles the process of writing poetry through the thoughts of Jack, a young boy who states, "boys don't write poetry./Girls do" (p. 1). Jack's teacher, Ms. Stretchberry, continues to give the class poetry assignments and arranges a visit from Walter Dean Myers. Gradually, Jack finds more and more to write about and finally produces a credible poem in imitation of Myers's poem "Love That Boy." This fresh look at the writing process will be an inspiration to both teachers and students.

At first glance, *Soda Jerk* (1990), by Cynthia Rylant with paintings by Peter Catalanotto, looks like a picture storybook for children. It is beautifully illustrated in a Norman Rockwell style, but the book is a story in poems for teens. A young man works in Maywell's Drugstore in Cheston, Virginia, where he makes sodas, fries, and hamburgers; pours coffee; and watches what customers buy and how they act. In 28 poems, readers learn about life in a small town where the soda jerk will not be needing "sexual aids" anytime soon, and "the tips are okay,/But the secrets are better" (p. 11).

Teens can discover one secret of poetry through these narratives: Like short stories and novels, narrative poetry offers readers satisfying stories for reading pleasure. For students who are reluctant to read and write poetry, when story is the key, the poetic form is seen as less of a barrier and more of an inviting pathway to literature.

Encouraging Involvement With Poetry

One of the easiest ways to get multiple students to peruse many poetry books is to have students participate in an activity called "Please Pass the Poetry." This is similar to the "Pass It On" activity presented in Teri Lesesne's chapter on "Biographies in the Classroom" (see Chapter 7 in this volume). Go to your school or public library (or both) and check out enough poetry collections so that each student in one class will have a book. Type up a list of the titles of the books and distribute it to your class. Briefly discuss prereading procedures, such as looking at the cover and reading the information on the dust jacket. Hand out one book to each student and set a timer for 1 or 2 minutes. Students have that amount of time to sample each book and check books on the list they are interested in reading. At the end of the session, every student will have looked at as many poetry books as you have students in the class. It is simple, it is effective, and students are introduced to a plethora of poems in a short span of time. Because poetry collections are not usually intended to be read straight through from cover to cover, this activity lends itself well to browsing.

There are other activities that can be effective in helping students learn to enjoy poetry without a complicated lesson. You can begin a class with a poem; you can announce, "Poetry Break!" and interrupt a lesson with a poem; you can end a lesson with a poem. Poems you present in a "poetry break" do not have to fit the current lesson or even the season of the year. Sometimes a contrast with what is happening in class provides the best break to change pace and to refresh one's thoughts. These "poetry breaks" can showcase poems you enthusiastically read aloud, particularly humorous and lighthearted poems. Also, you can reread your students' favorites aloud. To discover which poems are favorites, periodically find five new poems, read them aloud, and ask students to vote for the ones they prefer. Sometimes serious poems read aloud embarrass teens because of the intimate or intense nature of the subject, such as death and loss. To use serious poems for "poetry breaks," make copies of a poem and hand them out to students to read and keep.

Conclusion

Whether the poems are lighthearted or serious, modern poetry collections written specifically for teens are plentiful. The challenge is to gather poetry collections together and provide teens with enough choices so that they can find their own meaningful pathways to the enjoyment of poetry.

POETRY COLLECTIONS CITED

Grade ranges are provided to aid in determining the appropriateness of specific poetry collections.

Adoff, A. (1995). *Slow dance heart break blues*. Ill. W. Cotton. New York: Lothrop, Lee & Shepard. (Grades 7–10)

Adoff, A. (Ed.). (1997). *I am the darker brother: An anthology of modern poems by African Americans.* New York: Aladdin. (Grades 7–12)

Angelou, M. (1990). *I shall not be moved.* New York: Bantam. (Grades 9–12)

Carlson, L.M. (1994). *Cool salsa: Bilingual poems on growing up Latino in the United States.* New York: Henry Holt. (Grades 7–12)

Clinton, C. (Ed.). (1998). *I, too, sing America: Three centuries of African American poetry.* Ill. S. Alcorn. Boston: Houghton Mifflin. (Grades 5–7)

Creech, S. (2001). *Love that dog: A novel.* New York: Joanna Cotler Books. (Grades 3–7)

Duffy, C.A. (Sel.). (1996). *Stopping for death: Poems of death and loss.* Ill. T. Rafferty. New York: Henry Holt. (Grades 7–12)

Fletcher, R. (1994). *I am wings.* New York: Atheneum. (Grades 5–8)

Fletcher, R. (1996). *Buried alive: The elements of love.* New York: Atheneum. (Grades 5–8)

Glenn, M. (1982). *Class dismissed: High school poems.* Photo. M.J. Bernstein. New York: Clarion. (Grades 8–12)

Glenn, M. (1996). *Who killed Mr. Chippendale? A mystery in poems.* New York: Lodestar. (Grades 7–12)

Glenn, M. (1997a). *Jump ball: A basketball season in poems.* New York: Lodestar. (Grades 7–12)

Glenn, M. (1997b). *The taking of Room 114: A hostage drama in poems.* New York: Lodestar. (Grades 8–12)

Glenn, M. (1999). *Foreign exchange: A mystery in poems.* New York: Morrow. (Grades 7–12)

Glenn, M. (2000). *Split image: A story in poems.* New York: HarperCollins. (Grades 7–12)

Gordon, R. (Sel.). (1995). *Pierced by a ray of sun: Poems about the times we feel alone.* New York: HarperCollins. (Grades 7–12)

Hesse, K. (1997). *Out of the dust: A novel.* New York: Scholastic. (Grades 5–8)

Hughes, L. (1994). *The dream keeper and other poems.* Ill. B. Pinkney. New York: Knopf. (Grades 6–12)

Hughes, L. (1995). *The block.* Ill. R. Bearden. New York: Viking Children's Books. (Grades 6–12)

Janeczko, P.B. (Sel.). (1983). *Poetspeak: In their work, about their work.* New York: Atheneum. (Grades 8–12)

Janeczko, P.B. (Sel.). (1990). *The place my words are looking for: What poets say about and through their work.* New York: Atheneum. (Grades 5–8)

Janeczko, P.B. (Sel.). (1993). *Looking for your name: A collection of contemporary poems.* Danbury, CT: Orchard Books. (Grades 6–12)

Janeczko, P.B. (Sel.). (1995). *Wherever home begins: 100 contemporary poems.* Danbury, CT: Orchard Books. (Grades 8–12)

Johnson, D. (Ed.). (2000). *Movin': Teen poets take voice.* Ill. C. Raschka. Danbury, CT: Orchard Books. (Grades 6–10)

Mora, P. (2000). *My own true name: New and selected poems for young adults.* Houston: Arte Publico. (Grades 7–12)

Nye, N.S. (Sel.). (1999). *What have you lost?* Photo. M. Nye. New York: Greenwillow. (Grades 8–12)

Nye, N.S., & Janeczko, P.B. (Eds.). (1996). *I feel a little jumpy around you: A book of her poems & his poems collected in pairs.* New York: Simon & Schuster. (Grades 8–12)

Rochelle, B. (Sel.). (2001). *Words with wings: A treasury of African-American poetry and art.* New York: HarperCollins. (Grades 4–10)

Rosenberg, L. (Ed.). (2000). *Light-gathering poems.* New York: Henry Holt. (Grades 7–12)

Rylant, C. (1990). *Soda jerk.* Ill. P. Catalanotto. Danbury, CT: Orchard Books. (Grades 9–12)

Sones, S. (1999). *Stop pretending: What happened when my big sister went crazy.* New York: HarperCollins. (Grades 6–10)

Soto, G. (1990). *A fire in my hands: A book of poems.* New York: Scholastic. (Grades 6–12)

Turner, A. (1998). *A lion's hunger: Poems of first love.* Ill. M. Jimenez. Tarrytown, NY: Marshall Cavendish. (Grades 7–12)

Watson, E.P., & Todd, M. (Sel.). (2000). *The pain tree and other teenage angst-ridden poetry.* Boston: Houghton Mifflin. (Grades 7–12)

Willard, N. (Sel.). (1998). *Step lightly: Poems for the journey.* San Diego: Harcourt Brace. (Grades 7–12)

Wong, J.S. (1999). *Behind the wheel: Poems about driving.* New York: Margaret K. McElderry. (Grades 7–12)

YOUNG ADULT LITERATURE CITED

Angelou, M. (1997). *I know why the caged bird sings.* New York: Bantam.

Deuker, C. (1991). *On the devil's court.* New York: Flare.

Duncan, L. (1993). *Killing Mr. Griffin.* New York: Laurel Leaf.

Greenberg, J. (1984). *I never promised you a rose garden.* New York: New American Library.

CHAPTER 9

When I Hear a Poem, I Want to Write

Arlene Harris Mitchell

It doesn't always have to rhyme,
but there's the repeat of a beat, somewhere
an inner chime that makes you want to
tap your feet or swerve in a curve;
a lilt, a leap, a lightning-split:—
thunderstruck the consonants jut,
while the vowels open wide as waves in the noon-blue sea.

You hear with your heels, your eyes feel
what they never touched before:
fins on a bird, feathers on a deer;
taste all colors, inhale
memory and tomorrow and always the tang is today.

—"Inside a Poem" by Eve Merriam (1964, p. 3)

Poetry can be one of the most exciting genres to teach. Poetry stimulates critical thinking, generates creative thinking, celebrates diversity, makes meaningful linkages to other content areas, and promotes expressive writing. Most of all, it is a joy to teach and fun to learn.

When I work with teachers, however, they often explain that although they enjoy reading and writing poetry, their students do not. Poetry is a genre that can be used in every subject area and read at every age, yet it is a genre that most young adult readers and their teachers find challenging, and unfortunately, often boring. Something seems to happen between the fourth and sixth grades, and again between the ninth and eleventh grades, that interrupts the fun of learning poetry. Let's remedy that and return to the joy of teaching and learning poetry. Although not a complete panacea, writing poetry and writing about poetry are dynamic ways for students to elevate their thinking process. Most important, writing poetry and writing about poetry give students the opportunity to become involved in their instruction through interesting and meaningful participation.

This chapter concentrates on writing poetry and writing about poetry to enhance young adults' opportunities to appreciate, understand, and experience poetry. Writing does not happen in a vacuum. In order to give students experiences that lead to a deeper appreciation of poetry, we also need to pay attention to other elements of instruction that will lead to their readiness. Three stages I include as part of classroom teaching and learning poetry are (1) selecting poems and writing about poetry, (2) reading poems and writing about poetry, and (3) writing poems and exploring poetry. These lessons guide students to thinking that is creative and critical and to writing that is reflective and imaginative.

I have selected several poems to concentrate on throughout this chapter. These poems are part of "Mitchell's 200 Favorites," a personalized collection that I use in classes and workshops. The collection includes poems and poetry books that I can share across grade levels, and lists poems on a variety of subjects and forms. My list changes from time to time as I find new and interesting poems. The "favorites" selected for this chapter are easy to work with, capture students' interest, and provide a good introduction to various elements of poetry:

1. "Still I Rise" by Maya Angelou contains rhymes and repetition, as demonstrated in the following excerpt from *The Complete Collected Poems of Maya Angelou* (Angelou, 1994):

> Out of the huts of history's shame
> I rise
> Up from a past that's rooted in pain
> I rise
> I'm a black ocean, leaping and wide,
> Welling and swelling I bear in the tide. (pp. 163–164)

Many students will find it uplifting, and it is a good source when they begin to write poetry and write about poetry. Many students will recognize Angelou's name. She has become well known, first for her autobiography *I Know Why the Caged Bird Sings* (1970), and later as an outstanding poet. Just remember, you are introducing the poem, not the poet.

2. "Street Music" is published in an illustrated children's book of the same name by Arnold Adoff (1995). The arrangement of words and lack of punctuation help readers to visualize the subject. Following is an excerpt:

```
as        planes
   overhead
             roar
an
orchestra
of rolling drums
and battle blasts
assaulting
         my ears
```

Adoff has several original poetry books to his credit, as well as edited collections.

3. "Mending Wall" by Robert Frost is a "traditional" poem, which in this chapter means only that it has been published in many anthologies of poetry and literature. Students will probably recognize his poem "The Road Not Taken." Both poems appear in *The Poetry of Robert Frost* (Lathem, 1979). The form and simple words of "Mending Wall" will help students understand how poetry can create a story line, lend itself to describe personalities, and generate mood. Further, this poem is a good example of the use of lines without rhyme, as demonstrated by the following excerpt:

> There where it is we do not need the wall:
> He is all pine and I am apple orchard.
> My apple trees will never get across
> And eat the cones under his pines, I tell him.
> He only says, "Good fences make good neighbors." (p. 33)

4. "I Have Ten Legs" by Anna Swir, a Polish poet, provides a chance to bring an international poet into the classroom. Students can easily relate to the poem and think of sports or other things in their lives that help them to "exist." The poem, translated by Czeslaw Milosz and Leonard Nathan in *This Same Sky: A Collection of Poems from Around the World* (Nye, 1992), teaches students that poetry can relate to us across cultures and across oceans:

> When I run
> I laugh with my legs.
>
> When I run
> I swallow the world with my legs.

When I run
I have ten legs.
All my legs
shout.

I exist
only when running. (p. 167)

5. "Inside a Poem" by Eve Merriam, from the poet's collection *It Doesn't Always Have to Rhyme* (1964), appears at the opening of this chapter and is one example of the many poems she has written about poetry. It defines poetry in simple language and helps students feel free in their writing.

6. "Ode to Pablo's Tennis Shoes" by Gary Soto is a fun poem, simple to read and fun to hear. The following excerpt, taken from Soto's collection *Neighborhood Odes* (1992), demonstrates the imagery in this poem, which will help students find other items in their lives that they can choose as topics:

He wants to be
Like his shoes,
A little dirty
From the road,
A little worn
From racing to the drinking fountain
A hundred times in one day. (pp. 20–22)

Although I have given brief author information here, it is important, especially at the exploration stage, that author information is kept brief or to the poet's name only. Sometimes authors should even be presented as "anonymous" until the students have had a chance to work through the poem; otherwise, students may tend to limit their responses and interpretations based only on what they know about the author. For example, several students responding to "Mending Wall" may see it only as a rural setting instead of taking a broader view such as the sample given later in this chapter.

Selecting Poems and Writing About Poetry

Selecting poems and writing about poetry is often the stimulant that gets our students involved in wanting to read poetry. Most, if not all, of our students, preschool through adults, have had some experience with poetry, even if they have not looked at it and defined it as poetry. They listen to songs, sing jingles, hear stories in poetic form, and use figurative language daily. Yet for some reason, after fourth grade, students envision poetry as an abstract creature that is difficult to understand most of the time, and impossible to understand at other times.

One way to reintroduce students to poetry is to share a few colorful poems: those that use language in unique ways and those that create pictures or help readers visualize a scene or person through words, as if someone has drawn illustrations. Concrete poetry, which creates pictures with words, is generally fun to see and read. Choose poems that have words that keep bouncing around in our heads, which make us want to sing or dance or join in. Some of these may have interesting word patterns. Chances are, if you like the poem, your students will also like it.

We should not begin sharing poetry by asking our students to turn to a certain page in an anthology. Instead, we should share a few poems that are special to us or someone we know, that are illustrated in interesting ways, or that

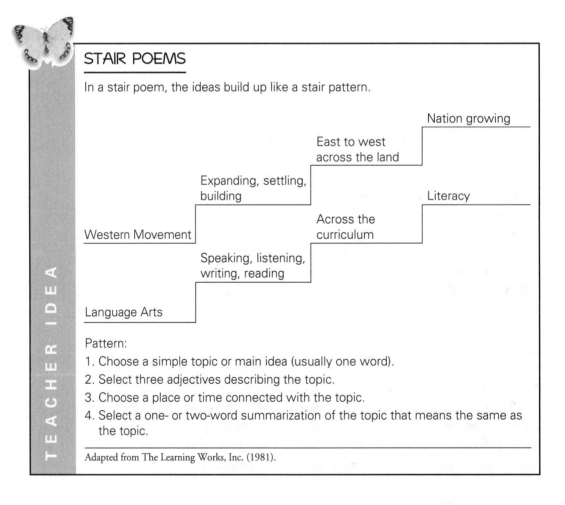

STAIR POEMS

In a stair poem, the ideas build up like a stair pattern.

Nation growing

East to west
across the land

Expanding, settling,
building

Literacy

Western Movement

Across the
curriculum

Speaking, listening,
writing, reading

Language Arts

Pattern:
1. Choose a simple topic or main idea (usually one word).
2. Select three adjectives describing the topic.
3. Choose a place or time connected with the topic.
4. Select a one- or two-word summarization of the topic that means the same as the topic.

Adapted from The Learning Works, Inc. (1981).

TEACHER IDEA

have a pleasant or interesting sound or form. Choose poems that students may have heard before and find familiar. Select poems that create a good feeling and that are short enough to allow two readings and a long look (if visual representation is available). Introduce the poem in a casual way, and do not ask "What does it mean?"

Sharing poems from an assigned text may intimidate students before they discover that poetry can be fun. If you find appropriate poems in the classroom anthology, copy them onto a separate piece of paper. You can always return to the text once you have helped students understand that poetry is not a demon. As well, when you revisit the poems in the text a second time, students will already have had some experience with them.

Next, encourage students to make their own selections. Selections can be integrated into your classroom routine over several days or several weeks as students search for and share their special finds. I like to encourage students to bring in poems throughout the year, even if I have concentrated on poetry as a genre for only a few days or weeks. This helps students see that poems, like essays and short stories, do not have start and end dates, but can be enjoyed over and over. Many young adult readers begin this process by selecting songs. Encourage students to bring in the actual format or the song itself. These can be used again in later sessions as you approach exploration.

Some students will bring in illustrated books of poetry with which they became familiar in earlier grades. This may be their comfort level, and we want them to be comfortable. From this beginning, we can move them to longer and more complex poems. Remember, we want students to feel comfortable, relaxed in sharing and responding to poetry, not challenged in trying to make sophisticated meanings unless the students themselves move to that point.

Today there are hundreds of poetry books that contain poems appropriate for young adult readers in Grade 7 and above. These books are contemporary with the times, include interesting poems about cities and rural living, represent cultural and racial diversity, and reintroduce traditional and contemporary poets. They are fun to read and interesting. Many are also easy to read, yet they hold deep meaning for discussion and a variety of forms for examples for writing. Unfortunately, their appearance is not always appealing to this older age group. Many are large books, illustrated in ways that are attractive but look juvenile. An introduction to these books by the teacher can alleviate the hesitation of students to bring these in for examples.

Bring an illustrated book such as Adoff's *Street Music: City Poems* (1995), which is housed for the juvenile curriculum but has beautiful pictures and interesting poems about the city. Carl Sandburg's poem "Arithmetic" can be read at any age and is often included in anthologies. The juvenile edition (Sandburg, 1993) is illustrated by Ted Rand and is fun to look at. It is also interesting to discuss when your students begin their process for analysis because of the way it is laid out across the pages. There are also many illustrated books of poets who generally write for older children and the content is appropriate for young adults (for example, Carl Sandburg, Maya Angelou, Robert Frost, Walt Whitman, Emily Dickinson).

Students and teacher should keep separate notebooks that they use only for poetry. They should attach copies of poems they want to remember, find interesting, or want to refer to later. This notebook also serves as their "personal poetry journal." It will include responses to prompts, as well as personal reflections and drafts of their original poems. It may have a separate section for homework and other assignments, which may be collected later.

Writing is integrated throughout the poetry lessons. In the beginning, the prompts are simple and not intrusive. Examples may include

- A poem I remember
- One of my favorite (or least favorite) poems
- When I think of poetry, I...
- If I drew a poem, it would look like...(illustrate)

Give students about 10 minutes to think about and begin writing on the prompt. I always write, too, usually while they are writing; sometimes I write before the class begins so I can walk around the room during the class and look at what the students are writing. Allow time to share responses, either with the full class or in small groups. Do not worry if their writings are incomplete; students can share portions of their response or all of it. We are building trust at this point, so I usually share my responses to model for students. We want to have fun. The more laughter there is, the better.

Reading Poems and Writing About Poetry

Reading poetry adds to the joy of teaching and exploring poetry. The expression on the readers' faces and the reaction of others to the reading add to the feelings that poetry evokes. Whenever possible, poetry should be read aloud. It is the magic of the words, the rhythm, the form, the images it creates that make it poetry. The more these experiences are shared, the more students begin to appreciate why it is poetry and what separates it from prose. But asking students "Why is this poetry?" can be as great a mistake as asking "What does it mean?" Instead, capitalize on this realization during later lessons.

When you and your students bring in selections, they should be read both silently and aloud. Reading poems silently allows students to get accustomed to the form and language, and to privately answer questions: Does it rhyme? Does it seem to continue from line to line without a break? Are there words I do not know or phrases that are odd? It is important, however, that students read poetry aloud and hear it to get a feel for the rhythm and to capture the best experience. Sometimes poems may be read to the full class. To save time, students can form groups of three or four and read to each other. From those readings, each group can then choose one "poem of the day" to be shared aloud or posted.

Three of the poems I listed earlier work well for reading aloud. Merriam's "Inside a Poem" is a simple poem about poetry and can set a positive mood. The internal rhyme in this poem may be missed when not read aloud, and the first line might suggest that there is no rhyme; however, look at the second line, "but there's the repeat of a beat, somewhere." Rhyme occurs in subsequent lines, as well. Adoff's "Street Music" and Soto's "Ode to Pablo's Tennis Shoes" are both fun to read and fun to hear. In addition, they are short enough for students to use in part of a class, to read several times, and to respond to in writing.

How a poem is read or heard influences how much the audience appreciates the poem or understands it, what images are created, and whether it soars as a poem or falls flat as words placed in lines. Invite students to read their choices aloud, just as you have done. Encourage them to practice reading their poems before they read them aloud to their class. You may need to give a few "general hints" about reading aloud, addressing voice tone, pitch, body language, and attention to punctuation or the lack of it.

As mentioned earlier, students often want to bring in songs they have selected. Introducing poetry with songs is a good strategy, and looking at song lyrics from time to time is also a good interlude for variety. Encourage your students to bring in the recorded version of the song, as well. This will help students understand that voice, pitch, and rhythm are important to poetry. They already understand that these elements are important in songs, and that knowledge will be transferred to the written words. It is an analogy that can be used throughout the year. Try to avoid the impulse to rely too heavily on this technique, however. Most of the poems that are used for instruction in schools are not songs, and students need to have opportunities to understand how to read lines and to get an understanding from them.

Before or after the reading, ask the students to explain briefly why they selected the song or poem. Explanations may be as simple as, "I read this in fifth grade, and I've liked it ever since." If their selection is an illustrated or a concrete poem, they can show the picture or the form. Their reading should be painless, because the students have chosen the ones they want to share. As teachers, we must be as nonjudgmental of their choices as possible. An easy way to turn off students is to concentrate on what is right and what is wrong. One of the joys of poetry is that the "right" and "wrong" are constructed between the writer and the reader. Louise Rosenblatt (1978) states that the transactional view "assumes close attention to the words of the text. But it assumes an equal closeness of attention to what that particular juxtaposition of words stirs up within each reader" (p. 137). The inner critic, evaluator, and interpreter may be invisible through most of these early experiences of instruction and learning.

The students' immersion in a variety of poems should lead to enjoyment and appreciation. Longer, more involved poems such as Frost's "Mending Wall" and Angelou's "Still I Rise" lend themselves to several readings and give students a feel of how to follow a longer poem. An introduction here will help for a more involved look later.

Prompt students to write a short list of words based on what they think about when they hear the poems. Prompts related to hearing or reading poems are often successful when they are related to feelings and imagery. Students might complete a sentence such as "When I heard…I felt…" or "The form used in…made me…because…."

Writing about poetry springs naturally from selecting and reading poems. In fact, hearing poems and writing *about* them is a good introduction to writing poetry. Often, after students listen to a poem, they are moved to write a poem themselves. Throughout this lesson, the class is not analyzing the poems nor attempting to write final drafts of poetry. The idea is for each student to begin to explore "what poetry means to me." The prompts should be simple:

- What do you think of when you think of poetry?
- Read or reread a favorite poem or listen to a favorite song and write why you would categorize it as "poetry" (as opposed to an essay).
- If you were writing a dictionary and could define poetry any way you wanted, what would be your definition?
- I like (or dislike) poetry or a specific poem because….

Students should spend about 15 minutes responding to prompts in their notebooks and then sharing with other students. Responses can refer to poems that are specifically about poetry, such as Merriam's "Inside a Poem" and other poems from books such as *Inner Chimes: Poems on Poetry* (Goldstein, 1992). Look for quotations from poets and other writers who address poetry, such as Gwendolyn Brooks, who says, "Do not be afraid to say something NEW. BE A LITTLE MYSTERIOUS! Surprise yourself and your reader" (Janeczko, 1990, p. 63). William Stafford states, "Talk with a little luck in it, that's what poetry is…" (Janeczko, 1990, p. 59). Encourage students to be creative in writing their definitions, descriptions, and notes. We do not want them to get bogged down with trying to make dictionary definitions. Poets and scholars disagree about what really makes it poetry, so do not expect your students to be uniform in their opinions.

Ask the students to look at several different poems by several different poets. For example, you might pair Swir's "I Have Ten Legs" with Frost's "Mending Wall" or Angelou's "Still I Rise" with Soto's "Ode to Pablo's Tennis Shoes." Then ask, What characteristics make each of these poetry: language, form, rhythm? How do they make you feel?

Because these poems are very different in form and in subject, the contrast should give students several characteristics to look at that will help them to formulate a working definition for themselves, broad enough that it will work for the two poems. It follows, therefore, that it may work for others, but perhaps not for all poetry. Students should share their definitions in groups and feel free to extend or qualify their own. They should revisit them as they write their own poems and read other types of poems so that they can revise, change to reflect their new knowledge, and/or validate what they have written. Encourage them to think also about the emotions that the poetry evokes and to include these thoughts into their definitions as well.

Other writings about poetry will come directly from the poems that are discussed in the class. Begin with something simple. Revisit poems brought in earlier during the selection and reading stages. Use appropriate poems from the anthology or the curricula if specific works or knowledge of terms are required. Students need the opportunity to move slowly and under planned instruction to be able to write well about poetry. In their poetry notebooks, students should write their first reactions and responses to the works used for the lesson. Encourage them to look for figurative language and to note where and how it is used. Then they can meet in small groups to brainstorm and discuss features about the style, form, and language used in the poem. Next, each student writes down his or her individual ideas about what the poem literally says. This step is completed before any attempt is made for students to interpret what the poem means. Some students, however, may naturally begin to give an interpretation of the poem.

Try to help your students follow the process by assuring them that they will have lots of time and opportunities to develop their interpretations and to formalize an analysis. This process will help them when the poems are unfamiliar or more complicated. For the poem "Mending Wall," for example, the first responses may look like the following:

Features of the poem (how the poem looks):

It doesn't rhyme.

The lines are long.

Some of the lines end sentences (or thoughts).

Some lines begin new ideas.

Language of the poem (include rhyme, figurative language, and interesting words):

The language is simple (I understood most of the words).

There's a conversation going on, although we don't hear much from the second person.

One person in the poem is the narrator.

Repetition of "Good fences make good neighbors."

Literal translation or summary in your (students') own words (What does it say?):

These two men get together each year and they mend the fence that divides their properties. One guy seems to want the fence and feels that it is necessary so they can be good neighbors. The other doesn't like fences and he wants to say things like elves don't like walls. [There are other things to be said here, and as the poem is revisited the student can elaborate.]

Relate to an experience you have had or an experience you can imagine:

Laura, a 10th grader, wrote, "Well, not really fences. But we have doors. My grandmother says we have to lock our doors now, but when she was growing up they just didn't lock the door at all. Our neighbors come over, but they always have to ring the bell for us to let them in—even when my friends come the door stays locked. I guess my grandmother would say that fences are not neighborly, but I know that doors keep us good neighbors and safe."

After students make these preliminary notes, they reread the poem and go back to identify words, phrases, punctuation, and form directly from the work that support their literal observations. Students should write questions about any language, words, or phrases that continue to puzzle them. If they think they have found or missed figurative language, they should note that. These questions and comments are discussed in their small groups. If the group cannot come to agreement, post the questions so that the teacher can respond to them. I usually have them write these on index cards and either visit the group about specific questions or extend explanations to the entire class if they seem to be problematic or interesting to several groups. Students revisit their responses and make any desired changes. This gives them a chance to find additional areas that they may have missed, and it also helps them get accustomed to validating their responses.

Writing a personal or related experience to the poem is an important step because it helps students understand that they have a relationship with the work. They need to know that what they bring to the meaning of the poem is as important as what others will offer. This is especially important as they get to the exploration stage, where we want them to interpret and analyze poetry and know how to validate their responses. Laura Robb, in her chapter "Thinking About Books on Paper," writes about students talking about books (see Chapter 2 in this volume). She notes that "a lively exchange of ideas will move students deeper and deeper into the meaning of a story" (see page 29). This holds just as true for developing ideas and meaning in poetry.

Writing Poems and Exploring Poetry

Writing poetry is a process in the same way that writing prose is a process. What makes a student's work poetry? Acceptance. If the student calls it poetry, we will accept it. Because many writers today do not use rhyme in their poetry, students learn very early that they do not need to rhyme their poetry. As a result, much of their initial poetry writing will be more prose than poetry. Remember, you will give lots of opportunities to read, talk about, listen to, and discuss all kinds of poetry. Your students will have opportunities to grow, learn, appreciate, and recognize when it is poetry and when it is prose, when it is good poetry and when it is bad poetry. They need opportunities to discuss with others openly. Students will begin to understand that it takes time for thinking, talking, writing drafts and making changes, editing, sharing, and reworking and recycling parts of this process again and again before making their poems public.

Prompts like the following usually spark students' creativity and get ideas flowing for their early drafts:

- Choose a word and develop a poem around it (e.g., *ain't, pretty,* or *play*).
- The color yellow makes me feel…but the color gray…
- Find an inanimate object in the room (such as a shoe, chair, picture) and compare it to something outside the room (such as an animal, a tree, a river).
- Study the form used by poet _____ and draft a poem that rhymes in the same way or choose a different rhyme scheme.

In addition to using prompts, we should also give our students an opportunity to write about their own topics. This allows them to pursue an idea that is important to them.

Bob, one of the students in a class with which I worked a few years ago, shared his notebook with me about halfway through the year. Some of the poems

A BAKER'S DOZEN WAYS TO RESPOND TO A POEM

TEACHER IDEA

1. Perform the poem in a dramatic presentation, with musical accompaniment, or direct yourself and friends in an arranged presentation.
2. Respond to the poem or a part of the poem in a journal entry.
3. Write a new poem modeling the form of the poem read.
4. Dramatize the poem.
5. Create a picture of an image or mood evoked by the poem. Write the poem or specific lines on the drawing.
6. Videotape images that illustrate the poem to an accompanying audio.
7. Make a picture book with lines or a stanza on each illustrated page.
8. Make a filmstrip of the poem.
9. Choreograph a dance that is performed to the oral reading of the poem.
10. Investigate the poet and share information with the class; include other poems written by the author.
11. Make a mobile with stanzas cut apart and hung together with illustrations.
12. "Can" or "box" a poem by decorating a container and inserting a copy of the poem and two items related to the poem.
13. Set the poem to music. Sing the poem or read it to musical accompaniment.

Joan B. Elliott is a professor at Indiana University of Pennsylvania, Indiana, Pennsylvania, USA.

were astonishing, insightful, and magical, displaying a wonderful use of language. Many of these had rhyme, internally and at the end of lines. Some of his poems did not rhyme and seemed to lack the music and the intricate use of words. I asked him which poems he liked best. Not to be taken in by this guest teacher, he responded by asking me which poems I preferred. I pointed out three poems that I really enjoyed reading, and I explained that they made me smile, even one of the serious ones, because they "moved." They had a rhythm that set moods that seemed to fit the subject, and words that set the tone. I explained how the length of the lines helped make this happen, but I added that the word choice completed the poems for me. He laughed. I had chosen two of his favorites in my three. He then told me that they had been easy for him to write and rewrite. I think that is the secret, the key to good poetry writing and to making poetry writing enjoyable. The topics, although they varied, meant something to him at the time he wrote them.

I had chosen only one poem that did not rhyme. He explained that it had come out of "doodling." I had asked the class to think of something interesting to them—a place, a person, an object, an animal, a relationship, a friend, a family member, a feeling. His poem began, "I'm really angry today." He continued with words that expressed the anger—*scared, lost, frustrated, furious*—but not the reason. It was probably the absence of the reason that made its impression on this reader. When I asked Bob about the poem, he explained,

> Usually, I prefer to write an essay rather than a poem that doesn't rhyme. I can't get into the poem when I don't rhyme. It becomes too long, and I need more time to express myself. But the poem on anger was real, and gave single words that described that feeling. I wasn't angry at the time, but I've been angry.

He liked this poem even though it did not rhyme because those words seemed to describe that anger for him. He had not thought about anger in those terms before.

I give this scenario for two reasons. First, Bob is not an exception to students or adults who try their hand at writing—whether poetry or short stories or plays. They need time and the room and the stimulus to get in touch with what they feel about their subject. Sometimes it comes quickly, but often it is a slow process. They need to write, write, write, even if it is "doodling," brain storming, or free and disconnected. Second, Bob's journey in writing a successful poem that does not rhyme shows how important it is to let students explore various forms of poetry and various ways to create them.

When we want students to write poetry, we must help them find their voice and their form. Many of their first drafts will begin as prose, loose forms, near rhymes, and attempts to imitate what they have seen or believe that poetry should be. Give them time to wrestle with words. Surround them with dictionaries, thesauruses, rhyming dictionaries, books, and poetry anthologies. Find interesting pictures that they can look through and make associations. That often motivates them to write.

Encourage students to share their writing with other classmates in small groups. Model for students how to give feedback that is constructive and to ask questions that will prompt the writers to look critically at their work. Their poetry notebooks should include room for revisions and drafts, as well as starts and stops. Students will be at different places in their work. Some will write profusely, but others will write less, taking longer to get into the mood.

Most students have written limericks or other rhymes. Encourage them to play with rhyme. Rhyming dictionaries help, but it is fun just to play with words. They may need to find synonyms for a word they want to use first in order to find a rhyming word that fits. Many students will need practice in using the writing process when they create their poems. Very often the poem is fine and only lacks syllables for rhythm or a few words for rhyme or a phrase that helps them complete the picture. But often it will need more work. Show them how to use appropriate stages of the writing process to meet their needs.

We want to encourage our students to try different forms until they find the one or ones they like—the ones that lend themselves to fit the voice of the writer. I have found that many students will write funny limericks very easily, yet they have a problem writing a-b-a-b rhymes. Sometimes our students who enjoy writing prose will immediately begin using free verse. They may find later, however, that this is not the form that suits their poetry voice best. There are students who will enjoy playing with words, and others who cannot economize and who use too many words, which interferes with the music or rhythm of the poem. Most students who are trying to write poetry for the first time in many years are skeptical about how their work will be received. For this reason, they may tend to write less, use a conservative form, and express themselves more timidly. Trust is important if you want them to write poetry.

Teachers can build trust by sharing their work with students. Some of our poetry writing is not easy, takes time, needs input. Share this with your students. Write with them. Join a group of students, if feasible, and be "a student" with them. Give ideas and receive ideas. My poem "If I Were a Poet" (see Mitchell, 1997) was worked through with students. Eve Merriam has a wonderful chapter called "Writing a Poem" in her book *A Sky Full of Poems* (1986), wherein she shows and discusses how she develops her poetry.

Final Thoughts

The poems cited in this chapter provide a good opportunity for your students to have examples of a range of poetry forms and topics. They can understand these poems immediately on a literal level. They can also understand and relate to these poems on a personal level and use that knowledge later as they move to writing their interpretations. These also lend very well to formulating the skills needed for higher level thinking, interpretation, analysis, and appreciation. Experiencing a range of poetic forms and subjects will help students to validate their own writings. Rosemary Chance, in her chapter "Poetry Pathways for Teens," has included an extensive list of poetry books that are a representation of poets across themes and across cultures (see Chapter 8). The list today is endless.

Exploring poetry can be the most interesting and enjoyable stage of studying and involving ourselves with poetry. It is also the most challenging. It is the stage that can affect whether or not students will want to study poetry in the future. It takes into consideration selecting, reading, and writing about poems, and creating our own poems. It adds dimensions for students to develop meaning to poetry in ways that will help them to cultivate an appreciation of the genre. This is important because students may not always like a poem or fully understand a poem, but they can still appreciate something about it—something about what the poet said, or how the poet used words, or how the poem looks. This is also the stage in which students will know to go back to the entire poem and use it to develop their understanding or to search for more validation of why it is not clear.

Adoff's poem "Street Music" and other poems from this book, as well as the illustrated poem "Arithmetic," can be helpful during the exploration lessons, because the illustrations help to bring an artistic interpretation. Discussing these illustrated books often helps students to picture the interpretation that they are trying to put into words. This may lead to sound arguments around their own interpretations in agreement or disagreement with the illustrator. I have read some very interesting analyses written by students when I use this technique. When it comes to teaching poetry, this is the point that we are expected to achieve in most of our curriculum objectives.

Too often in our curriculum, we expect students to analyze too soon. We have guides that seem to make the assumption that the writer of the guide also is the writer of the poem and has a specific interpretation in mind. That assumption is transferred to students, who generally seem to get it "wrong" based on these preconceived criteria.

I shared my poem "Whirlwinds," featured in *Best Poems of 1997* (Howard, 1997), with students from first "thinking" draft through final writing and then had them look at it at the exploration stage as a completed work. The interpretations were wonderful as they elaborated on their interpretations and analysis. I had in mind a poem churning in my mind when I wrote the words, "There's a whirlwind happening/picture images—life-like dreams" (p. 49), but these students found different ideas as they brought in their experiences. Some saw confusion or turmoil, whereas one saw fantasy. They could ask the writer what it meant, and when I responded that I was thinking about words to make a poem, they could accept and validate that; however, I made it clear that if I were not there to answer, they had made meaning for themselves that was valid.

Rosenblatt (1978) tells us that "the reader's attention to the text activates certain elements in his past experience—external reference, internal response. Meaning will emerge from a network of relationships among the things symbolized as he senses them" (p. 105). Indeed, as I read my poem a few months ago, it began to take on a different meaning for me based on what I was experiencing at the time.

Although the three stages of teaching and learning poetry in the classroom have been discussed in this chapter in a somewhat linear presentation, the process is circular, continuous, and sometimes spiral in its operation. Different stages are revisited from time to time as appropriate, especially as the works that we give students become more difficult and challenging for them.

At the exploration level, our students will develop notebooks full of ideas and examples. They will seek out poems that range as wide as their individual and collective tastes. Some poems will be special because they were recommended by someone, others because students heard them and liked the sound, still others because the poems helped students feel strong or happy or loved.

At the exploration level, students should revisit a poem such as "Still I Rise" and begin to go through their previous experiences reading and writing about the poem. They should begin to write about the poem in a personal way and to extend that to interpretation and analysis. From both an objective and a subjective standpoint, they can see many ways it can take on meaning. They can begin to interact with Angelou's words and extend them to their own lives or context and to the poet herself. They begin to understand the mix of the experiences of both poet-writer and poet-person, and add that they are reader-reader and reader-person. Personal exploration of poetry can make the reading and writing of and about poetry the most exciting or most boring and most difficult part of our lessons. Here, students make poetry their own, develop an appreciation for it, and understand that they have something valuable to say in their own poems and in the poems they study.

REFERENCES

Mitchell, A.H. (1997). If I were a poet, I'd say something beautiful. In N.J. Karolides (Ed.), *Reader response in elementary classrooms*. Mahwah, NJ: Erlbaum.

Rosenblatt, L.M. (1978). *The reader, the text, the poem: The transactional theory of the literary work*. Carbondale, IL: Southern Illinois University Press.

POETRY COLLECTIONS CITED

Adoff, A. (1995). *Street music: City poems*. Ill. K. Barbour. New York: HarperCollins.

Angelou, M. (1994). *The complete collected poems of Maya Angelou*. New York: Random House.

Goldstein, B.S. (Sel.). (1992). *Inner chimes: Poems on poetry*. Ill. J.B. Zalben. Honesdale, PA: Boyds Mills Press.

Howard, E. (Ed.). (1997). *Best poems of 1997*. Owings Mills, MD: National Library of Poetry.

Janeczko, P.B. (Sel.). (1990). *The place my words are looking for: What poets say about and through their work*. New York: Atheneum.

Lathem, E.C. (Ed.). (1979). *The poetry of Robert Frost*. New York: Henry Holt.

Merriam, E. (1986). *A sky full of poems*. Ill. Walter Gaffney-Kessell. New York: Dell.

Merriam, E. (1992). *It doesn't always have to rhyme*. New York: Atheneum.

Nye, N.S. (Sel.). (1992). *This same sky: A collection of poems from around the world*. New York: Aladdin/Simon & Schuster.

Sandburg, C. (1993). *Arithmetic*. Ill. T. Rand. San Diego: Harcourt.

Soto, G. (1992). *Neighborhood odes*. Ill. D. Diaz. San Diego: Harcourt.

YOUNG ADULT LITERATURE CITED

Angelou, M. (1970). *I know why the caged bird sings*. New York: Random House.

CHAPTER 10

Picture Books for Older Readers: Passports for Teaching and Learning Across the Curriculum

Carol J. Fuhler

I sit on the floor in my office surrounded by brand new picture books, stray bits of Styrofoam popcorn packing and a nearly empty cardboard carton at my knees. Even though I had ordered these titles and their impending arrival was no surprise, there is a sense of Christmas in the air, that anticipation of magic just ahead. Touching the covers of one stunning book and peeking quickly into another fuels my expectations of reading wonderful words and pictures in the upcoming hours. I reach for one book after another, delighting in the artwork, which is sometimes comical, at other times simply magnificent.

Finally, I am unable to leave *Vision of Beauty: The Story of Sarah Breedlove Walker* (Lasky, 2000). Voices of colleagues in the hallway dim as I slip into an engrossing biographical story world. The past flickers to life while I follow Sarah through the years, from the blistering cotton fields of her infancy and onward into adulthood. I marvel at Sarah's ingenuity as the author takes me through the doors of the Mme. C.J. Walker Manufacturing Company, Sarah's own company. A courageous African American woman, orphaned at a young age, Sarah never stopped dreaming. Fueled by a determination to build a better life for herself and for other African American women, she became one of the richest women of her time. I close the book, inspired by what dreams and an indomitable spirit can do, knowing that Sarah and I will meet again. Picture books—I cannot seem to live without them.

I am certainly not alone in this particular affliction; my college students, teachers-to-be, frequently stop by my office to borrow a book we have shared together. They gently probe, wondering aloud about what surprises I will bring to class next. It scarcely crosses their minds that picture books were once relegated to the domain of cozy bedtime stories or the much-anticipated storytime in primary grades. In our college classes, we learn together how to integrate these treasures of tale, art, and information into reading, certainly, but also into writing, social studies, art, and in an extended journey across the curriculum. It is critical to me, as a teacher, to model how picture books—in their myriad sizes, styles, and content—have appealed to me for years, and how I continually act on that love. My rationale is that I hope my students will gain such a comfort level with picture books that these books will eventually become an integral part of their future classrooms, prized by all students, regardless of age.

I have used a variety of picture books in the past to teach astonished eighth graders the rudiments of reading and writing. Today I find that I simply cannot teach my reading, language arts, or social studies methods courses without several illuminating titles at my fingertips. Periodically my colleagues and I meet in the hall to chat and to update each other on our latest finds. We enthusiastically join ranks with teachers in middle schools, high schools, and college classrooms across the country who understand that picture books have broken free of previous boundaries and now stretch across the curriculum, speaking to readers of all ages in the process.

And why not? Readers will quickly discover that some of today's best authors and illustrators devote a portion of their creative genius to enriching the world of picture books (Schwarcz & Schwarcz, 1991; Tunnell & Jacobs, 2000). Perhaps even more important is the fact that as an integral part of the world of literature, picture books enable readers to stretch their personal horizons as they contemplate the plights and pleasures bundled into 24 to 48 pages. Along with novels, these books present story worlds that are "intellectually provocative as well as humanizing, allowing us to use various angles of vision to examine thoughts, beliefs, and actions" (Langer, 1995, p. 5). There is much to be said for picture books as part of the upper-grade curriculum.

The Picture Book Defined

Opinions vary somewhat on the differences between a picture book, a picture storybook, and an illustrated book. Some experts in the field of children's literature say that any book containing pictures is a picture book. Others believe there is a distinct difference between a picture book and a picture storybook. The latter is a fictional story in which high-quality pictures and well-crafted words work interdependently to tell the story (Cullinan & Galda, 1998; Huck, Hepler,

Hickman, & Kiefer, 2001; Sims & Hickman, 1992). Based on this line of thinking, Graeme Base's alliterative *Animalia* (1987) would be classified as a picture book, because it does not relate a connected story, even though it cleverly highlights the letters of the alphabet. *Shibumi and the Kitemaker* by Mercer Mayer (1999), however, readily fits the criteria for a picture storybook. The reader watches Shibumi, the emperor's daughter, and an elderly kitemaker work together to ease the lives of the townspeople, who have been forced to endure

ALMOST FAMOUS DAISY! BY RICHARD KIDD

Daisy decides to enter a painting competition that requires her to paint her favorite things. In order to find her favorite things, she and her dog, Duggie, travel the world in a 1-week adventure, discovering famous artists and artwork along the way. At each stop, Daisy sends a postcard home detailing her adventure. Artists spotlighted in the book include Vincent Van Gogh, Claude Monet, Marc Chagall, Paul Gauguin, and Jackson Pollock.

Suggested Activities

• Prior to reading the story aloud, display a piece of artwork from each artist featured in the book. These can be found on museum sites on the Internet for easy printing. On colored cards, note the year of each painting, the artists' names, and the styles of the paintings. After reading the story, have the students recall each artist. Students can then try to discover which painting belongs to which artist. Introduce the style vocabulary and correctly label the painting. Finally, reveal the original years of the paintings to see which predictions were correct.

• Have students choose an artist not featured in the story. Ask them to create their own postcard with references to their artist. Topics they might want to investigate could include the location of the artist, themes from artwork, the time period, the artist's style, etc. They could gather information from library art books, Internet museum sites, or local museums. On the back of their postcard, students can draw their own "masterpiece" utilizing their artists' particular style. (Example: Using French pointillist Georges Seurat's style, have students design a picture using Q-tips or dots.)

Amy Jones is a teacher in the State College Area School District, State College, Pennsylvania, USA.

poverty in extreme contrast to life inside the palace walls. Stunning artwork and beautifully written text bring an imaginative province and its inhabitants to life, where they linger even after the book is completed.

Finally, if the illustrations merely function to decorate the story but do not extend the text in some important way, then the book is described as an illustrated book (Huck et al., 2001). In this type of book, the story can clearly stand alone, and the reader imaginatively supplies the majority of the pictures. The few illustrations that are available may help set the scene or highlight particular points in the story, but their primary role is to be aesthetically pleasing rather than to help tell the tale. A noteworthy example of an illustrated book is *The Deetkatoo: Native American Stories About Little People* (Bierhorst, 1998). The various tales are illustrated by Native American artist Ron Hilbert Coy, who perceptively extends the meaning of each tale with a single black-and-white illustration. Another exceptional illustrated book is the Coretta Scott King Honor winner *Her Stories: African American Folktales, Fairy Tales, and True Tales* (Hamilton, 1995), which has strong, provocative illustrations by Leo and Diane Dillon.

For our purposes in this chapter, the term "picture book" will reflect the definition of the picture storybook: the pictures and text work to present a unified whole, one enriching and blending smoothly with the other, resulting in a story that is somehow greater than the sum of its parts (Sims & Hickman, 1992). Consider, for example, *Faraway Home* (Kurtz, 2000). While Desta's father describes his life as a child in Ethiopia, the reader glimpses his memories through the lovely watercolor art by E.B. Lewis. The emotions of being caught between a new life in America and tender memories of his childhood home are poignantly described in text and pictures in a way that helps readers grasp what many immigrants have experienced. In addition, readers cannot help but empathize with Desta as she worries that her father might not come back to her. Although both words and pictures could probably stand on their own in this book, they are so much richer for their collaboration. As a result, so is the reader.

The length of picture books can vary from 24 to 48 pages. Unlike in an illustrated book, pictures take up appreciable space on every page, often with double-page spreads interspersed judiciously throughout the story. In some cases the text is relatively brief, although it tends to be longer in picture books targeted for older readers than for those more appropriate for primary grades. It is important to note, however, that the lines are blurred between books that are designated for one group or another. Depending on the reasons for their use, picture books that are written for younger readers can become perfect fare for upper grade readers as well.

Together, words and pictures recount a well-crafted story that ignites the reader's imagination, whether the student reads the book alone quietly or enjoys it as part of a classroom read-aloud. These books come in a variety of sizes and cover all the genres, including folk tales, fairy tales, fantasy, poetry, humorous or thought-provoking fiction or nonfiction, realistic or historical fiction, interesting nonfiction, eye-opening multicultural offerings, and intriguing biographies. Inventive and instructive, picture books are clearly compelling for the older reader.

The artwork that enhances each book covers a range of styles and a variety of media. The world of illustration has changed dramatically in the years since Comenius wrote *Orbis Pictus* ("The World in Pictures") in 1657. Advances in printing techniques and technology now allow publishers to reproduce complex original art beautifully. Picture book readers may find art that includes collage, watercolors, oils, photographs, cut paper, scratchboard, block prints, and more (Kiefer, 1995). What a pleasure it is to revel in contemporary illustrations. It can become a miniadventure in visual literacy for readers young and old.

An awe-inspiring example of a less common artistic technique appears in *The Paper Dragon* (Davol, 1997), illustrated by Robert Sabuda. Sabuda's work is done on delicate tissue paper, which he paints and then meticulously cuts to create the illustrations. It is truly lovely. The unusual gatefold pages open to stretch the illustrations across three pages in a book that begs the reader to spend special time with the artwork. The accompanying story in this Chinese tale relates the efforts of Mi Fei, a humble painter of scrolls, to subdue a fearsome, destructive dragon.

Quality picture books offer countless learning opportunities for older readers. When teachers select books carefully, students are treated to a combination of rich vocabulary, which broadens their language skills, and sparkling illustrations, which develop their taste in art (Schwarcz & Schwarcz, 1991). This, however, is just the beginning.

Strengthening Reader Response

Whatever the format, there are a number of reasons for middle school readers and young adults to be wrapped up in the world of the picture book. The first reason to have an accumulation of picture books on upper-grade classroom shelves is simply for pure enjoyment. During free time, students can select picture books for pleasurable reading, with no strings attached. This gives students a chance to savor the words, be tickled by the humor, contemplate the dilemmas presented, and study the artwork. Second, this is a time for facilitating "transactions" (Rosenblatt, 1983), special connections between a particular reader and a particular book. Such a connection is reader response in action as the student moves beyond mere "ink spots on a page" to create a live current between reader and text (Rosenblatt, 1983, p. 25). Such interactions happen with picture books just as they do with well-written novels. Third, because picture books are relatively easy to read and often packed with quick action, they attract the less able reader as well as those adept at deciphering print (Rief, 1992). In short, teachers can enhance a love of reading in students of all abilities by providing access to picture books. Without a doubt, these are books that are meant to be read, and then to be read again.

Kiefer (1995) notes, "The picture book is unique, and our experience of it will be something magical and personal, one that will change with each reading" (p. 6). To strengthen reader response, then, students can be encouraged to reread a book, spending some time reflecting on their reactions to revisiting a story. Sometimes, students' perceptions of a story change when they read a book, set it aside, and then read it again at a later date. The reason that reactions do not remain static lies within the interactions between readers and text. Langer (1995) refers to these interactions as "envisionments," which she describes as

> text-worlds in the mind, [which] differ from individual to individual. They are a function of one's personal and cultural experiences, one's relationship to the current experience, what one knows, how one feels, and what one is after. Envisionments are dynamic sets of related images, questions, disagreements, anticipations, arguments, and hunches that fill the mind during every reading, writing, speaking, or other experience when one gains, expresses, and shares thoughts and understandings. (p. 9)

Daily events, discussion, and changing perspectives are parts of the envisionment process and will affect a reader's interpretations of a book over time. Whether personal envisionments are developed as one interacts with picture books during free reading or are propelled along by animated discussions in large or small groups, they are a vital part of an individual's personal reading growth. Readers must connect with books if they are to build comprehension skills or ignite their imaginations. For a review of reader response and ways to encourage it, refer to Laura Robb's chapter, "Thinking About Books on Paper" (see Chapter 2), and Elizabeth Poe's host of ways to encourage response in "Reader Response, Process Writing, Young Adult Literature, and the Art of Book Reviewing" (see Chapter 1). The teacher facilitates personal envisionments by providing fabulous books, providing time to read and reread them, and allotting additional time to talk, talk, and talk about books and responses.

Enhancing Visual Literacy

Today's young adults have no shortage of visual stimuli in their daily lives. They are bombarded with videos, computer technology, and a formidable media blitz. However, the art savored in selected picture books may be the only quality art that some children see (Cullinan & Galda, 1998). Furthermore, students need help distinguishing varying degrees of quality. Picture books are an excellent way to help students learn to appreciate art and to hone their visual literacy skills (Galda, Ash, & Cullinan, 2000; Gambrell, 1996; Huck et al., 2001; Kiefer, 1995; Langer, 1995; Tunnell & Jacobs, 2000).

Begin by bringing in an inviting variety of books. Let the students study the pictures together, in small groups and individually, as you point out what makes the pictures special. Look for artwork that is unique, such as the illustrations in an old favorite, *Animalia* (Base, 1987), an alphabet book extraordinaire. Each full page is dedicated to a letter of the alphabet, and the illustrations accompany alliterative phrases such as "Diabolical dragons daintily devouring delicious delicacies." Every page lures readers to apply their visual literacy skills as they search for dozens of items within each picture that begin with the highlighted letter. Readers can even hunt for author-illustrator Graeme Base himself, represented by the little boy cleverly tucked away in the illustrations.

A natural extension of this particular book is to integrate reading, writing, and art to create a class version of *Animalia*. Ask students to select a letter and practice applying alliteration as they write a corresponding phrase or take on the extra challenge of devising a sensible sentence. Students should then illustrate their creative writing. Finished products can be shared with the class and bound into a book for future reading enjoyment. In the process of learning from Base, an expert writer and illustrator, students extend their creativity, develop their vocabulary, and possibly come to appreciate the value of the oft-ignored dictionary and thesaurus.

Another activity to help students focus on picture-book art is to compare illustrations filled with action and detail to those that are quiet and reflective. Read aloud Steven Kellogg's (1997) rollicking version of *The Three Little Pigs*. His cartoon art is so filled with vitality that one wonders how the characters stay on the page. Switch to *Grandad's Prayers of the Earth* (Wood, 1999) illustrated by P.J. Lynch. The soothing peace of an island in northern Minnesota emanates from every picture. Note the differences between these books together as a class or in small groups. Investigate Caldecott winners, like the unique *Snowflake Bentley* (Martin, 1998), which has unusual woodcuts meticulously crafted by Mary

Azarian. Offerings are so different—yet so effective—as illustrators and writers interweave their talents.

Examine other titles and discuss how the illustrations help establish the setting and delineate the characters. What is done to change the mood from title to title? To look at the numerous ways an illustrator works to extend the plot, share the illustrations of Caldecott winner Marc Simont in *The Stray Dog* (Sassa, 2001). In one brilliant spread of artwork, he moves readers through a whole week, using four related illustrations coupled with one sentence of text.

Not to be missed are nonfiction titles that can catch your eye. In Lois Ehlert's *Waiting for Wings* (2001), the author-illustrator portrays the life cycle of the butterfly through vivid collage illustrations, with smaller sized pages deftly tucked among larger pages. Fact filled and cleverly engineered, this book concludes with pertinent facts, also brightly highlighted.

Taking It One Step Further: Integrating Reading and Art

In an effort to help students understand what goes into illustrating a book and to bolster their experience in developing a discerning eye, invite the art teacher to collaborate on an integrated unit that includes art and reading. One approach might be to briefly introduce some of the masters in art and then look for similar styles used by a collection of today's superb illustrators of picture books. To begin, study the styles of expressionism, realism, surrealism, impressionism, and folk art. The art teacher shares knowledge about the work of selected masters; the reading teacher supplies stunning examples from picture books.

A number of picture books can serve as stepping-stones, and locating titles with strong illustrations is not a daunting task. One valuable resource is the award-winning *Talking With Artists* series, volumes 1 and 2 (Cummings, 1992, 1995). Another handy resource is *Adventuring With Books: A Booklist for Pre-K–Grade 6* (Pierce, Beck, & Koblitz, 1999), which contains hundreds of books for readers in kindergarten through sixth grade. For a focus on fine multicultural books, review *Kaleidoscope: A Multicultural Booklist for Grades K–8* (Yokota, 2001). Finally, teachers can work with the learning center director or local librarian to find additional examples of picture books that correspond with various artistic styles.

To help readers delve into impressionism, share *Linnea in Monet's Garden* (Bjork, 1985). Students can continue their exploration of this style by studying the pictures in *Virgie Goes to School With Us Boys* (Howard, 2000), illustrated by

E.B. Lewis. Switching gears, they might follow Cynthia Rubin (1989), who visited the National Gallery of Art to illustrate her colorful *ABC Americana From the National Gallery of Art*, a book highlighting the world of folk art. A lovely picture book follow-up is *This Land Is Your Land* (Guthrie, 1998), which includes charming, detail-filled folk art illustrations by Kathy Jakobsen.

Switching gears again, students can explore surrealism through the work of Anthony Browne, who stirs the imagination and adds a dash of humor in *Willy the Dreamer* (2000), in which he and his character Willy pay homage to a collection of famous painters in a most original manner. Similarly, in *The Math Curse* (1995), collaboration between the inventive author-illustrator team of Jon Scieszka and Lane Smith yields an amusing story with illustrations that push reality to the limits. In the same vein, readers might sample *Colors* (Nordine, 2000), in which Henrik Drescher, a New Zealand artist, presents a truly far-out extension of each poem. All of these illustrators clearly demonstrate how much fun one can have with art, and a leisurely inspection of these offerings is certainly warranted.

A memorable sampling of realism can be found in a variety of books. One especially appealing title is the previously mentioned *Grandad's Prayers of the Earth* (Wood, 1999), illustrated by P.J. Lynch. Light and detail are meticulously blended into soft scenes that reflect the tone of the story in a wonderful way. From there, note the rich, glowing tones and subtle shadings that bring the characters and setting realistically to life in a story within a story in *The Worry Stone* (Dengler, 1996), illustrated by Sibyl Graber Gerig. This is a special intergenerational story that should not be missed. Similarly, noted author-illustrator Lynne Cherry's fine watercolor work brims over with realistic detail throughout *Flute's Journey: The Life of a Wood Thrush* (1997). Intrigued readers follow Flute's migration from his threatened habitat in the Belt Woods in Maryland to Costa Rica and back again. Migrating songbirds grace the endpapers, which are lessons in themselves. Cherry's work, both text and pictures, is meticulously researched. No doubt this activity will be a journey of discovery for teachers, too, as they match styles and current illustrations for this particular activity, which enables art and understanding to work across the curriculum.

Depending on the amount of time available, teachers might continue the work by pointing out how the basic elements of art are used in picture-book illustration. Together, the class can look at line, shape, color, and texture. Because hands-on learning is particularly successful, ask students to experiment with several of the styles previously studied. With direction from the art teacher, invite budding artists to try various media or materials, including graphite/pencil, crayons, charcoal, pen and ink, acrylics, or watercolors. Then have them try interesting techniques or methods for creating unusual pictures, such as block prints, collage, photography, or folded or cut paper. When students are up to their elbows in the world of illustration, their visual learning is more effective. Once students have discovered a style and medium that is particularly their own, suggest that they use it to create their own picture storybook (Rief, 1992).

The Reading-Writing Connection: Creating a Picture Book of One's Own

Matching young adults with picture books is also a fine way to build general literacy skills. Students can review selected titles to learn how various literary elements (setting, characterization, plot, etc.) work, to study different writing techniques, and to notice how authors scrupulously work with words. Then students can create books of their own. Their audience will be based on personal choice—a book with a young adult focus or perhaps one designed for younger children.

Research has substantiated the fact that the average high school senior has a personal repertoire of 40,000 words at his or her fingertips (Beck & McKeown, 1991). To reach that average, students learn between 2,700 and 3,000 new words per year. Scanning that number of words and then finding the right combination for a picture storybook is a wonderful personal challenge for students in upper grade reading and language arts classes.

To begin this project, use a collection of quality picture books to review the literary elements and study the way words work to cleverly relate a story. Then support students as they write and eventually illustrate their own books. Explain that the basic literary elements are the same whether penning a novel or a picture book, but there are specific differences to note. Cullinan and Galda (1998) give the following useful guidelines when thinking about writing a fictional picture book:

- The setting (time and place) in which the story occurs should be quickly presented in the text and then extended through the illustrations. If writers choose to research and retell a different version of a popular folk tale, the setting should reflect the ethnic and cultural traditions associated with the particular origin of the tale.

- Characterization will vary depending on the genre. In folk tales and fairy tales, the characters are one-dimensional, flat, stereotypical individuals, with the good being really good and the bad being obviously bad. In a realistic fiction or fantasy story, the characters should have well-developed personalities and show some change or growth across the storyline. In addition, the reader ought to be able to relate to the feelings of the main character. Picture book characters actively solve some type of problem rather than passively experiencing the story world.

- The sequence of events, or plot, in the story is usually straightforward, presented in a chronological order. There is a problem to be solved or a conflict to be resolved, action peaks, and the story has a satisfying resolution. In these brief stories, foreshadowing may be used, but it is often done via the illustrations.

- When considering the story's theme, or its major idea or message, the writer should work to have the theme evolve naturally from the plot and the characters' actions. It should not be didactic or blatantly expressed.

- The style of writing is critical in a picture book. With relatively few words to work with, the choices must be rich and interesting. Internal rhythm is important, as is the melody of the words. The best test is to read the final draft aloud.

- Nonfiction text must be readable, with a smooth flow of information. Careful research must be done to present a current, accurate book.

To glimpse an author-illustrator in action, students will enjoy the informative and engaging *From Pictures to Words: A Book About Making a Book* by Janet Stevens (1995) or Aliki's interesting *How a Book Is Made* (1986). Introduce

TEACHER IDEA

A NEW LOOK TO AN OLD BOOK

Select several different books to share with the class for the purpose of discussing the cover design. Lead a discussion on how an author and illustrator decide what should be included on the cover of a book. Assign each student a book to read and then ask students to design a new cover for their book. This is a chance to reintroduce picture books to older students. Each new book jacket can be laminated and placed on the appropriate book. Students can then share new covers along with a brief summary of the book to support what they included on the cover.

Suzanne Mateer is a sixth-grade teacher in the Homer-Center School District, Homer City, Pennsylvania, USA.

several childhood stories from 10 well-known authors in *When I Was Your Age: Original Stories About Growing Up* (Ehrlich, 1996). These brief stories offer students a model to pursue, and reinforce the fact that these accomplished writers are normal people with a typical range of childhoods: If those writers can be successful, so can fledgling writers. For students who need just a little more moral support from the experts, suggest *Once Upon a Time* by Eve Bunting (1995) or Rafe Martin's (1992) *A Storyteller's Story.* Then, let the work begin.

Teachers will find Barbara Kiefer's *The Potential of Picture Books: From Visual Literacy to Aesthetic Understanding* (1995) an excellent support in this project. Topics include background information on picture books, creative ideas on how to complete a picture book, examples of how to lay out the book on a storyboard, instructions for making a "dummy" copy of the book, and directions for binding the final product. For the more enthusiastic bookmaker, instructions for making paper are included.

Although it is an ambitious project, developing a picture book of one's own brings students into the author-illustrator world as it integrates reading, writing, research, art, and creativity with a priceless final product. It becomes even more rewarding for author and listener alike if the completed books are shared with younger students.

Picture Books Across the Curriculum: Focus on Social Studies

Moving beyond visual literacy and writing, picture books for learners in the upper grades also facilitate students' comprehension. Used at the beginning of a reading lesson or in a content area such as social studies, these books can start a stimulating discussion that will activate background knowledge essential to the process of acquiring new knowledge.

Research emerging from work done by cognitive psychologists in the 1970s and 1980s has given educators a greater understanding of how comprehension works (Anderson & Pearson, 1984). One important theory growing out of that research is schema theory, which suggests that readers have a specific way of storing, retrieving, and expanding information—a personal filing system, so to speak. A schema could be likened to a file folder of knowledge about a particular topic. Each folder contains related concepts, events related to those concepts, emotions, and any roles attached to the topic, all uniquely colored by the individual's life experiences (Rumelhart, 1981). When presented with new knowledge about a topic, the learner quickly searches through those existing files for one containing any prior knowledge that might help in assimilating the new information. Then the new information is integrated with the old. Through this process, the learner's understanding is gradually broadened and deepened for innumerable topics as the individual matures.

This theory indicates that if comprehension is to be facilitated in the best possible manner, teachers must access students' prior knowledge before introducing a new topic or area of study. Barbara Illig-Avilés's chapter in this volume, "Great Moments in History: Engaging Young Adults Through Historical Fiction," presents a number of excellent books to help readers better relate to the Civil War (see Chapter 4). One way to introduce students to this turbulent period in U.S. history is through a picture book. Consider reading aloud *The Blue and the Gray* (Bunting, 1996a) or *Pink and Say* (Polacco, 1994). Then invite students to discuss the issues in either book, considering how those issues become integral to the war. This process taps prior knowledge and prepares fertile ground for further knowledge acquisition. Can you see how powerful cross-curricular connections can begin with a superb picture book? In this case, they offer an opportunity for discussion and an excellent transition into further historical fiction and nonfiction reading about the Civil War.

Let's look at an example social studies unit on immigration into the United States during the 19th and 20th centuries. Before beginning this unit, the teacher assesses individual knowledge by having each student fill in a K-W-L chart (Ogle, 1986). Learners fill in the What I *Know* column and some of the What I *Want* to Know column, leaving the What I *Learned*/Still Need to *Learn* column empty until the unit of study is completed. The class discusses individual charts, and the teacher records responses on a master K-W-L chart. The teacher addresses any emerging misconceptions at this point, or highlights them for special attention as the unit proceeds. One way to begin filling in any blanks in students' background knowledge is to introduce a selection of picture books. Once students have demonstrated an accurate foundation of background knowledge, study can proceed, with new concepts being attached to the old.

For this social studies unit, students need to discover what it was like to be an immigrant in the United States long ago and what it is like to immigrate to the United States today. This project complements ideas presented in Barbara Samuels's chapter in this volume, "Somewhere Over the Rainbow: Celebrating Diverse Voices in Young Adult Literature" (see Chapter 3). Beginning with picture books, students examine the wonderful mix of backgrounds and cultures that make up the United States, discovering more about who some of these people are and why they chose to come to America.

Read aloud Kurtz's *Faraway Home* (2000) and discuss it together as a whole class so that understandings are common among peers. Compare and contrast it with Woodruff's *The Memory Coat* (1999), the story of Russian Jews coming to the United States to escape persecution. Invite responses by posing questions like the following:

- How might you feel if you were one of the main characters? A parent?
- Have you ever moved before? What are your memories of that experience?
- Did you have worries that were similar to the characters in either of these books?

Other questions will evolve from the discussion, but it is sensible to have queries ready to keep a discussion moving. They might include the following:

- Why do people leave their homelands in the first place?
- Where did they come from?
- What were the promises that the United States seemed to hold?
- What was travel like for most people?
- What were the realities once immigrants arrived on U.S. shores?
- What has the impact of people from so many different countries been on the way the United States is today?

Discussion can continue in small groups fueled by individual titles chosen by group members. The Caldecott Honor Book *Peppe the Lamplighter* (Bartone, 1993) offers a slightly different perspective on the life of immigrants. A companion book is Bartone's *American Too* (1996), which illuminates Elsa's struggles to integrate her Italian ancestry with being a modern American girl. Allen Say (1993) relates how his grandfather's heart was divided between his home in Japan and his new life in California in *Grandfather's Journey*, and he shares some of his mother's experiences as a young woman in *Tea With Milk* (1999). In *Who Belongs Here? An American Story* (Knight, 1993), young Nary has come from a refugee camp in Thailand and is not finding the United States quite to his liking. A second storyline along the bottom of each page relates a brief history of U.S. immigration, beginning in 1892. This information will help students consider how immigrants may have influenced life as it is in the United States today.

Do not miss Aliki's *Marianthe's Story: Painted Words, Spoken Memories* (1998), in which two books are cleverly combined. Readers are treated to two stories in one as they get a sense of what it is like to be uprooted from one's home in another country and how much courage it takes to begin anew. These particular picture books and others like them can easily become catalysts to innumerable conversations that raise interest levels and urge students to dig further into a topic, talk more about it, and learn more in the process (Galda et al., 2000; Gambrell, 1996; Langer, 1995). This potent learning cycle begins with a deceptively simple picture book.

In another social studies unit, students could study the geography of the southwestern United States, focusing on Arizona, New Mexico, Oklahoma, and Texas. In this case, to assess students' prior knowledge, ask them to do a quick-write. Give them 3 to 5 minutes to jot down anything they can think of that is related to this part of the United States. Then invite them to share what they know. Record their information on a class chart to be posted for future reference. They will validate or correct this initial information in the ongoing course of study.

To continue, introduce each state in the region with a picture book. This helps students consider geographic topics to pursue through additional study (Fuhler, 1998). For example, *The Armadillo From Amarillo* (Cherry, 1994) encourages students to consider the placement of cities within Texas. The lesson can continue using a variety of fiction and nonfiction resources, but the picture book has hooked learners.

Similarly, a focus on what it is like to live in the southwestern United States can be introduced through *Cactus Poems* (Asch, 1998) or *Welcome to the Sea of Sand* (Yolen, 1996). Students can turn to the textbook and other informational resources to answer questions that result from initial investigations of what makes this region unique. Dynamic picture books can provide a jumping-off place for building geographic concepts and for learning about the five key geographic themes—location, place, human/environmental interactions, movement, and region (Joint Committee on Geographic Education, 1984)—as the quest for geographic knowledge becomes personal and memorable (Fuhler, 1998).

In her chapter on biography and autobiography, Teri Lesesne lauds the role of YA books to "provide students the chance to meet a wide range of people—people whose accomplishments might not warrant a footnote in a history, math, or science textbook, but people who reflect the rich diverse heritage of the United States" (see Chapter 7, p. 121). Picture books can entice students into further reading about the life of an individual whom they have met briefly within the pages of a picture book. For example, in *More Than Anything Else* (Bradby, 1995), readers meet Booker T. Washington as a young boy. As he labors beside his father in the salt works, he longs to be able to read. Who was this young boy, and what did he contribute as a result of learning to read? Another student might pick up *Hank Aaron: Brave in Every Way* (Golenbock, 2001) for an introduction to the man who broke Babe Ruth's legendary home run record. What did it take to achieve such a feat?

Determined and resourceful women are introduced through words and pictures as well. In *America's Champion Swimmer: Gertrude Ederle* (Adler, 2000), Ederle will inspire readers with her determination to swim the English Channel and to do so faster than any man. In *Wilma Unlimited: How Wilma Rudolph Became the World's Fastest Woman* (Krull, 2000), readers will discover that Rudolph saw polio not as an obstacle but as a challenge to overcome. She was so determined to run that she persevered until she won three gold medals in a single Olympics, the first woman to earn this acclaim. Similarly, overcoming the disdain of her people, Native American Maria Tallchief pursued her dreams to become an extraordinary ballerina (Tallchief, with Wells, 1999).

These are but a few exemplary picture book biographies and autobiographies that celebrate people from a variety of cultures. They have the potential to intrigue and encourage readers to reach for other resources about a person past or present with a real-life story to tell.

There are carefully researched, enticing picture books to introduce one topic after another in the social studies curriculum and to stretch the horizon of possibilities for each involved learner (Langer, 1995; Rief, 1992). Each year, look for the April/May issue of *Social Education* for an exceptional bibliography titled "Notable Children's Trade Books in the Field of Social Studies." This is a yearly list of outstanding books organized by categories conveniently keyed to the 10 thematic strands of the National Council of Social Studies Curriculum Standards. Fine selections of biographies, autobiographies, and historical fiction are cited and reviewed along with a variety of other genres.

In addition, when searching for books on a particular topic, another practical resource is *Book Links*, a journal by the American Library Association. Articles and related books are organized according to timely themes. Interesting interviews with authors and illustrators are also included. Obviously, picture books spur on learning in science and math as they do in social studies, and these curricular areas receive attention in *Book Links* as well. For additional reader-tested titles, watch for selected issues of *The Reading Teacher* that feature Children's Choices and Teachers' Choices lists. The Children's Choices list reflects favorites from newly published children's and young adults trade books, voted on by 10,000 children in five different regions of the United States. Librarians and teachers across the United States field test hundreds of newly published books each year to select the Teachers'

Choices. Travel the Web and investigate the sites listed at the end of this chapter. All of these resources will support the fact that there is little doubt about how picture books are on the move across the curriculum.

Connecting Picture Books and Young Adult Literature

A final suggestion involves an intriguing partnership that pairs a quality picture book with a novel from one of the Young Adults' Choices lists, a collection of books read and voted on yearly by readers in upper middle school classrooms through high school. This annual list appears in the *Journal of Adolescent & Adult Literacy*. With this process, if students enjoy the subject of the picture book, they can move on to an award-winning novel.

To begin, a teacher could capitalize on the perennial fascination with the sinking of the *Titanic* by introducing students to *Polar: The Titanic Bear* (Spedden, 1994). Readers of all ages will be intrigued by this story, which is based on a wealthy East Coast family's history and relates an eyewitness account of the sinking of the *Titanic*. Actual photographs of the family at home and on vacations are effectively interspersed with McGaw's lovely illustrations. The YA companion to this picture book could be *SOS Titanic* (Bunting, 1996b), an easy-to-read novel from the 1998 Young Adults' Choices list, or *On Board the Titanic: What Is Was Like When the Great Liner Sank* (Tanaka, 1996), a drama-packed book also from the 1998 list. Among the three titles, readers will surely have a sense of what people experienced as the *Titanic* slipped beneath the sea.

Lovers of fantasy know that Brian Jacques's Redwall series is a treasure. Readers who know the characters well eagerly await each new novel. They will delight in the picture book by Jacques titled *The Great Redwall Feast* (1996a). Within its pages, readers find many familiar figures, who "bustled and hustled...hurried and scurried, flittered and skittered and skipped" in the preparation of a fabulous surprise feast for the abbey's beloved Father Abbot. The artwork is simply charming, and the book is an irresistible invitation to read the 1998 Young Adults' Choice *The Outcast of Redwall* (Jacques, 1996b), the eighth volume in this popular series. What a pleasing way to lure new readers into the realm of Redwall Abbey.

On a much more somber note, Tom Feelings's 1997 Young Adult Choice, *The Middle Passage: White Ships Black Cargo* (1995), is an almost painful wordless picture book to read. Feelings chronicles the voyage of slave ships, including the indignities and agonies suffered by the passengers on those ships, many of whom did not survive. This book will certainly open discussions on the topic of slavery. Readers can move from this picture book to a 1998 Young Adults' Choice, *True North: A Novel of the Underground Railroad* (Lasky, 1996). They will quickly be caught up in the story told by two main characters, Lucy, an abolitionist's granddaughter, and Africka, an escaped slave traveling alone on the Underground Railroad. This pairing would make an excellent addition to the social studies curriculum as well as the reading curriculum.

When studying the Caldecott Honor winner *Harlem* (Myers, 1997), readers glimpse the hopes and dreams of the African American culture in more contemporary terms. Another contemporary option is *The Paperboy* (Pilkey, 1996), a 1997 Caldecott Honor picture book. To move from these picture books to a young adult novel that gives some insight into family life in the 1960s, readers can select the sometimes amusing, sometimes bleak 1997 Young Adults' Choices selection and Newbery Honor novel *The Watsons Go to Birmingham— 1963* (Curtis, 1995). Another excellent selection by the same author is the Newbery winner *Bud, Not Buddy* (1999). By mixing and matching these titles and participating in lively discussions based on their reactions, readers may gain some understanding of life in a different but parallel culture. They will have the opportunity to ponder the progress and setbacks of the African American population in the United States over the years. As Langer (1995) notes,

> Through literary experience, teachers can help students become aware of and use their various cultural selves to make connections, explore relationships, examine conflicts, and search for understandings through the literature they read and the interactions they have. (p. 38)

These pairings can go on and on, including each year's current YA favorites. Fired by the imagination of the teacher and the goals for learning across the curriculum, some memorable partnerships will be formed. Teachers can also invite students to match books they have enjoyed and then share them with their classmates. It is possible that such picture-book companions will provide a year of quality reading.

Conclusion

Picture books have a varied but vital role in the reading and learning lives of young adults. It is exciting to watch imaginative teachers integrate these books into their reading and content area curriculum with a wise eye and a knowing heart. Tricia Crockett, an eighth-grade student in one of noted educator Linda

Rief's middle school classes, explains the value of picture books from a young adult's perspective:

> We've been given our eyes to see and react to life, and words to pass what we've seen on to others. Picture books are able to combine both of these. When we're little, we like books for the pictures of animals and the stories. But when we get older, we can find more meaning in the words. The pictures don't just visualize what the words are saying, instead they go beyond the words giving clues to the depths of meaning in words. These picture books can never be outgrown. (Crockett & Wiedhaas, 1992, p. 67)

In the hands of an enterprising teacher, picture books do become a powerful addition to the classroom fare. They are truly passports for teaching and learning across the curriculum.

REFERENCES

Anderson, R.C., & Pearson, P.D. (1984). A schema theoretic view of the basic processes in reading comprehension. In P.D. Pearson (Ed.), *Handbook of reading research* (pp. 255–291). New York: Longman.

Beck, I.L., & McKeown, M. (1991). Conditions of vocabulary acquisition. In R. Barr, M.L. Kamil, P. Mosenthal, & P.D. Pearson (Eds.), *Handbook of reading research* (Vol. II, pp. 789–814). White Plains, NY: Longman.

Crockett, T., & Weidhaas, S. (1992). Scribbling down the pictures. In S. Benedict & L. Carlisle (Eds.), *Beyond words: Picture books for older readers and writers* (pp. 59–67). Portsmouth, NH: Heinemann.

Cullinan, B.E., & Galda, L. (1998). *Literature and the child* (4th ed.). New York: Harcourt Brace.

Cummings, P. (1992). *Talking with artists: Conversations with Victoria Chess, Pat Cummings, Leo and Diane Dillon, Richard Egielski, Lois Ehlert, Lisa Campbell Ernst, Tom Feelings, Steven Kellogg, Jerry Pinkney, Amy Schwartz, Lane Smith, Chris Van Allsburg, and David Wiesner*. New York: Simon & Schuster.

Cummings, P. (1995). *Talking with artists, volume two: Conversations with Thomas B. Allen, Mary Jane Begin, Floyd Cooper, Julie Downing, Denise Fleming, Sheila Hamanaka, Kevin Henkes, William Joyce, Maira Kalman, Deborah Nourse Lattimore, Brian Pinkney, Vera B. Williams, and David Wisniewski*. New York: Simon & Schuster.

Fuhler, C.J. (1998). *Discovering geography of North America with books kids love*. Ill. A. Loyal. Colorado Springs, CO: Fulcrum.

Galda, L., Ash, G.E., & Cullinan, B.E. (2000). Children's literature. In M.L. Kamil, P.B. Mosenthal, P.D. Pearson, & R. Barr (Eds.), *Handbook of reading research* (Vol. III, pp. 361–379). Mahwah, NJ: Erlbaum.

Gambrell, L.B. (1996). What research reveals about discussion. In L.B. Gambrell & J.F Almasi (Eds.), *Lively discussions! Fostering engaged reading* (pp. 25–38). Newark, DE: International Reading Association.

Huck, C.S., Hepler, S., Hickman, J., & Kiefer, B. (2001). *Children's literature in the elementary school* (7th ed.). New York: McGraw-Hill.

Joint Committee on Geographic Education. (1984). *Guidelines for geographic education: Elementary and secondary schools.* Washington, DC: Association of American Geographers and the National Council for Geographic Education.

Kiefer, B.Z. (1995). *The potential of picture books: From visual literacy to aesthetic understanding.* Englewood Cliffs, NJ: Merrill.

Langer, J.A. (1995). *Envisioning literature: Literary understanding and literature instruction.* New York: Teachers College Press.

Ogle, D. (1986). K-W-L: A teaching model that develops active reading of expository text. *The Reading Teacher, 39,* 564–570.

Pierce, K.M., Beck, C., & Koblitz, D. (1999). *Adventuring with books: A booklist for pre-K–grade 6* (12th ed.). Urbana, IL: National Council of Teachers of English.

Rief, L. (1992). Good children's literature is for everyone, even especially adolescents. In S. Benedict & L. Carlisle (Eds.), *Beyond words: Picture books for older readers and writers* (pp. 69–87). Portsmouth, NH: Heinemann.

Rosenblatt, L.M. (1983). *Literature as exploration.* New York: Modern Language Association of America. (Original work published 1938)

Rumelhart, D.E. (1981). Schemata: The building blocks of cognition. In J.T. Guthrie (Ed.), *Comprehension and teaching: Research reviews* (pp. 3–26). Newark, DE: International Reading Association.

Schwarcz, J.H., & Schwarcz, C. (1991). *The picture book comes of age: Looking at childhood through the art of illustration.* Chicago: American Library Association.

Sims, R.S., & Hickman, J. (1992). Four or fourteen or forty: Picture books are for everyone. In S. Benedict & L. Carlisle (Eds.), *Beyond words: Picture books for older readers and writers* (pp. 1–10). Portsmouth, NH: Heinemann.

Tunnell, M.O., & Jacobs, L. (2000). *Children's literature, briefly* (2nd ed.). Englewood Cliffs, NJ: Prentice Hall.

Yokota, J. (Ed.). (2001). *Kaleidoscope: A multicultural booklist for grades K–8* (3rd ed.). Urbana, IL: National Council of Teachers of English.

YOUNG ADULT LITERATURE CITED

Adler, D. (2000). *America's champion swimmer: Gertrude Ederle.* Ill. T. Widener. San Diego: Harcourt Brace.

Aliki. (1986). *How a book is made.* San Diego: Harcourt Brace.

Aliki. (1998). *Marianthe's story: Painted words, spoken memories.* New York: Greenwillow.

Asch, F. (1998). *Cactus poems.* Photog. T. Levin. San Diego: Harcourt Brace.

Bartone, E. (1993). *Peppe the lamplighter.* Ill. T. Lewin. New York: Scholastic.

Bartone, E. (1996). *American too.* Ill. T. Lewin. New York: Lothrop, Lee & Shepard.

Base, G. (1987). *Animalia.* New York: Harry N. Abrams.

Bierhorst, J. (Ed.). (1998). *The Deetkatoo: Native American stories about little people.* Ill. R.H. Coy. New York: William Morrow.

Bjork, C. (1985). *Linnea in Monet's garden.* Ill. L. Anderson. New York: R&S Books.

Bradby, M. (1995). *More than anything else.* Ill. C. Soentpiet. New York: Orchard.

Browne, A. (2000). *Willy the dreamer.* Cambridge, MA: Candlewick.

Bunting, E. (1995) *Once upon a time.* Katonah, NY: Richard C. Owen.

Bunting, E. (1996a). *The blue and the gray.* Ill. N. Bittinger. New York: Scholastic.

Bunting, E. (1996b). *SOS Titanic.* San Diego: Harcourt Brace.

Cherry, L. (1994). *The armadillo from Amarillo.* San Diego: Harcourt Brace.

Cherry, L. (1997). *Flute's journey: The life of a wood thrush.* New York: Gulliver Green.

Curtis, C.P. (1995). *The Watsons go to Birmingham—1963.* New York: Bantam Doubleday Dell.

Curtis, C.P. (1999). *Bud, not Buddy.* New York: Delacorte.

Davol, M. (1997). *The paper dragon.* Ill. R. Sabuda. New York: Atheneum.

Dengler, M. (1996). *The worry stone.* Ill. S.G. Gerig. Flagstaff, AZ: Northland Publishing.

Ehlert, L. (2001). *Waiting for wings.* San Diego: Harcourt Brace.

Ehrlich, A. (Ed.). (1996). *When I was your age: Original stories about growing up.* Cambridge, MA: Candlewick.

Feelings, T. (1995). *The middle passage: White ships black cargo.* New York: Dial.

Golenbock, P. (2001). *Hank Aaron: Brave in every way.* Ill. P. Lee. San Diego: Harcourt Brace.

Guthrie, W. (1998). *This land is your land.* Ill. K. Jakobsen. Boston: Little, Brown.

Hamilton, V. (1995). *Her stories: African American folktales, fairy tales, and true tales.* Ill. L. Dillon & D. Dillon. New York: Scholastic.

Howard, E.F. (2000). *Virgie goes to school with us boys.* Ill. E.B. Lewis. New York: Simon & Schuster.

Jacques, B. (1996a). *The great Redwall feast.* Ill. C. Denise. New York: Philomel.

Jacques, B. (1996b). *The outcast of Redwall.* New York: Philomel.

Kellogg, S. (1997). *The three little pigs.* New York: Morrow Junior Books.

Knight, M.B. (1993). *Who belongs here? An American story.* Ill. A.S. O'Brien. Gardiner, ME: Tilbury House.

Krull, K. (2000). *Wilma unlimited: How Wilma Rudolph became the world's fastest woman.* Ill. D. Diaz. San Diego: Harcourt Brace.

Kurtz, J. (2000). *Faraway home.* Ill. E.B. Lewis. San Diego: Harcourt Brace.

Lasky, K. (1996). *True north: A novel of the Underground Railroad.* New York: Scholastic.

Lasky, K. (2000). *Vision of beauty: The story of Sarah Breedlove Walker.* Ill. N. Bennett. Cambridge, MA: Candlewick Press.

Martin, J.B. (1998). *Snowflake Bentley.* Ill. M. Azarian. Boston: Houghton Mifflin.

Martin, R. (1992). *A storyteller's story.* Katonah, NY: Richard C. Owen.

Mayer, M. (1999). *Shibumi and the kitemaker.* New York: Marshall Cavendish.

Myers, W.D. (1997). *Harlem.* Ill. C. Myers. New York: Scholastic.

Nordine, K. (2000). *Colors*. Ill. H. Drescher. San Diego: Harcourt Brace.

Pilkey, D. (1996). *The paperboy*. New York: Jackson/Orchard.

Polacco, P. (1994). *Pink and Say*. New York: Philomel.

Rubin, C. (1989). *ABC Americana from the National Gallery of Art*. Orlando, FL: Harcourt Brace.

Sassa, R. (2001). *The stray dog*. Ill. M. Simont. New York: HarperCollins.

Say, A. (1993). *Grandfather's journey*. Boston: Houghton Mifflin.

Say, A. (1999). *Tea with milk*. Boston: Houghton Mifflin.

Scieszka, J. (1995). *The math curse*. Ill. L. Smith. New York: Viking.

Spedden, D.C. (1994). *Polar: The Titanic bear*. Ill. L. McGaw. Boston: Little, Brown.

Stevens, J. (1995). *From pictures to words: A book about making a book*. New York: Holiday House.

Tallchief, M. (with Wells, R.). (1999). *Tallchief: America's prima ballerina*. Ill. G. Kelley. New York: Viking.

Tanaka, S. (1996). *On board the Titanic: What is was like when the great liner sank*. New York: Hyperion.

Wood, D. (1999). *Grandad's prayers of the Earth*. Ill. P.J. Lynch. Cambridge, MA: Candlewick.

Woodruff, E. (1999). *The memory coat*. Ill. M. Dooling. New York: Scholastic.

Yolen, J. (1996). *Welcome to the sea of sand*. Ill. L. Regan. New York: Putnam.

PERTINENT JOURNALS

The ALAN Review
Assembly on Literature for Adolescents
National Council of Teachers of English
1111 West Kenyon Road
Urbana, IL 61801

Book Links: Connecting Books, Libraries, and Classrooms
Book Links
P.O. Box 615
Mt. Morris, IL 61054-7564
Phone: 888-350-0950

Social Education: The Official Journal of the National Council for the Social Studies
NCSS Headquarters Office
3501 Newark Street NW
Washington, DC 20016
E-mail: socialed@ncss.org

USEFUL WEBSITES

Brian Jacques's Website

http://www.redwall.org/dave/jacques.html

> An exciting website that includes biographical information, answers to frequently asked questions, and passages about the author's writing habits.

Carol Hurst's Children's Literature Site

http://www.carolhurst.com

> Information is plentiful on this site, including children's and YA literature, book reviews, author biographies, teaching materials, and suggestions for integrating books across the curriculum.

Children's Book Council

http://www.cbcbooks.org

> This site contains a wealth of information, including poetry suggestions; books hot off the press; pages relating to publishers, teachers, and librarians; books awards; and a forum for discussing topics relevant to children's literature.

Children's Literature Web Guide

http://www.ucalgary.ca/~dkbrown/index.html

> This easy-to-use site contains a wealth of information, including links to children's publishers and booksellers, upcoming conferences and book-related events, children's writing, children's literature discussion groups, journals, book reviews, and numerous resources for parents, teachers, writers, and illustrators.

Children's Picture Books Database at Miami University

http://www.lib.muohio.edu/pictbks

> Find over 4,500 picture book abstracts at this site. Weblinks are available to connect content area interests and related picture books.

Choices Booklists Home Page

http://www.reading.org/choices

> Learn more about Young Adults' Choices, Children's Choices, and Teachers' Choices. Lists of winners for the past 3 years are available to download.

The Internet Public Library

http://www.ipl.org

> Teen readers and their interests are thoroughly addressed through a number of sites and resources.

Kay Vandergrift's Special Home Page

http://www.scils.rutgers.edu/special/kay/

> This online resource offers extensive materials on how to use children's and YA literature across the curriculum. In addition, you will find sample syllabi, information on censorship, and numerous topics related to YA literature.

Studying Authors

Author studies and author visits remain popular and effective ways to maintain and extend students' interest in reading. Chapter 11 takes us through the process for an author study. The final chapter can help teachers plan an author visit and make it effective for students, teachers, parents, and the community.

Empowering Young Adult Readers and Writers Through Author Study

Lynne R. Dorfman

One of the best strategies for developing committed, empowered readers and writers in your classroom is to make students aware of the authors and illustrators who create quality literature. I have been fortunate to hear Mem Fox, a noted children's author, discuss the qualities of a good book. She talked about books that have subtle signposts to living in a social world, characters who readers can care deeply about, perfect words in perfect places, and an emotional impact that will change the reader. Teachers, particularly teachers of middle school students, need to find authors who write quality literature. Their stories should have multiple life lessons and characters who struggle with the same issues with which their readers struggle. In order to maximize the benefits of author study for students, teachers should search for authors whose craft is worth examining and whose stories are worth reading.

I began to notice that many titles in my classroom collection clustered around authors such as S.E. Hinton, Mildred Taylor, Gary Paulsen, Jerry Spinelli, Laurence Yep, Jane Yolen, Laurie Halse Anderson, Jean Craighead George, Lois Lowry, and Patricia Polacco, to name a few. I also recognized that these books were not the typical series book collections that so many adolescent students seem to find on their own. Why did I choose these books, and why do young adults choose certain books? In 1998, while teaching a graduate course titled "Writing and Children's Literature" for the Pennsylvania Writing and Literature Project, I asked teachers to create a list of reasons why they thought children chose one book over another. Teachers cited action/excitement, characters, genre, authors, powerful language, predictability, repetition, humor, imagination/fantasy, level of difficulty/number of pages, illustrations, availability, recommendations, catchy and intriguing titles, and classroom read-alouds.

As I examined the list, I realized that most of the reasons have something to do with what students and adults expect from authors—the way they tell a story, their point of view, the genre they use, their choice of words, their choice of characters, their voice, and their own intentions. Young people develop a taste for certain authors, and they read their favorites with confidence, enjoyment, and a higher degree of critical understandings.

There are many different ways to engage young adults with literature, but probably one of the most effective ways to develop readers and writers is to engage students in author studies. These studies usually involve reading, listening to, discussing, and writing about books written by the same author. According to Jenkins (1999), author studies revolve around biographical, critical, and aesthetic response to an author's works. Many times young adults love to find out about the real lives of the authors through the author websites, videos, biographies, autobiographies, and articles. For example, in *Firetalking* (1994), Polacco admits she did not do well in school because she had difficulty with reading. Students will find more clues in her books, particularly *Thank You, Mr. Falker* (1998). Through a critical stance, students examine literary elements. Polacco's themes run throughout her books, often developing around a cross-generational tie and deep sense of pride in one's heritage. Often her themes resonate in morality— questions of what is right and wrong. Aesthetic response allows the reader to make personal connections, often transporting a character's problems, struggles, and goals and applying them to real life. Here, what readers learn about the characters and events in a story helps them learn more about themselves.

The rationale for author study is clear: Author study gives students a chance to think about books and develop thoughtful, creative responses. Reading and sharing books by the same author helps young adults gain a deeper understanding of those books and a greater enthusiasm for them. Learning about an author's life helps young people understand the author's purpose, setting, characters, tone, and word choice. Understanding authors will deepen students' comprehension and help them read to make meaning. It will also help to develop their own skills as young authors.

Ann Lammot, author of *Bird by Bird: Some Instructions on Writing and Life* (1994), tells us that books are filled with things we do not get in real life. She talks about author's craft, an excellent reason to create author studies in the classroom:

They [books] are full of all the things that you don't get in real life—wonderful lyrical language, for instance right off the bat. And quality of attention: we may notice details during the course of the day but we rarely let ourselves stop and pay attention. An author makes you notice, makes you pay attention, and this is a great fight. (p. 15)

Author studies can often center around themes, genres, or areas of the curriculum. Author studies will make students want to read more as they become familiar with the author's voice, characters, settings, themes, and sometimes illustrations. For example, it is as easy to identify author-illustrator Patricia Polacco for the pictures she paints as for the stories she weaves, and later in this chapter, we will describe how Polacco's books, though picture books for young children, can be used successfully in an author study in classrooms of older students.

As students read and share books by the same author, they develop a sense of confidence that allows them to take risks, ask questions, and solve problems. As they share insights about an author by comparing and contrasting his or her books, they find new layers of meaning. Author studies can change your students by renewing their interest in reading and writing and by developing their engagement as readers who continue to question, predict, reflect, and problem solve before, during, and after reading.

TRADING CARDS

- Students should research author Web pages to choose an author they would like to use to make a trading card.

- Distribute a 4-by-6-inch blank index card to each student.

- On one side of the card, the students should either draw a picture of the author or print a picture from the author's Web page and glue it to the card.

- The back of the card should include important facts and information about the author. Examples might be birth date, birthplace, title of their first book, interests, hobbies, etc.

- You can turn this learning activity into a fun trading game by having students determine which cards are more "valuable" by the demand during trading. Students can determine the rules of the game: how often trading is allowed, who can trade, how many cards can be traded at once, etc.

TEACHER IDEA

Joan B. Elliott is a professor at Indiana University of Pennsylvania, Indiana, Pennsylvania, USA.

Engaging Students With Literature Through Author Studies

There are many ways to engage young adults with literature. Providing read-alouds, developing classroom libraries, allowing time for independent reading, and encouraging personal response benefits all readers in a classroom. Also, using literature circles and introducing companion pieces to young adult literature such as picture books develop students' interest in reading and help learners grow (see Chapter 10 for suggestions of picture books appropriate for young adult students). All of these things can be used in an author study.

The Read-Aloud

During read-alouds, wonderful words fall softly as spring rain or like torrential sheets of summer storms. Reading aloud is a powerful way to introduce an unfamiliar author and make connections with familiar authors and themes. Teachers can ask students to listen for the author's voice, strategies, and scaffolds the author uses repeatedly to craft the reader's experience. Because all the students have the same experience through the read-aloud, regardless of reading level, the teacher can create a host of minilessons that will help students make reading-writing connections and revise their own writing. The minilessons also can be used as topics for future small-group author study discussions. More often than not, students will independently reread a book that a teacher has read to the class or will finish a story that a teacher has started but very purposefully stopped at a riveting moment. Reading aloud is a way to honor genres, authors, cultures, and even dreams. It is a teacher's way to "hook" students on books and authors.

Classroom Library and Time for Independent Reading

Another way to engage students with literature is to create a classroom library that contains a variety of books reflecting different genres and reading levels, as well as multiple works by individual authors. Daily time—if only 10 to 15 minutes—for book selection and independent reading is a crucial part of the literature experience. Students read independently to find biographical information on websites or to read one or several chapters to be discussed in their author study group. Even if some or most reading is assigned for homework, teachers will have more success if they can develop a reading habit by allowing some daily independent reading time in class. Whenever possible, students should have some choice in author selection, their peer group, or the book they will read by the selected author. With more ownership and choice, students will be willing to invest more effort and time.

Personal Response

In *Envisioning Literature: Literacy Understanding and Literature Instruction* (1995), Judith Langer states that all literature gives us a way to imagine human potential. It provides us with ways to see ourselves and rewrite ourselves. Basically, personal response can center around three facets: perceptions, associations, and affect. First, readers often respond to literature by talking about their perceptions—what they find to be surprising, confusing, or important in the story. This response is their point of view, their opinion, and their way of "owning" the story. A second way readers make meaning and assume ownership is by making connections or associations with their own personal experiences and the experiences of the people around them as they relate to the literature. Finally, the third element involves affect—what readers are thinking and feeling when they are reading the story. These elements are what Rosenblatt (1991) refers to as the aesthetic stance in her reader response theory. Rosenblatt explains that this stance allows readers to journey with the characters—relive life through the pages of a book. She states that this "lived-through" experience also helps readers remember and apply efferent information. Author study is a good way to use aesthetic stance because students become familiar with the author's style and often reread to compare the characters from several different books and how they solve the problems they encounter. In rereading and citing evidence from text to illustrate points made during small or large group discussions, the students learn the content, or efferent information.

Although there have been criticisms of reader response theory, it has been my experience with students of all ages that a book takes on a new life and new meaning in the hands of a reader, and particularly in the hands of a community of readers. For instance, at a seminar with participants of the Pennsylvania Writing and Literature Project Summer Institute on the Teaching of Writing, author-illustrator Peter Catalanotto told an anecdote about his original intentions for the watercolors that accompany the story in *Cecil's Story* (Lyon, 1995), a narrative set in Civil War times: When he dripped water on his work, Catalanotto decided he liked the way the mistake turned out, so he added more. Later on, a reader told him that she loved the way he had painted the story, especially the drippings that would remind the readers of the blood, sweat, and tears shed during a brutal time in America's history. His intent? Not at all! Yet he wishes it had been his original intent. As Jenkins (1999) explains, "The life of a book is in the hands of the reader, not the author" (p. 38).

Further, it is important for students to feel that readers play a part in the meaning, not just teachers or the text alone. Very often, their interpretations grow in sophistication as they work together to make connections. These students also learn to appreciate other interpretations that may differ from theirs, and they begin to develop an aptitude for monitoring their own reading and learning (Spiegel, 1998).

Literature Circles

Literature circles are small, temporary discussion groups whose members have all chosen to read the same story, poem, article, or book. Participants also can be grouped by theme, such as courage or friendship; by genre, such as mystery or science fiction; and by author, such as Patricia Polacco or Gary Paulsen. Group members usually meet to predetermine how much will be read and what roles or specific responsibilities each member will be prepared to take on in the upcoming discussion. There are many ways to use literature circles during author study. One sensible way to begin is to start with the entire class reading the same book. Then offer a variety of titles and allow children to break into small groups by choice or teacher assignment. Another variation would be to offer the chance to form several new author studies, but focus on one genre. Although Daniels (1994) outlines roles such as "Passage Picker, Discussion Director, Vocabulary Enricher, and Connector," these roles are not necessary to maintain after the students have had an adequate time for practice. (See also Chapter 5 of this volume for more on roles in literature circles.)

Literature circles help validate the importance of reader response as a natural consequence. We enjoy talking about movies, plays, books, and authored pieces with others. Response is absolutely essential to help build the common literary ground that binds a community of readers together. Literature circles also allow teachers to sit as outside observers and evaluate or predict students' reading processes. Circles allow readers many opportunities to reevaluate their lives through the experience of a text.

Perhaps one of the most striking aspects of literature circles is that they encourage students to ask questions that promote higher order thinking skills. Before students get together into their groups, it is a good idea to present a minilesson on literature circle questions. When using literature circles in an author study, ask students to consider the following questions:

- How does the author build suspense or "take your breath away" during the story?

- How does the author let you know what any particular character is thinking?

- If you could talk with the author, what questions would you ask? What would you tell the author?

- What techniques does the author use that you find interesting? How will you incorporate this information into your own writing?

- How does the author set the mood or tone?

- Does the author let you know what she or he thinks or feels about this subject?

- Does the story remind you of anything in the author's life? Of your own life? How does this information help your understanding or change your interpretation of the story?

- What new and interesting words did you learn from this book?

- Are special categories of words found throughout the author's work, such as terms from another language or culture?

- What are some powerful sentences that illustrate how the author uses word choice and/or figurative language to paint pictures in your mind or make you linger on a passage?

Companion Pieces: Picture Books

In Chapter 10 in this volume, Carol Fuhler suggests that partnerships of a quality picture book and a novel from the Young Adults' Choices lists can begin with a picture book that speaks to a theme, event in history, or particular culture or tradition. Fuhler suggests that we allow our students to find the pairs or sets, read them, and share with their classmates. This idea carries over to author studies, especially in cases where the author being studied has written both young adult novels and picture books. For instance, an author study on Patricia Polacco might involve pairing her picture book *The Butterfly* (2000) with a complementary novel.

In *The Butterfly*, Polacco's aunt tells her the story of her mother, Marcel, who was part of the French resistance before the Nazis arrived. Monique discovers that her mother has been hiding Jewish families from the Nazis in their basement. She becomes friends with Sevrine, a Jewish girl who eventually escapes to safety with her parents. To this day, Marcel's daughter remains friends with Sevrine, now a grown woman who lives in Israel. In the story, Polacco creates powerful images that linger with the reader for a long time after the book is finished. Monique watches as a Nazi soldier grasps a butterfly in his gloved hand and squeezes it. In this one action, Polacco gives the reader the cruelty and injustice of that time as well as the fragility of beauty and life itself.

Activities for an Author Study

Author Quilt

Students will enjoy making a class quilt of memories or characters from the author's books or capturing some powerful prose accompanied by an illustration. Students also can create a four-square quilt (larger for older children) of their own memories of family and home to help make personal connections with the literature. An extension would be to have each child research family traditions and the traditional dress, food, and customs of one country linked to a parent, grandparent, or great-grandparent and display the information quilt-style. To make a "quilt," take each written piece and mount on a colored construction square. Use a binding machine to make holes around the edges of the construction paper. Give the children four pieces of yarn and have them thread the yarn through the holes. Tie the ends into bows. Mount the colored squares on butcher block paper to hang.

To help students create individual family quilts using writing, offer these guidelines:

- Indent to begin your paragraph and write your lead. (For example, "My grandfather is a very special person.")
- Write several sentences to describe what your person looks like.
- Tell how the person spends his or her free time: sports, hobbies, other activities.
- Tell about one of the following: the funniest, most embarrassing, happiest, or most frightening moment in this person's life.
- Tell any interesting or unusual thing about this person.
- Write a paragraph that begins "I remember when…and I…."
- Tell why this person is special to you.

Analyze an Author

Students benefit from analyzing authors because they need to read and reread carefully for varying purposes; thus, comprehension is layered and richer. Often they will be able to imitate the author in different ways within their own writing. Ask students to read the selections in the set. To analyze the author, students should think about the books in the set and answer the following questions:

- What ideas, themes, characters, or plots do the author's books have in common?
- What interesting or unusual things did you notice about the illustrations?
- In your opinion, does the author have a certain message he or she is trying to communicate to readers? Explain your answer.
- What is your favorite book by this author? Explain.
- Which character is most like you? Or, which character would you like to meet? Why?
- On a scale of 1 (low) to 10 (high), give this author a rating and a recommendation for other readers.

Students may answer these questions in small- or whole-group discussions. They can mark key pages with adhesive notes and write a word, phrase, or sentence on the note as a memory jogger. When the discussions are rich and comprehensive, there probably is little need to write the answers somewhere else. Sometimes, however, they may respond in a written response in a reading response journal or literature notebook, especially if the teacher has given the students a rubric with specific information to include for evaluation purposes.

TEACHER IDEA

LITERARY REPORT CARD

Title of Book _____

Characters	Letter Grade	Reasons

Students discuss the main characters in the story they have read, then give each character a letter grade. They should explain why they gave the grades. (Discuss in small groups, then share with the class.)

Joan B. Elliott is a professor at Indiana University of Pennsylvania, Indiana, Pennsylvania, USA.

Writing Autobiographies and Author Profiles

At the beginning of the school year, students can write a short autobiography about themselves as writers, sharing their successes and failures. These short pieces help alleviate stress by sharing the frustrations and difficulties they may have experienced in the past. Getting it out in the open and finding other peers who have had similar experiences helps to build community and establish trust, especially if the teacher also shares his or her own writing successes and failures. The autobiographies also provide the teacher with important insights about the writers in the class, especially their writing behaviors and their attitudes toward writing. A good way to begin is to share a short autobiography about someone who became an author. For instance, Polacco's *Firetalking* (1994a) discusses her process, her struggles, and her successes.

In Chapter 7 of this volume, "Whose Life Is It, Anyway? Biographies in the Classroom," Teri Lesesne suggests having students create their own reading autobiographies and share them anonymously. The chapter also details an activity called "A Profile of Me," which could be applied to authors the students have studied or would like to study (see page 129). For example, students can read author profiles that note the author's hobbies, talents, pets, favorites, and difficulties in order to decide which author appeals to them. Students can create author cards with pertinent, interesting facts. When laminated, these cards can be used year after year as a motivator or link to help children choose an appropriate author to study. This activity can make a wonderful introduction to author studies in a middle school classroom.

About the Characters

HOW THE AUTHOR REVEALS THE CHARACTERS. An interesting activity that teachers can use with any author study involves helping students discover how the author reveals his or her characters to the reader. Teachers should guide students to examine the stories to look for these points about a main character:

- description of the character
- conversation—what the character says
- conversation—what other characters say about the character being studied
- actions—what the character does
- what the character is thinking and feeling
- what other characters are thinking and feeling about that character
- what the illustrations reveal

Students can add passages to their literature notebooks directly from the text that illustrate the way an author reveals the characters to the reader. The students can refer to these examples to help them in their own writing and as signposts to an author's style. Does the author rely heavily on physical descriptions? On dialogue? On thought shots? On actions?

BOOK CHARACTER PARTIES. For a book character party, divide students into small groups and ask each member of the group to choose a character from one of the author's stories. Students then create a clever, inexpensive gift and card based on events and general knowledge of the characters and how they would behave and act. At the party, one student role-plays the recipient, opens each gift, and responds to each of the other student-characters in kind. Reactions are mainly a matter of interpretation, but should remain authentic and true to the character the author has created. If appropriate, students could respond with an expression or line the character actually says in the text.

CHARACTER PROBLEM-SOLVING TECHNIQUES. For a third character-based activity, make a chart with a title such as "It's All Part of Growing Up." Each group can list problems that the author's characters have faced and the solutions the characters discovered. Finally, each student makes personal connections with the problems and talks about how they solved similar problems in real life. Teachers can choose to have students respond in reader response journals, literature circles, or whole-group discussions.

Potpourri

Here's a list of additional activities that would be appropriate for an author study:

- Encourage students to create a banner for a book or an author.
- Ask students to decorate a T-shirt or your classroom door to represent the author being studied.
- As a class, vote for your favorite book by the featured author and graph the results.
- Place a comment page or booklet into the books the students read and allow each reader to write a personal response.
- As a class, begin to create a list of characteristics that make the author unique. (For example, is the artwork realistic or cartoon-like?)

Sample Author Study: Patricia Polacco

About the Author

Patricia Polacco's rich background is the source for many of her wonderful stories. She was born in Lansing, Michigan, USA, and grew up in both California and Michigan. Stories such as *Meteor!* (1987), *My Ol' Man* (1995), *The Trees of the Dancing Goats* (1996b), and *Boat Ride With Lillian Two Blossom* (1988a) take place in and around the village of Williamson outside of Lansing, Michigan. *Tikvah Means Hope* (1994c) is a heartwarming story that takes place in Oakland, California, during the time of the great fires that left several thousand families homeless in a matter of hours. This and other stories such as *Rechenka's Eggs* (1988c), *Chicken Sunday* (1992a), *Welcome Comfort* (1999), and *Mrs. Katz and Tush* (1992b) allow us to catch glimpses of family customs and traditions.

Although Polacco's early school years were difficult and somewhat frustrating for her, she earned an M.F.A. and a Ph.D. in art history and has acted as a museum consultant in the restoration of icons. Polacco has participated in exchange programs for writers and illustrators and has traveled throughout Russia and former Soviet republics. Her interest in fostering mutual respect and tolerance has also led her to become involved with inner-city projects in the United States that promote peaceful resolution of conflict and encourage art and literacy programs.

A good place to start is by reading aloud from *Firetalking* (1994a), Polacco's autobiography for children, in which the author reveals her process—how she does not always get her drawings or stories right the first time. She admits that as a child, reading was difficult for her because she processed information differently. Her dyslexia was not diagnosed right away, and she had many painful moments in school. As an adult, she starts her day by sitting in a rocking chair and listening to music. She explains, "When I rock, my thoughts boil in my head. They catch the air and fly. The images and stories come with fury and energy" (p. 25). Polacco tells us that she has rockers in every room of her house.

Before I read *Firetalking* to my students, they had believed that writers did not have much difficulty getting their thoughts down on paper or expressing themselves when they were in school. Now they were able to identify with Polacco's struggles and realize that authors need to use many strategies to get themselves started.

In the video titled *Dream Keeper* (1996a), Polacco discusses her use of music to create a dream state that helps her keep writing. When she goes to a rocking chair and rocks, she says this is where the dream begins, "and of course a book is a dream." Indeed, the ideas of dreams, magic, and miracles appear often in her stories, such as *Appelemando's Dream* (1991), *Rechenka's Eggs* (1988c), *Boat Ride With Lillian Two Blossom* (1988a), *Welcome Comfort* (1999), and *Babushka's Doll* (1990a). These books would be good choices to have in the classroom library for students to read independently. Polacco says that the wonderful thing about writing and reading is that anything is possible. Readers get to go anywhere the writer can take them.

SENTENCE STEM SCRAMBLE

This activity uses sentence stems to allow students to consider their personal values, opinions, and ideas on a particular book or author. Write sentence stems on separate pieces of newsprint, and hang the papers at stations throughout the room. Divide students into the same number of groups as there are sentence stems. Each group begins at a different sentence stem and has 1 minute for the members of the group to write responses on the newsprint. All group members respond at the same time, and no one is allowed to stop and read what other group members have written. Groups then rotate to the next sentence stem. After students have responded to all of the sentence stems, each group again moves to each station to read everyone's reactions.

To process this activity, each group stops at one sentence stem, discusses it, and writes a brief summary of the comments on the newsprint. A spokesperson from each group discusses the summaries and the teacher facilitates discussion of common themes and points of disagreement.

Example

Encourage students to consider their opinions and ideas about the characters, plot, and gender messages in *Out of the Dust* (Hesse, 1997) through sentence stems such as

> Billie Jo could be described as...
>
> Billie Jo demonstrated bravery by...
>
> Billie Jo's mother sacrificed by...
>
> If I were Billie Jo, I would...
>
> Billie Jo's family life...
>
> Billie Jo's father demonstrated sensitivity when he...
>
> Living during the Dust Bowl would be like...

Modified from Rose-Colley, Bechtel, & Cinelli (1994) by Kay A. Chick, Assistant Professor of Curriculum and Instruction at Penn State-Altoona, Altoona, Pennsylvania, USA.

TEACHER IDEA

Polacco talks about absolute mutual respect in which people experience joy in being around people who are different from themselves. Most of Polacco's books take on some multicultural aspect, partly because of her own rich heritage and the background of friends and neighbors where she actually lived. In today's changing and all too often violent world, it is important to develop a sense of ethnic pride while simultaneously developing an awareness and understanding of other cultures. In *Mr. Lincoln's Way* (2001b), Polacco's characters, a principal and a tough sixth grader named Eugene, find answers to difficult questions. Mr. Lincoln provides the reader with a subtle role model for human kindness while addressing issues of prejudice that sometimes accompany children to school from home. The mutual respect and intercultural friendship that develop in *Pink and Say* (1994b), the story of Polacco's great grandmother arriving at Ellis Island, and the making of the "keeping quilt" in *The Keeping Quilt* (1988b) are things that middle schoolers can respond to aesthetically as well as critically.

Polacco Picture Books for Young Adults

Although her stories are considered to be picture books, Polacco's themes and life lessons are particularly appropriate for young teens to explore. Another plus for teachers is the availability of many of Polacco's books in paperback, making it possible to purchase multiple copies for literature circles. Students can pair or form groups to read the same book, several books by theme, or books from different years to watch an author change and grow. *Rechenka's Eggs* (1988c) and *Chicken Sunday* (1992a) are both about the quality of being noble and giving, centering on the act of human kindness when it is bestowed unselfishly upon another person. In *Babushka Baba Yaga* (1993), Polacco shows us how people need each other, the terrible loneliness that can result from being "different" from everyone else, and how the young and innocent are without the prejudice and preconceived notions of adults. It is a story that teaches tolerance and ends with a compelling thought as one of the babushkas takes the hand of Baba Yaga and declares, "Those who judge one another on what they hear or see, and not on what they know of them in their hearts, are fools indeed!"

In *Pink and Say* (1994b), there are also many lessons to be learned. The book addresses prejudice, injustices, and courage. It shows us a mother's love and exemplary friendship, and it reveals our human frailties. *Thunder Cake* (1990b) is a story about confronting our fears and mustering up our courage. It places a grandmother in the role of a teacher who coaxes her granddaughter to make some positive discoveries about herself.

In a recent story, *The Butterfly* (2000), Polacco takes us to France during the Nazi occupation in World War II. She explores the role that a family played to hide Jewish families and help them escape to freedom. The author's note explains to the reader that the story is absolutely true. Although Sevrine and Polacco's Aunt Monique have remained friends to this day, the author tells us that Sevrine's own parents did not escape to safety. Again, the theme of human kindness—first by Monique's own mother, who offered her home as a sanctuary, and later by Monique, herself, when she gives up her cat, Pinouff, to Sevrine as a token of her friendship—is a theme Polacco has used before. Polacco nudges us toward tolerance and an understanding of others as gently as the butterfly's wings brush against Monique's cheek like a kiss. *The Butterfly* shows us that the act of being human means we are often our best when times are at their worst. It is a wonderful companion piece for a book such as *Anne Frank: The Diary of a Young Girl* (Frank, 1993), Karen Ackerman's *The Night Crossing* (1995), and other Holocaust stories.

In another recent story, *Betty Doll* (2001a), Polacco uses a letter as a vehicle to tell the story. It is a collection of moments in her mother's life, all intertwined with her favorite handmade doll, Betty Doll, which her mother credits with many things, including the rescue of herself and her two brothers during a December blizzard. Her mother recalls the times she loaned Betty Doll to Polacco when she needed her. In the letter, which the author discovered along with the doll a year after her mother's death, she tells Polacco, "She'll help you remember such warm things. But most of all, when you look into her face, I want you to remember how much I love you."

Final Thoughts

Evelyn Krieger (1997) talks about an author's "special effects" that help the reader to become a better writer. She explains how to train our students to use their ears and eyes to spot examples of effective writing. Similarly, Jenkins (1999) refers to the critical response, which involves training students to read like writers and linger over passages in which the writer paints pictures with words. These are all things that can be accomplished through author study.

This chapter has focused on Patricia Polacco as an example of author study, even though most of Polacco's books are picture books. Polacco's stories are wonderful and appropriate for young teenagers because their characters show strength, courage, human kindness, and wisdom to do the right thing. Perhaps the most important aspect of Polacco's work is the celebration of differences and the way she creates excitement for storytelling and enthusiasm for traditions, family, and life itself. Her books also give dignity and new respect for senior citizens, honoring their important place in the lives of children. Polacco gets us to consider becoming a storyteller of our own family's history and traditions. She gives young writers permission to "tweak the truth" to make their stories work. In general, students benefit from an author study because they

- develop personal interpretations of a piece of literature;
- practice an aesthetic stance of reading, as well as an efferent stance;
- read and understand a variety of material;
- develop a sense of ownership, personal involvement, and an active engagement in the act of reading;
- develop skills in all the communication areas, including reading, writing, speaking, and listening;
- are supported and encouraged to write;
- gain self-confidence and self-assurance; and
- learn to take responsible learning risks.

Conducting author studies with young adult students will allow us to get closer to our goal of creating lifelong readers and writers. Young adult students, especially, need the familiarity and comfort of voices they have come to know and love, and that nudge them into reevaluating their lives in the light of literary experiences.

REFERENCES

Daniels, H. (1994). *Literature circles: Voice and choice in the student-centered classroom.* York, ME: Stenhouse.

Jenkins, C.B. (1999). *The allure of authors: Author studies in the elementary classroom.* Portsmouth, NH: Heinemann.

Krieger, E. (1997). *Developing reading and writing through author awareness: Grades 4–8.* Boston: Allyn & Bacon.

Lammot, A. (1994). *Bird by bird: Some instructions on writing and life.* New York: Pantheon.

Langer, J.A. (1995). *Envisioning literature: Literacy understanding and literature instruction.* New York: Teachers College Press; Newark, DE: International Reading Association.

Rosenblatt, L.M. (1991, October). Literature-S.O.S.! *Language Arts, 68,* 444–448.

Spiegel, D.L. (1998). Reader response approaches and the growth of readers. *Language Arts, 76,* 41–48.

YOUNG ADULT LITERATURE CITED

Ackerman, K. (1995). *The night crossing*. New York: Random House.

Frank, A. (1993). *Anne Frank: The diary of a young girl*. Englewood Cliffs, NJ: Prentice Hall.

Lyon, G.E. (1995). *Cecil's story*. Ill. P. Catalanotto. Danbury, CT: Orchard Books.

Polacco, P. (1987). *Meteor!* New York: Dodd.

Polacco, P. (1988a). *Boat ride with Lillian Two Blossom*. New York: Philomel.

Polacco, P. (1988b). *The keeping quilt*. New York: Simon & Schuster.

Polacco, P. (1988c). *Rechenka's eggs*. New York: Philomel.

Polacco, P. (1990a). *Babushka's doll*. New York: Simon & Schuster.

Polacco, P. (1990b). *Thunder cake*. New York: Philomel.

Polacco, P. (1991). *Appelemando's dreams*. New York: Philomel.

Polacco, P. (1992a). *Chicken Sunday*. New York: Philomel.

Polacco, P. (1992b). *Mrs. Katz and Tush*. New York: Bantam.

Polacco, P. (1993). *Babushka Baba Yaga*. New York: Philomel.

Polacco, P. (1994a). *Firetalking*. Katonah, NY: Richard C. Owen.

Polacco, P. (1994b). *Pink and Say*. New York: Philomel.

Polacco, P. (1994c). *Tikvah means hope*. New York: Doubleday.

Polacco, P. (1995). *My Ol' Man*. New York: Philomel.

Polacco, P. (1996a). *Dream keeper* [Video]. New York: Philomel.

Polacco, P. (1996b). *The trees of the dancing goats*. New York: Simon & Schuster.

Polacco, P. (1998). *Thank you, Mr. Falker*. New York: Philomel.

Polacco, P. (1999). *Welcome comfort*. New York: Philomel.

Polacco, P. (2000). *The butterfly*. New York: Philomel.

Polacco, P. (2001a). *Betty Doll*. New York: Philomel.

Polacco, P. (2001b). *Mr. Lincoln's way*. New York: Philomel.

CHAPTER 12

Getting the Most Out of an Author's Visit: Multiple Perspectives

Joan B. Elliott and Suzanne Mateer,
with Jerry Spinelli and Jan Cheripko

Inviting an author to visit your school should be an exciting and educational time for everyone, both young adult students and their teachers. It affords a direct experience with an author in which questions about reading and writing can be addressed. Having a direct acquaintance with an author leads young adults to understand why the book was especially written for their interests. In many cases, an author's visit motivates young adult readers to pursue reading other books by the same author (see Chapter 11 in this volume for an exploration of author study). In addition, students may elect to model the author's writing in their own original creations.

The author's visit, to conserve time and energy, should be a district-wide visit for all young adult students. The first section in this chapter offers a plan to help teachers balance organization and enthusiasm in designing and implementing a successful visit. In the second section, Jerry Spinelli, a well-known author and winner of the 1991 Newbery Award for *Maniac Magee* (1990), provides a unique perspective on how to ensure a successful author visit. Next, Jan Cheripko, an author who also has experience in the publishing industry, contributes his thoughts and personal insights on how to enhance an author's visit. He provides suggestions for teachers in promoting a worthwhile and memorable experience for teachers of young adult literature and their students.

The objectives of an author's visit for young adult readers include the following:

1. Motivating young adults to read through having direct contact with an author.

2. Having greater comprehension of the author's work after hearing the author talk about his or her book(s).

3. Enabling students to gain techniques that help them to understand the writing process and how they can apply it.

Planning for an Author's Visit

The time and effort put forth for a single author's visit is rewarding and worthwhile. With serious thought, planning, and commitment, an author's visit can add enrichment and excitement to school curriculum. As you begin to plan an author's visit, be sure to involve administrators, teachers, and students. This

TEACHER IDEA

READ A BOOK IN AN HOUR

1. Tear a paperback book into chapters.
2. The teacher reads the first and last chapters, or the first and second chapter, as well as the last two chapters.
3. Give each student a chapter and the table of contents, and have each student read and take notes on his or her chapter.
4. Students then get into a circle and summarize their chapters with everyone listening.
5. Students can take notes on each chapter if desired.
6. The class can write a summary when the discussion is through.

Guidelines As You Prepare for Presentation
1. Tell a short summary of what happens in the chapter. Be sure to include information about characters, especially if they are new.
2. Try to make a prediction of what you think is going to happen in the chapter.
3. Share three new vocabulary words in context and their meanings.
4. Pick out the one or two main ideas of the plot that the class should try to remember and possibly write down.
5. Write one or two questions that you may have that you would like answered in later chapters.

Adapted from Vacca, R.T. (1983). The book an hour strategy. *Middle School Journal, 14,* 17–19.

teamwork will enrich the curriculum and enhance student learning. Even well-known authors need the assurance that they have the support and preparation of the faculty and students if their visit is to be a smashing success.

Organization and enthusiasm can go hand in hand when designing and implementing a successful visit. Refer to the following guidelines to ensure that the author's visit will be an experience students will always remember.

Before the Visit

One Year in Advance

- Select who or what type of author to invite. Consider recommendations from teachers and students. Check website information on authors, and contact their publisher as to availability.

- Determine funding for the event. What financial resources do you have available? Write grants, or consider fundraisers such as book fairs, books for sale by the visiting author, and so forth.

- Set dates and times with the school calendar and the author. Discuss possible evening activities to involve the author with the community and with parents.

- Send a letter of agreement to the author including the date, time, sessions, and costs to be covered for the visit.

Two to Three Months in Advance

- Order books written by the author to sell to students and faculty for autographing during the author's visit. Books may be ordered directly from the publisher, a book distributor, and/or a local bookstore. Provide a sheet listing the titles and prices of each book.

- Contact the author and/or publisher(s) for biographical information, photographs, and any curriculum material that might be available.

- Determine any equipment or materials the author may need for the visit.

- Prepare a teacher packet, which may include titles of the author's books, videos, websites, activity ideas, and other available information.

- Begin to have the students read books by the author and participate in related activities or projects. To have a successful visit, it is crucial for teachers and students to be truly familiar with the author's work.

One Month in Advance

- Display announcements on bulletin boards, on posters, and in the hallways and library to make students aware of the author's upcoming arrival.

- Place an announcement in the local paper or on the local radio stations about the author's visit.
- Consider planning a staff luncheon or dinner with the author.

Two Weeks in Advance

- Purchase or make gifts for the author.
- Plan for autographing books. Students who wish to have an autographed book should print their name on an adhesive note and place it on the inside cover of each book they wish to purchase. This enables the author to sign the book(s) at his or her leisure or the evening before the visit. Then the books are distributed to each student during the author's visit. If sufficient time is available at the presentation for autographing at a signing table, it is still necessary for the student to write his or her name on paper and hand the book to the author for autographing.
- Finalize the schedule in cooperation with the other faculty members, determining the number of presentations and the length of each presentation. Be careful not to exhaust the author. It is a good idea to allow approximately a 20-minute break between presentations. If possible, schedule a time in the day for the author to interact with students at multi-young-adult age levels, or arrange for some students to participate in an informal discussion with the author.
- Send the final schedule of events to the author to preview before his or her arrival.
- Arrange with the author his or her expectations of travel arrangements.
- Send an invitation and the final schedule of events to all faculty.

One Week in Advance

- Help the students generate a list of questions to ask the author. Focus on asking specific questions that relate to the books the author has written.
- Hang "Welcome" banners and student projects throughout the hallways to build anticipation and excitement.

Prior to the Presentation

- Set up audiovisual equipment and test it to allow time for adjustments. Have media support personnel ready to solve any problems.
- Provide a pitcher of water and a glass for the author.
- Set up a table for late book sales and autographing.

During the Visit

- When the author arrives, faculty members and student ambassadors should meet and greet him or her. A smile, a warm welcome, and a cup of tea or coffee will begin the day on a positive note.
- Remind and encourage all faculty to attend the author's presentation.
- A hospitality team should be ready to escort the author to the various events of the day.

After the Visit

- Follow up the author's visit by continuing to read his or her works and participating in related activities.
- Students and faculty should write thank-you notes to express appreciation to the author. Some follow-up activities could also be sent. These should be collected and sent to the author in one large envelope. This may also include any publicity materials from the newspaper or any other sources.
- Teacher surveys are helpful. The following are some sample questions that could be used to receive feedback from the faculty:

1. What did you like best about the author's visit?
2. What part of the presentation was most effective in relating the importance of reading and writing to your students?
3. If your students participated in a small-group discussion, how did they share what they learned with the other students?
4. What would you do differently to improve upon an author's visit?
5. Which authors would you like to invite to visit our school in the future?

Advice for Teachers From Jerry Spinelli

Query 10 authors about the Do's and Don'ts of school visits and you will get 10 different lists. I would bet, however, that at least one DO would appear on every list: DO make sure that the students are familiar with the author's work.

There is good reason for this. Though an author's presentation may be informative and even entertaining in and of itself, an audience of knowledgeable readers adds a dimension that the author alone cannot provide.

In the weeks before the visit, have the students read—or read to them—one or more of the author's books. Discuss them in class. Maybe assign essays or other projects. The purpose of this activity is not merely to educate, but also to prime the students. It is the literary equivalent of a football pep rally. In fact, why not have a classroom pep rally for an author or book? ("Gimme an A!")

Whatever form your previsit activity takes, your goal is to have students looking forward to the day when the writer comes to school. Primed, prepared readers will help make your author's visit a meeting, an interaction, rather than a one-person show. And the author will take his or her proper place as the pièce de résistance of a process that began weeks before with the opening of a single book.

Of course, despite these plans, there are bound to be students who decline to jump aboard the bandwagon. Call them "reluctant readers" or just not interested, they will occupy a seat, but that is all. (Unless you have got a bold inquirer, like the kid in the back of the library where I was speaking one day who called out, "Who are you and what are you doing here?")

Facing such students may be more confrontation than interaction, but that does not mean the cause is lost. There is still hope that the author may, by an entertaining presentation or by sheer force of personality, say something that inspires the student to someday open a book or darken the doorway of a library.

There are many other aspects to hosting an author, but the preceding, I believe, is most important. Prime the students to participate with interested, knowledgeable questions—not just raised hands—and pray that your author will smite with inspiration those who evade your efforts. Doing so will maximize your author's contribution to the larger objective that guides us all: to encourage young

TEACHER IDEA

ALPHABET BOOK

Write a profile about a favorite author you are studying or an author who will be visiting your school. Use each letter of the alphabet once to tell either a fact you discovered during your research, a book the author has written, or a character the author has used in a book.

Example (The ABC's of Louis Sachar)

A   A Newbery winner

B   *There's A Boy in the Girls' Bathroom*

C   Comical writer

D   …

Joan B. Elliott is a professor at Indiana University of Pennsylvania, Indiana, Pennsylvania, USA.

people to continue to read—willingly and enthusiastically—once they enter the world beyond the classroom.

And because a reader's favorite author may never come to school, it is good to know that fan mail offers another way to communicate. Most letter-writers hope for a reply. If they do not get one, they tend to assume that the author never answers mail. This may not be the case. I, for one, answer all of my mail. Yet sometimes a fan fails to get a reply. How can this be? Well, sometimes a letter gets lost at the publishing house before it is passed on to me. Or it winds up by mistake in another author's mailbox and is not rerouted. Or it does get to me, but even though the reader pleads, "Please write back," he or she fails to include a return address. Or the address is illegible. Or wrong. (A reply of mine recently came back with "No Such Address" stamped on it. The sender probably thinks I am an old meanie who never answers mail.)

And then there is the author's universal pet peeve: letters that do not arrive in one batch. Arriving over a period of several days, these letters all come from the same place, same school, same classroom. Thirty of them, all wanting, all expecting an individual, customized reply. How much happier I and my writing time and postage budget would be if they all arrived in a one-envelope batch. Remember this: Your favorite author has already communicated with your students in the best way he or she knows how—by writing a book. Most authors love to open a letter and read that someone loves their writing. Know what we love almost as much? Finding that the fan letter comes with a stamped, self-addressed envelope.

Advice for Teachers From Jan Cheripko

One day, back in ninth grade, a teacher pulled me aside after class and told me that I had talent as a writer. Here was an adult, a teacher, a man I respected and admired, articulating for me what my hidden sense of myself was. I did think that I had talent. That day back in ninth grade, thanks to Bob Ciganek, my freshman English teacher, I decided to be a writer.

An author's visit can do for students what my teacher did for me: validate the hopes and dreams of a young person. It may not be that he or she will decide to be a writer or an illustrator, but it could be that an author just may say something that gives that young person hope, insight, vision, or direction. It is because of that possibility that I think author's visits are important.

For the past 11 years I worked as Assistant to the Publisher of Boyds Mills Press, a children's book publishing company owned by *Highlights for Children.* I worked with many authors and illustrators, primarily helping them and their books become known by teachers and librarians. Additionally, for the past 17 years I have been a teacher of high school English at a private school for young people in trouble. Recently, I left publishing to go back to teaching full time. I have had the good fortune to have three of my books published and have been asked to speak at schools and conferences throughout the United States and internationally. I have worked with dozens of authors and watched them present. As a teacher, author, and former assistant to a publisher, I have had some experience with author visits. Here are a few suggestions for teachers that I hope might be helpful:

Suggestion One: For the beginning teacher who has never had an author visit his or her classroom, talk with teachers who have. They will have plenty of stories about what worked and what did not. Then talk to your librarian. I have found that author visits are always more successful when the teachers work closely with librarians. Then talk with your local bookstore owner. Many have personal relationships with authors and could be helpful in finding the right author for your needs and in getting you in touch with him or her. Finally, attend conferences sponsored by organizations such as the National Council of Teachers of English, the International Reading Association, or the American Library Association. These conferences will give you opportunity to preview presentations of authors and perhaps make direct contact with them.

Suggestion Two: Authors and teachers should discuss what the classroom teachers expect and how the presentation could dovetail with the material being covered by the teachers. For example, one of our authors has written a number of nonfiction books about his trips on rivers throughout the world. Because the New York state social studies curriculum covers state history in fourth and eighth grades, if the teacher preferred, this author might gear his slide presentations to emphasize his river trips on the Hudson River and the Erie Canal when he is speaking to New York state students.

Suggestion Three: Communicate! I know this has been covered earlier in this chapter, but it is a key point. Get the details of the visit spelled out in writing. This will avoid confusion and bad feelings. Directions, meals, fees, overnight accommodations, number of presentations, audience age, audience size, book sales, contact person, and breaks all need to be clear ahead of time.

Suggestion Four: Teachers should make sure that they and their students have read the works of the author. If you think it is a good experience to have an author visit your classroom, then make the most of it by being familiar with the books of the author. Every year, I visit a school in upstate New York. The first year I was there, the teacher presented me with a large piece of paper signed by all of the students who had read my novel *Imitate the Tiger* (1996). Of 125 students, nearly 100 had read the book. It was one of the best experiences I have ever had as an author. The students had numerous thoughtful, insightful questions and comments. I go back to that classroom every year because the teacher prepared the students so well for my visit.

BOOK DETECTIVES

This is a scavenger hunt type of activity based on a main character from any piece of literature. Each student has a copy of the list and is encouraged to obtain the autograph of a real person (family member, friend, teacher, etc.) who fits the description. The activity helps to set a purpose for reading, provides clues to the main character, and leads to some interesting predictions and comments. Students can create their own people scavenger hunts based on other novels and stories.

Example

Use the following scavenger list prior to reading *Maniac Magee* (1990) by Jerry Spinelli:

Find someone who...

1. has a nickname.
2. has eaten a Tastykake Butterscotch Krimpet.
3. knows someone who is adopted.
4. has a friend from a different race.
5. has pitched baseball.
6. has read part of the encyclopedia.
7. has slept outside.
8. is allergic to pizza.
9. can untangle knots.
10. has a home address.

Audrey M. Quinlan is a doctoral candidate at Indiana University of Pennsylvania, Indiana, Pennsylvania, USA.

TEACHER IDEA

Suggestion Five: Please do not stand in the back of the room correcting papers. Grading papers and talking during a presentation is not only bad manners, but it sends the wrong message to your students.

Suggestion Six: Roll with the punches, because things do not always go as planned. Have a Plan B. If an author is doing a slide presentation, sometimes the bulb burns out. Who fixes it? At one school I visited, the principal told me he had three slide projectors ready just in case something went wrong. Once, when I was in Panama with some other authors, I had to do a slide presentation outside. You cannot very well turn out the lights and pull down the shades to make the room dark. Then, in the middle of the presentation, the students were suddenly in a bit of an uproar and moved to one side of the porch. I looked up and saw a 4-foot-long iguana perched on the beam at the top of the porch covering. It was time for "Plan B." I looked up "What to do when an iguana threatens your presentation" in my mental book of Plan Bs, but there was nothing there. The teacher and I quickly agreed that it was time to end the presentation.

Suggestion Seven: Authors and teachers should not worry about book sales. The success of an author's visit is not determined by the number of books sold. Success, I suspect, has more to do with touching the hearts and minds of young people.

Suggestion Eight: Teachers should make sure the books are available for the visit. Often, a bookstore in the local area can facilitate getting the books to the school in time for the presentation. Selling books is their profession—why not let them handle that detail?

Suggestion Nine: Match the right author with the right audience. Do not assume that simply because an author is coming to your school that he or she can speak to all age groups. Like many authors, I have had experiences when I was with my right audience and when I was mismatched. There have been occasions when I have faced an assembly of second to eighth graders at one time. Although I do have books that are written for different age groups, it is difficult to reach such a diverse audience with one presentation. On the other hand, during a visit to an alternative school in Queens, New York, a tough-looking boy, dressed in gang colors, came up to me after I had finished talking. He grabbed my hand with a firm handshake. He looked at me hard, straight in the eyes, so that he knew I was concentrating only on him. "Yo, man," he said. "I never read a book in my whole life, but I read yours, all the way through. It was my story. Thanks." As an author, there are few experiences better than having connected with your audience, one on one.

Final Thoughts

An author's visit can be a successful and worthwhile experience for students, teachers, and the author if organizers follow the suggested planning sequence at the beginning of this chapter. A successful visit enables teachers to provide young adults with an opportunity to meet authors who can enrich their experiences and knowledge about the author and his or her books. Meeting an author motivates young adults to read a book with increased awareness and interest, and it enables them to gain the author's perspective by seeing the author reading his or her work. Bringing authors into the classroom helps to encourage students to continue reading and loving young adult literature.

YOUNG ADULT LITERATURE CITED

Cheripko, J. (1996). *Imitate the tiger*. New York: St. Martin's Press.
Spinelli, J. (1990). *Maniac Magee*. Boston: Little, Brown.

Young Adult Literature Resources on the Web

Aaron Shepard's RT Page

http://www.aaronshep.com/rt

> This site contains scripts and tips for Readers Theatre, recommended script collections and other books for Readers Theatre, and more.

Amazon.com Children's Books

http://www.amazon.com/childrens

> This site allows searches for books according to age level, highlights new books, and lists books for purchase.

American Library Association, ALSC Awards and Grants

http://www.ala.org/alsc/awards.html

> This site offers lists of books that have won awards (Newbery, Caldecott, etc.), Children's Notables (present and past), professional awards, grants and fellowships, and scholarships.

The Big Busy School House

http://www.harperchildrens.com/schoolhouse/index.htm

> This site is a resource center for children's books for early childhood and K–8 educators. It includes information about newsletters, author/illustrator school visits, teacher's guides, *Little House* books, *Math Start*, *I Can Read* programs, and more.

Bookwire

http://www.bookwire.com/bookwire

> This site contains information on authors of interest, publishers' home pages, and other useful materials for studying young readers' books.

Carol Hurst's Children's Literature Site

http://www.carolhurst.com

> This site offers reviews of books that can be searched by title, author, or grade level. An online newsletter also gives in-depth information about authors.

Children's Book Council

http://www.cbcbooks.org/

> This site contains links to authors' and illustrators' websites, with books ranging from preschool through eighth grade.

Children's Literature: Beyond Basals
http://www.beyondbasals.com
> This site contains guides for using children's literature in K–12 classrooms, links for the best sites for children's literature, and Young Reader's Choice Award (YRCA).

The Children's Literature Web Guide
http://www.acs.ucalgary.ca/~dkbrown/authors.html
> This site contains information about authors' personal websites and websites maintained by fans, scholars, and readers.

Children's/Young Adult Literature
http://www.washburn.edu/services/mabee/crc/ed325.html
> This site contains links to children's literature sites and awards, young adult literature and awards, and information about censorship.

Choices Booklists
http://www.reading.org/choices/index.html
> This site includes the Young Adults', Children's, and Teachers' Choices annotated booklists published annually by the International Reading Association. The lists include favorite recently published books selected by young adults, children, teachers, and librarians throughout the United States.

Electronic Poetry Center
http://wings.buffalo.edu/epc
> This site contains information on authors, e-poetry, links, poetry magazines, and information about the State University of New York at Buffalo poetics program.

Index to Internet Sites: Children's and Young Adults' Authors & Illustrators
http://falcon.jmu.edu/~ramseyil/biochildhome.htm
> This site is an index to author and illustrator sites through the Internet School Library Media Center. This meta-site makes it easier to access curriculum-related sites for teachers, school librarians, parents, and students.

Interesting Personal WWW Sites of Authors and Illustrators
http://www.underdown.org/topsites.htm
> This site offers links to authors' and illustrators' personal sites that go beyond simply listing a biography and a list of books written.

Kathy Schrock's Guide for Educators
http://school.discovery.com/schrockguide
> This site provides links to other sites, such as Ask the Young Adult Author, American Verse projects, Aesop's Fables Online Exhibit, Children's Literature Web Guide, and much more.

Poetry for Kids
http://www.poetry4kids.com/poems.html

This site exposes students to poetry and includes instruction and tips on how to write poetry. Ken Nesbitt posts his updated works continually.

The Reading Corner
http://www.carr.org/read/YA.htm

This site for teenage readers contains reviews by teenage readers and a listing of books chosen as winners of the Margaret Alexander Edwards Award.

Young Adult Library Service Association (YALSA) Winning Titles
http://www.ala.org/yalsa/booklists/index.html

This site offers information on award lists, nomination forms for awards, and links to current and previous award winners or lists of titles. Some examples are Alex Awards, Best Books for Young Adults, Quick Picks for Reluctant Young Adult Readers, and more.

GLOSSARY OF TEACHER IDEAS

A to Z Book Activities. Interesting ways for students to respond to a book for every letter of the alphabet. page 20

Almost Famous Daisy. Two activities that correspond to the book *Almost Famous Daisy* include guessing-the-artist game and researching artists' styles to create postcards. page 172

Alphabet Book. Using all the letters of the alphabet, students list facts about authors and their books. page 216

Anticipation Guide. Students respond to a list of questions or factual statements before and after reading. page 92

A Baker's Dozen Ways to Respond to a Poem. Thirteen unique ways to have students respond to poetry, from drama to music. page 164

Bio-Cube. Students analyze a character by illustrating that character's traits using appropriate colors, fonts, and drawings on the sides of a cube. page 124

Biography Collage. Elements of literature are displayed using a magazine collage technique. page 132

Body Biography. A character study in which students create body silhouettes and place pertinent facts from the character's life on appropriate body areas. page 120

Book Detectives. Used to introduce a book, this scavenger hunt activity has students obtaining the signatures of people who match a character trait or an experience from the book. page 219

Breaker. Three activities for the book *Breaker* are "object analysis"—students analyze objects important in the book; "picture analysis"—students write a diary entry or a description of action, moods, or dreams based on pictures in the book; and "timeline"—students create a timeline of a character's life using specific parts of the book as supporting evidence. page 72

Can It! Objects to represent story events are placed in a decorated coffee can and presented to the class. page 100

Clerihews. A four-line humorous poem is used to describe a famous person, place, or author. page 147

Comic Strips. Responding to a nonfiction book, students use a comic strip format to deliver facts from the book. page 97

Commemorative Coin. Students follow criteria to design a commemorative coin based on a character in the book. page 76

Descriptive Poem. A five-line poem with specific guidelines is created based on the characters, setting, and conflict of a story. page 22

Dinner and Conversation. A character from a book is invited to the student's home for dinner, where menu choices and conversation topics are determined. page 30

Graffiti. A "wall" of paper is provided for students to write unique events or favorite parts of a story. page 15

Literary Report Card. Each character from the book is evaluated by being given a letter grade along with the reasons for the grade. page 202

Movies, Here We Come! A persuasive letter is created to convince a producer why a specific book should become a movie. page 37

A New Look to An Old Book. Students design a new book jacket for a book they have read. page 180

Postcards. Students design and write postcards based on characters and settings in a book. page 52

Read a Book in an Hour. Students use notetaking and summary skills as they each read only one chapter of a book and retell it in numerical order until they reach the final chapter, which is read aloud. page 212

Research Mania. Provides four alternatives to a research paper that include writing a fiction story based on an issue of concern, presenting information on endangered animals, designing a career brochure, or creating a poster to describe a person, event, or topic. page 110

Sentence Stem Scramble. Students write opinioned responses to sentence stems that are written on chart paper hung around the room. page 206

Stair Poems. Using a stair pattern graphic organizer, students follow a specific step format for creating a stair poem. page 156

Teaching Free Verse and Nontraditional Poetry. Using teacher prompts on notecards, students create a free verse or nontraditional poem. page 142

Top 10 List. Using the idea of a late-night television program, students create their own Top 10 lists of clever and humorous reasons why they like a book. page 46

Trading Cards. Students research authors and create "trading cards" for them with biographical facts and illustrations. page 196

Whip Around. Following reading, each student is given the opportunity for quick response to a specific query as the teacher "whips around" the class or row. page 60

CREDITS

We thank the following poets, publishers, and agents for the use of copyrighted material as listed. Every effort has been made to contact copyright holders for permission to reprint poetry in this volume, as required. The author and publisher regret any oversights that may have occurred and will be pleased to rectify them in future printings.

page 139   Excerpted from "Buried Alive" in *Buried Alive* by Ralph Fletcher. Copyright ©1996 Ralph Fletcher. Used by permission of Marian Reiner.

page 140   "Forgotten" from *Waiting to Waltz* by Cynthia Rylant. Copyright ©1984 Cynthia Rylant. Reprinted with the permission of Simon & Schuster Books for Young Readers, an imprint of Simon & Schuster Children's Publishing Division.

page 141   "Restraint" from *Behind the Wheel* by Janet S. Wong. Copyright ©1999 Janet S. Wong. Reprinted with the permission of Margaret K. McElderry Books, an imprint of Simon & Schuster Children's Publishing Division.

page 144   "Dreams" from *The Collected Poems of Langston Hughes* by Langston Hughes. Copyright ©1994 The Estate of Langston Hughes. Used by permission of Alfred A. Knopf, a division of Random House, Inc.

page 145   "Teenagers" by Pat Mora is reprinted with permission from the publisher of *My Own True Name: New and Selected Poems for Young Adults* (Houston: Arte Publico Press—University of Houston, 2000).

page 146   Excerpted from "Sister's in the Psycho Ward" in *Stop Pretending* by Sonya Sones. Used by permission of HarperCollins Publishers.

page 152   "Inside a Poem" from *It Doesn't Always Have to Rhyme* by Eve Merriam. Copyright ©1964, 1992 Eve Merriam. Used by permission of Marian Reiner.

page 154   Excerpted from "Street Music" in *Street Music: City Poems* by Arnold Adoff. Copyright ©1995 Arnold Adoff. Used by permission of HarperCollins Publishers.

page 154   "I Have Ten Legs" by Ann Swir reprinted with permission of translators Czeslaw Milosz and Leonard Nathan.

page 155   Excerpted from "Ode to Pablo's Tennis Shoes" in *Neighborhood Odes* by Gary Soto. Copyright ©1992 Gary Soto. Reprinted by permission of Harcourt, Inc.

AUTHOR INDEX

Note: References followed by *f* indicate figures.

A

ABRAHAMSON, R.F., 88, 101
ALLINGTON, R., 90
ALTENBAUGH, R.J., 89
ANDERSON, R.C., 71, 181
ANDERSON, T., 91
AOKI, E., 61
APPLEBEE, A., 121
ARMBRUSTER, B., 91
ASH, G.E., 176, 184

B

BARRERA, R.B., 54
BEACH, R., 88
BECK, C., 177
BECK, I.L., 179
BEERS, K., 89
BERKOWITZ, R.E., 111
BISHOP, R.S., 47, 53
BROWN, J.E., 49
BURKE, C., 31, 39

C

CAISSY, G.A., 71
CAMPBELL, J.R., 88
CARLSEN, G.R., 126
CARTER, B., 88, 101
CHAMBERS, A., 101
CULLINAN, B.E., 171, 176, 179, 184
CUMMINGS, P., 177

D

DANIELS, H., 101, 199
DAY, F.A., 47, 49
DEWEY, J., 77
DONAHUE, P.L., 88
DRESANG, E.T., 3

E

EGAN, K., 90
EISENBERG, M.B., 111
ELKIND, D., 70
ENGEL, D.E., 90
ERICKSON, L., 76

F

FINK, R.P., 90
FUHLER, C.J., 184

G

GALDA, L., 171, 176, 177, 184
GAMBRELL, L.B., 176, 184

H

HARMIN, M., 60*f*
HARRIS, V., 47
HARSTE, J.C., 31, 39
HARVEY, S., 108
HEPLER, S., 171, 176
HICKMAN, J., 172, 173, 176

Note: References followed by *f* indicate figures.

A

ACKERMAN, K., 208
ADLER, D., 185
ADOFF, A., 139, 143, 154, 157, 159, 167
ALIKI, 180, 183
ALLENDE, I., 57
ALVEREZ, J., 56
ANAYA, R., 54
ANDERSON, D., 109
ANDERSON, L.H., 194
ANGELOU, M., 143, 153, 158, 160, 161
ARDLEY, N., 96
ASCH, F., 184
ASHABRANNER, B., 96
AVI, 73, 74, 85
AYRES, K., 85–86

B

BALLARD, R., 90, 102, 104
BANK, L.R., 58
BARTOLETTI, S.C., 93
BARTONE, E., 183
BASE, G., 172, 176
BAT-AMI, M., 75*f*, 86
BEALS, M.P., 136
BEATTIE, O., 102
BEATTY, P., 75
BERTRAND, D.G., 57
BIERHORST, J., 173
BJORK, C., 177
BODE, J., 90, 96

BOO, M., 109
BRADBY, M., 184
BRIDGES, R., 90
BRILL, M.T., 82
BROOKS, G., 144, 161
BROWNE, A., 178
BRUCHAC, J., 59, 86
BUNTING, E., 181, 182, 186

C

CADUTO, M.J., 59
CARLSON, L.M., 145
CARR, T., 94
CHANG, I., 75
CHERPIKO, J., 7, 211, 217–220
CHERRY, L., 178, 184
CISNEROS, S., 56
CLINTON, C., 144
COERR, E., 121, 136
COFER, J.O., 56
COLLIER, C., 75
COLLIER, J., 75
CONE, M., 98
COOK, N., 109
COVILLE, B., 23
CREECH, S., 148
CREW, L., 63
CURTIS, C.P., 187
CUSHMAN, K., 86

D

Danziger, P., 12, 14, 17, 23, 133
Davol, M., 174
Delaney, B., 144
Dengler, M., 178
Desouza, P., 83
Deuker, C., 146
Dickens, C., 2
Dickinson, E., 158
Dorris, M., 61, 75*f*
Duffy, C.A., 139
Dunbar, P., 144
Duncan, L., 146
Dunn, W., 136
Durrant, L., 86
Dyer, D., 96

E

Ehlert, L., 177
Ehrlich, A., 181
Erikson, J., 23

F

Feelings, T., 186
Fleischman, P., 75–76, 75*f,* 82–83
Fletcher, R., 139
Fox, M., 194
Fox, P., 83
Frank, A., 99, 136, 208
Freedman, R., 93, 96, 102, 131–132
Fritz, J., 124–125, 130–131
Frost, R., 154, 158, 160–161

G

Gallo, D., 10, 50
Garland, S., 63
Geiger, J., 102
George, J.C., 194
Giblin, J.C., 99
Giovanni, N., 144

G (cont.)

Gleitzman, M., 18, 23–24
Glenn, M., 146
Goldstein, B.S., 161
Golenbock, P., 185
Gordon, R., 140
Gorrell, G., 75
Greenberg, J., 148
Guthrie, W., 178

H

Hahn, M.D., 75*f*
Hamilton, J., 109
Hamilton, V., 50, 173
Hampton, W., 96
Hansen, J., 75
Haskins, J., 132
Haynes, B., 24
Hesse, K., 75*f,* 78*f,* 146, 206*f*
Hickam, H., 90
Hickman, J., 74
Highwater, J., 59–61
Hinton, S.E., 52, 194
Howard, E., 168
Howard, E.F., 177
Hughes, L., 143–144
Hunt, I., 83
Hunter, M., 86

I–J

Islas, A., 57
Jacques, B., 186
Janeczko, P.B., 141–143, 161
Johnson, A., 52–53
Johnson, D., 143

K

Kalergis, M.M., 96
Karr, K., 86
Kellogg, S., 176
Kidd, R., 172*f*
Kiefer, B., 181

KNIGHT, M.B., 183
KONIGSBURG, E.L., 24, 99
KORMAN, G., 12, 16, 24–25
KRAKAUER, J., 90
KRULL, K., 96, 133, 185
KURTZ, J., 173, 183

L

LACHTMAN, O.D., 57
LANGLEY, A., 83
LASKY, K., 170, 187
LATHEM, E.C., 154
LAUBER, P., 94, 96
LAWSON, D., 96
LEE, H., 33
LESTER, J., 98
LEVIN, T., 184
LEVINE, E., 136
LISLE, J.T., 75*f*
LOBEL, A., 136
LONDON, J., 90
LOWRY, L., 194
LYON, G.E., 198

M

MacCAULEY, D., 96, 99
MACK, S., 96
MANES, S., 12, 25
MARQUEZ, G.G., 57
MARRIN, A., 94
MARSHALL, J., 37
MARTIN, J.B., 176
MARTIN, R., 181
MARTINEZ, V., 55–56
MAYER, M., 172
McCAMPBELL, D., 49–50
MELTZER, M., 136
MERRIAM, E., 152, 155, 159, 161,
    166–167
MITCHELL, A.H., 153, 166, 168
MORA, P., 145–146

MOREY, J., 136
MORI, K., 63–64
MOSS, M., 82
MUNSON, S., 121, 137
MURPHY, J., 75, 94, 95, 103
MYERS, W.D., 50–52, 96, 148, 187

N

NAMIOKA, L., 62
NAYLOR, P.R., 16, 25
NORDINE, K., 178
NYE, N.S., 140, 143, 154–155

O–P

OSBORNE, M.P., 82, 87
PATERSON, K., 75*f*
PAULSEN, G., 87, 90, 98, 122, 137, 194,
    199
PECK, R., 41
PEREZ, N.A., 72*f,* 83
PILKEY, D., 187
PINKWATER, D., 25
POLACCO, P., 182, 194, 195, 196, 199,
    200–201, 205–209
POWELL, A., 83

R

RAFFERTY, T., 139
REEDER, C., 87
RINALDI, A., 87
ROBINET, H.G., 75*f*
ROBINSON, B., 26
ROCHELLE, B., 144
ROCHMAN, H., 49
RODOWSKY, C., 39
ROSENBERG, L., 141
ROTH, S.L., 90
RUBIN, C., 178
RYAN, P.M., 56–57
RYLANT, C., 140, 148

S

Sachar, L., 12, 26
Salisbury, G., 75f, 87
Sandburg, C., 158
Sassa, R., 177
Say, A., 183
Scieszka, J., 12, 18, 19, 26, 178
Sims, R., 53
Singer, M., 50
Sneve, V.D.H., 59
Sones, S., 146
Soto, G., 26, 32, 54–55, 145, 155, 159, 161
Speare, E.G., 58
Spedden, D.C., 186
Spinelli, J., 7, 26, 194, 211, 215–217, 219f
Stafford, W., 161
Stanley, D., 129, 133–134
Stanley, J., 93, 102
Steele, P., 83
Stevens, J., 180
Sutton, R., 95
Swir, A., 154–155, 161

T

Tallchief, M., 185
Tan, A., 64
Tanaka, S., 102, 186
Tate, E., 53
Taylor, M., 53, 194
Taylor, T., 75f
Teague, S., 26
Thomas, J.C., 49, 53
Tillage, L.W., 90
Todd, M., 143
Tsuchiya, Y., 92f
Twain, M., 2

U–V

Uchida, Y., 62
Valdes, G., 145
Van der Rol, R., 97, 99
Vennema, P., 133
Verhoeven, R., 97, 99
Villasenor, V., 57
Vuong, L.D., 49

W

Walker, A., 144–145
Watson, E.P., 143
Wells, R., 185
White, R., 137
Whitman, W., 158
Wilder, L.I., 58
Willard, N., 141
Williams-Garcia, R., 53
Wisler, G.C., 75
Wong, J.S., 141
Wood, D., 176, 178
Woodruff, E., 183
Woodson, J., 52
Wrede, P.C., 17, 27
Wright, R., 99

Y

Yep, L., 61–62, 194
Yolen, J., 14, 184

Z

Zeinert, K., 75
Zindel, P., 27

SUBJECT INDEX

Note: Page numbers followed by *f* indicate figures.

A

B

I

IDENTITY, quest for, 70

ILLUSTRATED BOOKS, vs. picture books, 173

INDEPENDENT READING: nonfiction trade books for, 95–96; time for, 197–198

INQUIRY GROUPS, nonfiction trade books for, 99–100

INTERNATIONAL READING ASSOCIATION (IRA), 10

INTERNET RESOURCES, 192, 223–225

I-SEARCH BIBLIOGRAPHY SHEET, 111, 115*f*

I-SEARCH NOTECARDS, 114*f*

I-SEARCH RUBRIC, 113*f*

I-SEARCH TIMETABLE, 112*f*

J

JOURNAL OF ADOLESCENT & ADULT LITERACY, 93

JOURNALS, reader, 103–104, 103*f*

K–L

K-W-L CHART, 111, 182

LATINOS/LATINAS: books about, 47, 53–57; poetry of, 145; *See also* diversity

LIBRARY, classroom, 197

LITERARY REPORT CARD, 202

LITERATURE CIRCLES, 199–200; for nonfiction trade books, 101–102

LITERATURE NOTEBOOKS, 31, 34–36; fast-writes in, 34, 35; modeling for, 37; pause points and, 30; for reluctant writers, 30, 36; self-censorship in, 35; sharing of, 36; teacher comments on, 36

LIVING ILLUSTRATIONS, 79–80

M

MEXICAN AMERICANS: books about, 47, 53–57; poetry of, 145; *See also* diversity

MODELING, for literature notebook, 37

MOTIVATIONAL ACTIVITIES, for reluctant readers, 89

MOVIES HERE WE COME!, 37

MULTICULTURALISM. *See* diversity

MULTICULTURAL LITERATURE, 45–65; authenticity of, 47–48; benefits of, 64–65; biographies/autobiographies as, 121–122, 131–133; folk tales as, 49; nonfiction trade books as, 91–92; by outsiders, 47–48; picture books as, 177, 182–185; poetry as, 143–145; selection of, 47–64; short story collections as, 49–50

MURDOCK, STEVE, 45

N

NARRATIVE POETRY, 146–148